9th e-Learning Excellence Awards 2023

An Anthology of Case Histories

Edited by Shawren Singh

9th e-Learning Excellence Awards: An Anthology of Case Histories

Copyright © 2023 The authors

First published October 2023

All rights reserved. Except for the quotation of short passages for the purposes of critical review, no part of this publication may be reproduced in any material form (including photocopying or storing in any medium by electronic means and whether or not transiently or incidentally to some other use of this publication) without the written permission of the copyright holder except in accordance with the provisions of the Copyright Designs and Patents Act 1988, or under the terms of a licence issued by the Copyright Licensing Agency Ltd, Saffron House, 6-10 Kirby Street, London EC1N 8TS. Applications for the copyright holder's written permission to reproduce any part of this publication should be addressed to the publishers.

Disclaimer: While every effort has been made by the editor, authors and the publishers to ensure that all the material in this book is accurate and correct at the time of going to press, any error made by readers as a result of any of the material, formulae or other information in this book is the sole responsibility of the reader. Readers should be aware that the URLs quoted in the book may change or be damaged by malware between the time of publishing and accessing by readers.

Note to readers: Some papers have been written by authors who use the American form of spelling and some use the British. These two different approaches have been left unchanged.

ISBN: 978-1-914587-84-9 (Print)
ISBN: 978-1-914587-85-6 (pdf)

Published by: Academic Conferences International Limited, Reading, United Kingdom, info@academic-conferences.org

Available from www.academic-bookshop.com

Table of Contents

Bridging the Gap: A Collaborative International e-Learning Initiative for Developing Global Business Skills (BIG-BIZ) 1
   Rosalina Babo and Scott Bingley

Know Yourself, Grow Your Wealth®: A Case Study on the Design, Development, Implementation, and Impact of a Free Online Financial Literacy Program 11
   Valencia L. Gabay, Timi J. Jorgensen, Martha Fulk, Grady L. Batchelor, Jr

The C-4X Protocol for Remote Instructional Support for Physical Classrooms: An e-Learning Model for the Revitalization of Teacher Education and Classroom Instruction 29
   F. Todd Goodson, Eileen Wertzberger, Debbie Mercer and Tracey Conway

Diagnosis Zombie: An Interactive Lesson on Brain and Behaviour 45
   Jane Guiller, Alex Oliver, Ken Rice, Emma Gibson and Jordyn McNally

Digital Presentations in Higher Education: An Australian Perspective..... 59
   Tomayess Issa and Dr Mahnaz Hall

uQualio Video4Learning 75
   Hatla Færch Johnsen, Christian Bjerre Nielsen, John Gage

Blended Learning UK (James Paget University Hospital NHS FT) 91
   Tom King, James Pereira, S.J. Leinister, Sue Down and A.D. Simpson

Towards building a sustainable community through social platforms 105
   Sweta Patnaik and Nadine Sonnenberg

Student teachers use of an ePortfolio for authentic assessment................ 121
   Sibongile Simelane-Mnisi

ECS1500: An Economics Module to Accommodate Diverse Learning Needs of Young Adults 135
   Cecilia J. van Zyl

Unlocking Potential: Creating an innovative learning platform to foster digital skills of educators 151
Georg Winder, Andrea Kern, Karin Zehetner, Dr. Josef Buchner

DP Education: Equitable Access to Free Quality Online Learning 167
Kawshi Amarasinghe, Dhammika Perera, Dhivyaluckshanna Chandrasegar, Loodeesha Ekanayake, Rambukka Maha Vidyalaya

LivePBL Liking Vocal Education through Project-Based Learning: A Music-led Hybrid Sino-International Social Learning Community 189
Ying Liu, Andy Hogg, Yuanyuan Li, Lian Sun, Ting Zhao, Jing Geng Xiang Li, Zhinan Zhu, Yasmin Mirza

Inclusive e-Learning for Marginalized Communities: The Mobile Learning Center Initiative 209
Mahmoud Hawamdeh, Bayan Shoubaki, Nisreen Awadallah, Saeda Abu Halaweh

Acknowledgements

We would like to thank the judges, who initially read the abstracts of the case histories submitted to the competition and discussed these to select those to be submitted as full case histories. They subsequently performed double-blind evaluations of the entries and made further selections to produce the finalists who are published in this book.

Paula Charbonneau Gowdy is Associate Professor in English as a Foreign Language Teacher Education at the Universidad Andres Bello in Santiago, Chile and formerly Senior Advisor in Learning and Technology to the Government of Canada. Her research interests lie in the sociocultural implications of online learning for teaching, learning and learners.

Susan Crichton is an emeritus professor in Educational Technologies at the University of British Columbia, Canada. She is currently a consultant who has been working to support educators in the K-12 sector, as well as post-secondary trades training and university to respond to the challenges posed by COVID 19.

Colin Loughlin is the Learning Technology Manager at the University of Surrey (UK) and a PhD candidate with Lund University (Sweden). His research interests are related to large class teaching and the impact of educational theory on classroom practice. Recently published: 'Reclaiming Constructive Alignment' (bit.ly/reclaimingCA).

Shawren Singh is an Associate Professor at the School of Computing at the University of South Africa, he has spent more than 20 years teaching and researching in the Information Systems space. In 2014 he obtained his PhD, based on research into eGovernment in South Africa, from the University of the Witwatersrand. His current research has focused on digital scholarship and e-Government, his research has been published internationally and he has presented papers at several conferences.

Introduction

e-Learning and indeed blended learning are now established integral ways in which education and training are managed and delivered across all levels of education and in the workplace. The International e-Learning Excellence Awards provides an opportunity for individuals and groups to consider new and innovative ways of using this method of learning.

The response this year to the nineth International e-Learning Excellence Awards reflects the continuing innovation being practised in many parts of the world. With 24 initial submissions from 12 countries, 20 competitors were invited to send in a full case history describing their initiative. The range of subjects written about in the case histories has certainly been extensive and the panel of expert judges had their job cut out for them during the blind reviewing process to find the most interesting case histories and short list them to the finalists published in this anthology.

14 authors or groups of authors have been invited to present their work in the final rounds of this competition at the 2023 European Conference on e-Learning, being held at the University of South Africa (UNISA) in Pretoria, South Africa, and as finalists these initiatives are published in this book of case histories. The topics to be addressed are listed in the Contents page of this book and represent projects from Australia, China, Palestine, Portugal, Sri Lanka, South Africa, Switzerland, the United Kingdom and the United States.

The presentation of these cases at UNISA is of special significance as the university celebrates its 150th anniversary. UNISA has been a pioneer in first distance and now e-Learning.

I would like to thank all the contributors to the book for the excellent work which has been done towards developing new and interesting ways of applying e-Learning. And of course, it is also important to thank the individuals who constituted our panel of expert judges.

Dr Shawren Singh
October 2023

Bridging the Gap:
A Collaborative International e-Learning Initiative for Developing Global Business Skills (BIG-BIZ)

Rosalina Babo[1] and Scott Bingley[2]
[1]Polytechnic University of Porto (P.Porto)/ Porto Accounting and Business School (ISCAP), Portugal
[2]Victoria University (VU), Melbourne, Australia
babo@iscap.ipp.pt
scott.bingley@vu.edu.au

Abstract: With globalization, international experiences and skills have become increasingly important. Companies value employees who can adapt to different cultural contexts, collaborate across geographical boundaries, and navigate diverse business environments. Strong collaboration, communication, and digital literacy skills are crucial for success in a globalized and remote work environment. Therefore, universities need to equip their students to work in international settings by providing them opportunities to develop critical skills needed to thrive in the interconnected world of work. This experimental educational initiative brought together by two higher education institutions from different parts of the planet: Victoria University (VU), Australia, and Porto Accounting and Business School (IPP-ISCAP), Portugal. The initiative had students from both universities working collaboratively to solve a real-world industry problem through their SAP Next Gen labs. The goals were to promote the building of knowledge, the acquisition of business practices, and the development of crucial soft and technical skills. The main challenges were the differences in timezones and language. Considering the ten-hour gap between countries, it was troublesome to schedule meetings, when real time meetings were necessary to coordinate efforts to develop a project. Also, English was the language used to carry the project and communication within the groups, thus the Portuguese students had to be proficient in that language. The outcomes of this initiative were very positive on the student learning journey. Surveys distributed at the end of each project (or Semester) revealed that most of the students find that this international project helped them further develop their technical and soft skills. They also learnt to apply these skills in a more complex landscape of international borders and different cultures. This initiative has already had two editions and the universities involved are making plans for future editions.

1. Introduction

Globalisation allow the world to be more connected and the growth of online work enable the collaboration between people from different backgrounds and countries, drawing the attention of business and academic institutions. International experiences and skills have become increasingly important, and companies value employees who can adapt to different cultural contexts, collaborate across geographical boundaries, and navigate diverse business environments. Strong collaboration, communication, and digital literacy skills are crucial for success in a globalized and remote work environment.

It has become important that workers be able to work in teams with people from around the globe. These Global Virtual Teams (GVT) allows for a shared flow of knowledge and the creation of circumstances where all team members gain with international network. These teams enable organizations to have access to specialists, regardless of their geographical location, and enhance productivity (Jimenez *et al.*, 2017; Amaratunga, Liyanage and Haigh, 2018; Chen, Zhang and Fu, 2019; Glikson and Erez, 2020).

The use of GVT in the context of higher education can providing the students with opportunities to develop critical skills needed to thrive in the interconnected world of work. Higher education institutions have started to recognise the significance of teaching their students to work collaboratively to solve real and complex problems. These teachings, however, generally only occur within the same subject and within the same university. Students' interaction can foster the building of knowledge and the acquisition and development of crucial business skills necessary as 21st century citizens (Le, Janssen and Wubbels, 2017; Muukkonen *et al.*, 2019; Herrera-Pavo, 2021).

Le et al. (2017, pp. 103–104) stated that collaborative learning happens when the teachers promote their "teaching and learning strategies" by having groups of students complete a set of activities that can "optimise their own and each other's learning". This interaction exposes students to other people, environments, and cultures, and consequently allows them to develop their social and cultural viewpoints (Le, Janssen and Wubbels, 2017; Herrera-Pavo, 2021).

However, despite the advantages of these practices, some issues can also incur. The main issue is related to the lack of collaborative skills in students, which can impact and hinder their collaborative learning experience. Another issue, related to the actual collaboration nature, is communication problems which may inhibit the engagement with the group work and limit their contribution to the outcomes. According to Le et al. (2017, pp. 115–116), there are four main barriers to an effective collaborative learning experience: "students' lack of collaborative skills, free-riding, competence status, and friendship" (Le et al., 2017).

The initiative presented here took into account the need to empower the students with an international experience, where they could collaborate with students from another country to achieve a common goal. Therefore, Victoria University (VU), in Melbourne, Australia, and Porto Accounting and Business School (ISCAP|P.Porto), from Porto, Portugal, have started an experimental educational initiative.

This initiative has already two editions with different industry sponsored problems, that the students had to undertake, as well as different team settings. It started in 2021, with Case A and in 2022 was conducted case B. Both cases involved the students with real case scenarios from industry companies where they had to build a solution with an Enterprise Resource Planning (ERP) system, namely SAP.

Case A concerned a company, with over 25 years of experience in digital transformation projects, focuses on consulting services to assist clients with ERP system functionalities, based in Melbourne, Australia. The goal was to propose a resolution and prototype for the specific business problem which involved issues related to ERP implementation in a manufacturing organization. The company was collaborating with a large agricultural business that used sorting machines without integration to standard operating systems or computer networks.

The proposed solution involved developing SAP Fiori apps to read and organize batch reports into a database. The students from the two universities had to collaborated in the project development, enhancing the SAP Fiori apps with visualizations, additional features, and innovative ideas. There were two groups composed of students from both universities, who worked together to develop the project.

The industry company in Case B is an international glass container manufacturing organization that utilizes SAP for its operations. The proposed problem is related to changes in certain departments, where some processes have been implemented outside of SAP using Excel and Word. The organization has 26,500 employees across 78 plants in 23 countries, and aims to enhance its internal processes, particularly in the HR Department, by building data science and business analytics dashboards.

To achieve this, the organization provided the students with Excel files downloaded from their ERP and other systems to analyse and create dashboards using SAP Cloud Analytics. The students had to answer various workforce-related questions, such as headcount across countries, turnover rates in different departments or locations, trends in internal employee movements, average time in roles before movement, the gap between new hires and leavers, age and gender distribution, absenteeism patterns, and the potential link between absenteeism and overtime worked. This case used only one team of six students, four from Portugal and two from Australia, where they had to collaborated, while receiving feedback from their supervisors on their individual work, culminating in a joint presentation of their results.

2. The infrastructure

This initiative involved two higher education institutions (ISCAP and VU) around a project where the students had to use an SAP application to solve a real-world industry problem. In this project, the students worked in teams to solve an industry sponsored problem. The first higher education institution involved is ISCAP|P.Porto, located in Porto, Portugal. P.Porto is one of Portugal's largest and most prestigious public Polytechnic Institutes and has about 19.211 students. ISCAP is housed within P.Porto and offers its 4,500-strong student population a range of innovative undergraduate and graduate programs. P.Porto is ranked 301-350 in young universities on the Times Education Ranking (Times Higher Education, n.d. a).

The other university is VU, located in Melbourne, Australia. VU has over 40,000 students enrolled in higher education, and vocational education and training students studying on their campuses. VU houses the VU Business School. This university is ranked at equal 77th in young universities on the Times Education Ranking (Times Higher Education, n.d. b)).

The initiative had teams composed of both members based in Porto, Portugal, and in Melbourne, Australia (approximately 17,716 km and 10-hour time difference apart).

SAP software is also an important part of this initiative infrastructure. It is one of the biggest software companies in the world that develops business management solutions to assist organizations in processing data and information in an effective way. This software is used by businesses and organizations of various sizes and industries. SAP applications are widely known for their high level of complexity with several programs and subprograms. It has four modules, namely Financial, Logistical, Human Resource, and Cross-Application. These cover almost every aspect of the "business management and work in a collaborative fashion on a single platform." ((*What is SAP?*, no date; Welz and Rosenberg, 2018; Savchuk and Kirsta, 2019, p. 1468)

SAP software is one of the leading ERP software providers and is used to collect and process data, from raw material, on one platform. Their solutions can enable businesses to better understand and respond to their customers. In turn, the organizations can run their operations in a profitably way, easily adapt to the environment and thus sustainably grow (*What is SAP?*, no date; Welz and Rosenberg, 2018).

Within SAP, they have an area called SAP Next Gen. This is a community for youth driven by purpose and innovation to support SAP's customers from all industries in more than 180 countries. SAP Next-Gen labs assist in bringing ideas to the market by educating students in digital skills and prepare them for the industry. There are around 111 of these innovation labs around the world. IPP and VU both have one of these SAP Next Gen Labs (*What is SAP?*, no date; Welz and Rosenberg, 2018).

3. The challenges

Considering this initiative was unprecedented in both institutions, it was conducted with a small group of participants, and it has only undergone two editions. Several factors contributed to the limited sample size. Firstly, the recruitment process relied on sending emails to students in courses where the initiative could be applied, and it relied on volunteers who expressed interest. This method, while effective in this context, naturally limited the number of participants.

There were several challenges that needed to be overcome and the lecturers involved took several months of planning and designing the experience. Some aspects to take into account were the different backgrounds of the students, both undergraduate and graduate programs, and their motivations to participate in the initiative. The task distribution to ensure equal participation and contribution from all members was also a crucial aspect that required careful attention. This was done by creating a list of foreseeable tasks and distributing them by the students/groups. The distribution ensure equity amongst the students in terms of workload.

Another challenge was the adaptation of the evaluation system, since the two institutions had different assessment criteria and methods that had to be coordinated. Also, logistical considerations, such as finding a suitable schedule for collaborative work had to be surpassed. Both parties required careful organization and flexibility to allow successful communications. The knowledge from these challenges was retained by the lecturers, which led them to change and improve some aspects of the project in the second edition.

The students also expressed that the difference in timezones was challenging. Considering the eleven-hour gap between countries, arranging real time meetings, necessary to coordinate efforts to develop a project, was troublesome. The students felt it was not easy to schedule meeting times with their group members.

Also, the cultural and religious differences caused some issues for the students. When there is a small window to schedule meetings, students try to schedule these to days when they do have classes, normally the weekend days. However, students stated that scheduling meeting times with group members was difficult and expressed the difficulty in figuring out time to schedule these.

Another challenge of the project was the communication within the groups, where English was the language used. Even though the students from both countries spoke English, the Portuguese students were especially put to test. They had to be proficient in the English language, unlike the Australian students whose official language is English.

It is also important to state that this project demanded a lot of time from the responsible teachers as well. They had to be available for the students in case of any question and doubt, as well as to keep them motivated when faced with innumerable challenges.

4. Participants' perceptions and Learning outcomes

At the end of each project, the students involved were asked to answer a survey about experience. The overall results show that the participants have a positive perception about the initiative. This leads to the conclusion that the students involved in the innovative project were pleased with how the project was carried out.

In the first edition of the project, the students were very enthusiastic to be part of an international project. The teachers' responsible by the project were likewise motivated with the initiative and may have transmitted all this energy to the group of students. The opinions on the second edition were better, which may be due to the experience gained by the lectures during the first interaction. The lecturers also retained new knowledge from the challenges of the first edition, which led them to change and improve some aspects of the project.

The students felt that the project boosted their enthusiasm for studying and they were more motivated to learn. They also expressed that the international project made them more interested in the topics taught and assisted in improving their technical and soft skills, namely problem-solving skills, autonomy, responsibility, and time management. Likewise, they stated that this initiative allows them to learn to apply these skills in a more complex landscape of international borders and different cultures.

Given the constraints faced, this initiative was seen to be successful on many fronts, both the students and the industry companies involved benefited. As a project, the company had several different solutions to view, and 'cherry-pick' the best ideas, and insights, in implement into their business. The students also benefited by working in much the same many a consultant would. In working on a project, they are not familiar with, in an industry they are not familiar with, and with software they might not be familiar with. The project allowed the students to use an ERP and contact with a real-world industry project. Which, as expressed by them, allowed to grasp an idea of professional context.

This initiative has been proved as a valuable asset for the students involved. These students were able to work in a global virtual project which has help them gain important collaborative skills to face the world of work. Also, since SAP software was used to carry the project and it is widely used by businesses worldwide, for the students to have the practical experience with it, is a great advantage in their future.

5. Plans for the future

This initiative has already had two editions and the universities involved are making plans for future editions. Thanks to initiatives such as exchange programs and Erasmus+, international experiences are more common. These initiatives are helpful for personal and professional development, as they expose students to other environments and cultures, thereby developing their social and cultural perspective.

However, not all students have the opportunity or means to participate. Thus, initiatives like the international industry project presented here can give real meaning to students' lives and act as a means of partially replacing these experiences. Therefore, this initiative is ongoing between the two universities.

The teaching model of this initiative is scalable, but it does require additional resources in terms of teaching time and workload allocation compared to a traditional lecture/tutorial approach. Since this model emphasizes student consultation over lectures and tutorials, it is somewhat more labour-intensive. Each student group will have a weekly meeting with the lecturer to discuss their project progress. Additionally, incorporating an international component adds an extra layer of intensity to the process. However, the flexibility and engagement fostered by this model make it well-suited for adaptation to other contexts, larger groups of students, and collaboration with different international organisations.

Acknowledgement

This work is financed by Portuguese national funds through FCT – Fundação para a Ciência e Tecnologia, under the project UIDB/05422/2020

References

Amaratunga, D., Liyanage, C. and Haigh, R. (2018) 'A Study into the Role of International Collaborations in Higher Education to Enhance Research Capacity for Disaster Resilience', Procedia Engineering, 212, pp. 1233–1240. Available at: https://doi.org/10.1016/J.PROENG.2018.01.159.

Chen, K., Zhang, Y. and Fu, X. (2019) 'International research collaboration: An emerging domain of innovation studies?', Research Policy, 48(1), pp. 149–168. Available at: https://doi.org/10.1016/J.RESPOL.2018.08.005.

Glikson, E. and Erez, M. (2020) 'The emergence of a communication climate in global virtual teams', Journal of World Business, 55(6), pp. 1–10. Available at: https://doi.org/10.1016/j.jwb.2019.101001.

Herrera-Pavo, M.Á. (2021) 'Collaborative learning for virtual higher education', Learning, Culture and Social Interaction, 28, p. 100437. Available at: https://doi.org/10.1016/J.LCSI.2020.100437.

Jimenez, A. et al. (2017) 'Working Across Boundaries: Current and Future Perspectives on Global Virtual Teams', Journal of International Management, 23(4), pp. 341–349. Available at: https://doi.org/10.1016/j.intman.2017.05.001.

Le, H., Janssen, J. and Wubbels, T. (2017) 'Collaborative learning practices: teacher and student perceived obstacles to effective student collaboration', Cambridge Journal of Education, 48(1), pp. 103–122. Available at: https://doi.org/10.1080/0305764X.2016.1259389.

Muukkonen, H. et al. (2019) 'Assessing the Development of Collaborative Knowledge Work Competence: Scales for Higher Education Course Contexts', https://doi.org/10.1080/00313831.2019.1647284, 64(7), pp. 1071–1089. Available at: https://doi.org/10.1080/00313831.2019.1647284.

Savchuk, R.R. and Kirsta, N.A. (2019) 'Managing of the Business Processes in Enterprise by Moving to SAP ERP System', in 2019 IEEE Conference of Russian Young Researchers in Electrical and Electronic Engineering (ElConRus). IEEE, pp. 1467–1470. Available at: https://doi.org/10.1109/EIConRus.2019.8657213.

Times Higher Education (no date a). Polytechnic Institute of Porto. Available at: https://www.timeshighereducation.com/world-university-rankings/polytechnic-institute-porto (Accessed: 12 April 2022)

Times Higher Education (no date b). Victoria University. Available at: https://www.timeshighereducation.com/world-university-rankings/victoria-university (Accessed: 12 April 2022)

Welz, B. and Rosenberg, A. (2018) SAP Next-Gen: Innovation with purpose, SAP Next-Gen: Innovation with Purpose. Springer International Publishing. Available at: https://doi.org/10.1007/978-3-319-72574-1.

What is SAP? (no date) SAP. Available at: https://www.sap.com/about/company/what-is-sap.html (Accessed: 10 August 2021).

Author Biographies

Rosalina Babo is a Coordinator Professor of Information Systems Department at ISCAP/P.Porto. Rosalina is the Director of SAP University Alliance at P.Porto. Among other functions she was Head of the IS Department (+20 years), member of the university scientific board (12 years), founder of CEOS.PP (former CEISE STI) research centre and its director (5 years).

Scott Bingley is a senior lecturer, researcher in Information Systems, and programme director of SAP at Victoria University. In recent years he has published in highly ranked Q1 journals. Scott has lectured, coordinated, and tutored in undergraduate and postgraduate subjects both in Melbourne and overseas. Scott is the

Rosalina Babo and Scott Bingley

Director of Victoria University's SAP Next-Gen Lab and Director of VU's SAP Academic Competence Centre - APJ region.

Know Yourself, Grow Your Wealth®:
A Case Study on the Design, Development, Implementation, and Impact of a Free Online Financial Literacy Program

Valencia L. Gabay, Timi J. Jorgensen, Martha Fulk, Grady L. Batchelor, Jr
The American College of Financial Services, King of Prussia, Pennsylvania, USA

valencia.gabay@theamericancollege.edu
timi.jorgensen@theamericancollege.edu
martha.fulk@theamericancollege.edu
grady.batchelor@theamericancollege.edu

Abstract: The study examined the creation and impact of Know Yourself, Grow Your Wealth®1 (KYGYW), an online self-paced financial literacy program, launched across 38 Historically Black Colleges and Universities (HBCUs). This personalized, gamified e-Learning platform aimed to deliver financial education that addressed the systemic barriers to financial wellness. Program goals included: deliver culturally relevant content, increase applied financial knowledge, improve financial well-being, and provide an engaging and inclusive learning environment. The key performance indicators used to measure program success were registration, commencement, completion, increased knowledge, and improved financial well-being. The study, which employed a single-case, holistic design included mixed methods using qualitative and quantitative analysis to evaluate and report on the learning experience. This reporting was based on observations, pre-and-post-program assessments, knowledge checks and end-of-course questionnaires. The results indicated enhanced financial knowledge and confidence, reduced financial stress, and above-average online completion rates for learners.

1. Introduction

The Center for Consumer Financial Education at The American College of Financial Services (TAC) helps individual consumers improve their financial wellness through culturally relevant financial education courses designed to increase financial knowledge and skills and decrease financial stress and anxiety while boosting financial confidence. In 2022, the Center launched the *KYGYW* program, a self-paced, e-Learning, financial education certificate program to foster consumer financial empowerment. Utilizing gamification, modularization, and personalization learning design strategies focused on promoting behavior change and continuous learning, the program delivers digestible, targeted, and on-demand financial education content that positively impacts learners financial knowledge and wellbeing.

Unlike other financial education programs, we designed KYGYW with the learner in mind. The program's holistic approach to financial education begins with learners challenging their thoughts, feelings, and espoused beliefs about money through self-reflective and metacognitive exercises. As learners advance through the program, they engage with basic financial education concepts, create new knowledge, and set realistic financial goals based on their core values. Learners assess their gains in financial knowledge throughout the program and determine their growth areas. This approach allows learners to create mindset shifts and develop new financial behaviors.

Figure 1 outlines the full learner progression. Learners start the program by completing a 30-question pre-program survey before gaining access to 13 e-Learning modules where they engage with financial education concepts (earning, spending, budgeting, and saving). Learners assess their knowledge of these concepts by completing module level assessments. Before earning their certificate of completion, learners must complete a post-program survey and a program experience questionnaire.

Figure 1. Learner Progression

2. Learning Experience Goals

We deliver the 13-module program with four learning experience goals: provide culturally relevant content, increase financial knowledge, improve financial well-being, and empower and engage learners through a nurturing and inclusive learning environment. Knowing that cultural and social identity impact financial matters (Gudmunson & Danes, 2011), it was essential for learners to reflect on their worldviews to develop a more informed learner experience. According to Engerman and Otto (2020), the combination of culturally relevant pedagogy, interactive, and interdependent online learning is essential to learner empowerment. Financial education serves as a tool to increase financial knowledge; as such, we designed the program to enhance objective financial knowledge and self-reported financial knowledge and skills. Arriving at financial wellness differs for everyone, as learners' financial situations and circumstances vary. Considering the variances in financial conditions and circumstances, the program outcomes include strategies to reduce financial stress and anxiety (Gidley et al., 2010; Jorgensen, 2022). Finally, community and peer-to-peer engagement must support discussing financial concepts and encourage a change in financial behavior. Therefore, the program has a nurturing and inclusive learning environment where learners engage with others and foster collective knowledge through discussion forums.

3. The Infrastructure

The *Know Yourself, Grow Your Wealth®* (KYGYW) platform is a custom-built eLearning infrastructure that utilizes eLearnCommerce™ (https://elearncommerce.com/) and Active Campaign (https://www.activecampaiogn.com/) to create a dynamic learning experience. eLearnCommerce™ is a proprietary infrastructure used to deliver KYGYW on a WordPress backend. eLearnCommerce™ provides several core platform features like classroom dashboards, content delivery, and assessments. Additional custom applications include unique join links, badging, multi-level leaderboards, grade books, and interactive forums. These features collectively create a tailored, modularized, and gamified learning experience.

Active Campaign is a customer automation software integrated with the KYGYW platform to deliver email notifications throughout the learner journey. Automated emails include personalized welcome messages after learner enrollment, notifications prompting learners to engage and re-engage with the learning content, and congratulatory notifications at key learning milestones. The use of eLearnCommerce™ and Active Campaign, collectively, created a vibrant learning infrastructure that allowed learners to feel connected and thrive in the online setting.

4. The Learner Journey

Learners begin their learning journey in KYGYW by enrolling on the platform using a specialized join link unique to different audiences. The platform, supplied with integrated gaming mechanics, automated communications, and discussion forums, creates an engaging and inclusive online classroom that fosters feelings of personal accomplishment and promotes behavior change, and it is easy for staff and facilitators to manage. The program offers financial education in various formats, including videos, infographics, handouts, worksheets, and dialogue simulation.

Learners accumulate points on the leaderboard week-to-week for completing program activities. Game elements like leaderboards augment motivation and program participation (Na & Han, 2023). Program achievements are embedded throughout the learning journey using digital badging to celebrate learner milestones. Modules are grouped into four badges: Financial

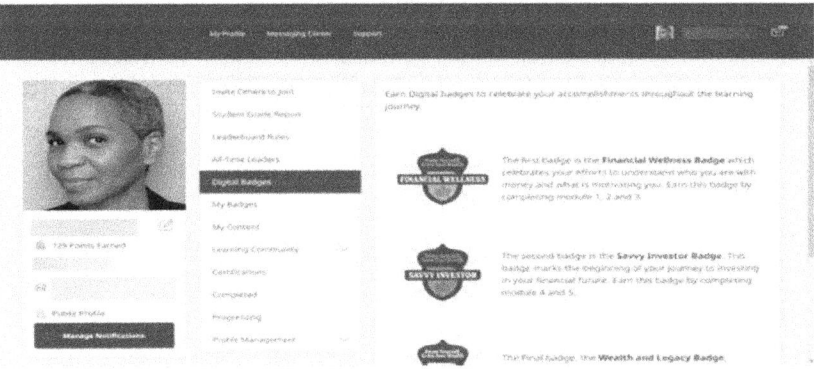

Figure 2. Know Yourself, Grow Your Wealth® Program Achievements Page

Wellness, Brilliant Borrower, Savvy Investor, and Wealth Legacy. The badges celebrate learners' achievements in understanding their self-motivations relating to financial matters, making smart borrowing decisions, investing as a vehicle to grow their money, and defining wealth on their terms. Once learners satisfactorily complete module knowledge checks to earn a badge, a badge is presented to the learner as a digital download. We encourage learners to share their badges on social media (see Figures 2 and 3). Upon completion of the program, learners download their certificates.

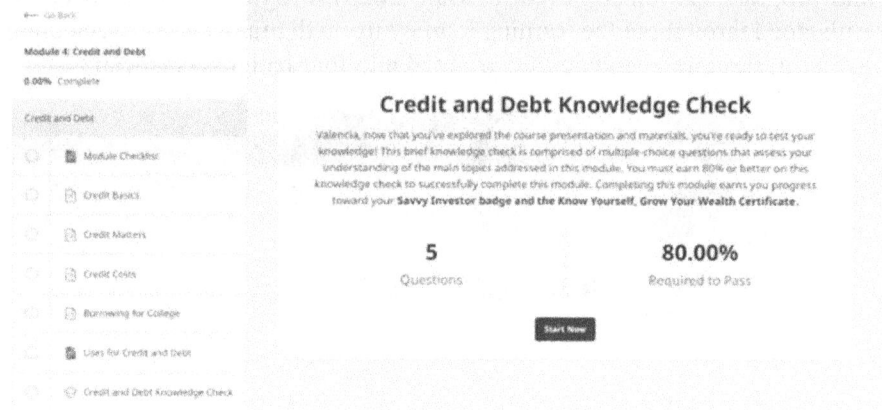

Figure 3. Know Yourself, Grow Your Wealth® Knowledge Check

5. The Challenges

With individual and corporate donor funding, KYGYW is freely accessible to students at 38 HBCUs nationwide. Instructors and leaders at select campuses facilitate the program as a capstone to personal finance and introductory business courses at colleges and universities. Student support services programs, including financial aid, career services, academic advising, and other student assistance groups, offer KYGYW as a resource. The program is also available to employees and their families at nonprofit organizations through employee wellness initiatives, professional development, and corporate learning networks.

A contributing factor to the successful implementation and delivery of the program included our four-step program advocacy approach. We designed this approach based on our partner engagement experiences. The steps include:

1. leverage partner academic/organizational leaders as program champions to promote and validate the program benefits and learning outcomes,
2. customize enrollment plans to meet the specific needs of each organizational partner,
3. provide training to boost facilitation practices and utilization of reporting dashboards to capture learning enrollments and

completions, and maintain an active presence in the community and effectively manage partnerships.

While the program advocacy approach was instrumental in boosting program engagement among most corporate entities, we experienced challenges in advancing program rollouts across academic institutions to reach diverse learner groups. These challenges included: (a) changes in the partner organization's structure or climate, (b) the inability to quickly identify key stakeholders and decision-makers to promote and champion the program's implementation and delivery, and (c) partner's lack of in-depth knowledge about the learner's experience. As a solution, our implementation and delivery methods now include a required in-depth two-week training and targeted partnership experience. This experience begins with the organization identifying key stakeholders and primary decision-makers to be program champions and participate in the required training. Second, these individuals must complete the KYGYW program and earn their certificate. Finally, they must adhere to a comprehensive timeline for scoping and ideation around a sustainable implementation and delivery plan. The goal is for these program champions to become better advocates for the program within their organization and community.

6. The Learning Outcomes

We used a single-case holistic design (Remenyi, 2013), including mixed methods using qualitative and quantitative analysis to evaluate and report on the learning experience holistically. The course employed standard pre-and-post-surveys to establish a baseline and comparative measures of the effectiveness of the course in its primary learning outcome goals. Each module included a short, five- to seven-question knowledge check requiring a score of 80% or higher to pass. Students could take these knowledge checks as many times as necessary to get a passing score because the goal is for the students to learn. The final component was a qualitative questionnaire given to students during the last module that asked specific questions with open-ended responses. Those qualitative responses were coded using AtlasTI and thematic analysis coding practices at the end of the initial implementation term. These qualitative themes were the benchmarks for subsequent analysis and have guided program updates and content additions. After each update to the course, the thematic analysis has been evaluated to determine if there has been a negative impact on any of the four qualitative measurements of success.

7. Qualitative Analysis

The program had four main qualitative measurements of success: culturally relevant content, increased financial knowledge, improved financial well-being, and an empowering and engaging learning experience. We tested culturally relevant content using engagement and completion metrics and qualitative feedback from learners. Increased financial knowledge was measured using validated measures of objective financial knowledge, subjective financial knowledge, and financial skills and capabilities. In addition, these scores were cross-examined with the qualitative feedback and thematic analysis of reported knowledge increase from learners. Improved financial well-being was measured using validated scales of financial stress, financial anxiety, financial confidence, and satisfaction.

These quantitative measures were cross-examined with qualitative feedback and reports of decreased stress and increased confidence in the end of course survey. The empowering and engaging learning experience was measured using the following engagement goals based on industry standards of excellence:

- Goal: >60% of learners who registered for the program continued and engaged with the program.
- Goal: >75% of learners completed the course after starting the first module.
- Goal: >50% of learners completed the course once they registered on the platform.

The Inclusive Financial Well-being & Empowerment Model guided these metrics (Jorgensen, 2020).

7.1 Qualitative Results

1. **Culturally Relevant:** Through qualitative feedback, learners identified the content as culturally relevant: "I liked all the African American representation throughout the presentation. It made the information more relatable and easier to digest." Because this was a design goal of the program, rather than solicit feedback that could bias these comments, all comments were coded with the theme "cultural relevance".
2. **Increase Financial Knowledge:** To receive the KYGYW Certificate, learners must have scored 80% or higher on all module-level knowledge checks. Cumulatively, this resulted in a minimum of

32 correct answers out of 40 questions for 100% of learners. Further analysis of pre-and-post-surveys showed that 90% of learners reported an increase in their subjective financial knowledge when asked, "On a scale of 1 to 10, how would you assess your overall financial knowledge?"

From the pre-survey to the post-survey, 58% of learners showed an increase in the specific five-question financial knowledge scale. Beyond knowledge, 63% of learners showed increased financial skills related to the time value of money, diversification and risk, and inflation and cost of living. When questioned about actual changes in financial behaviors, 48.6% said they had paid down credit cards since the completion of the course, and 53.8% said they had saved more money because of the course.

Qualitative responses around increased knowledge were the most powerful theme:

"My financial understanding was pretty low when I first began this course. As I progressed throughout each module, I learned so much more than I started with. I also expanded my knowledge on prior topics I thought I knew a lot about, such as budgeting, stocks, and bonds."

1. **Improve Financial Well-being:** Between pre-surveys and post-surveys, 86.5% of learners reported increased financial satisfaction, and 86.2% reported increased financial confidence. Regarding the financial wellness scale, there was a 58.8% increase from pre- to post-survey results. The mean overall financial wellness score increased by 10% for the entire population during the course.

The second most robust theme was qualitative responses focused on stress reduction and increased confidence. One example is, "I was stressing about financial issues and knowing about debt and credit, as these are things I have not been taught successfully before now.

2. **Empowering and Engaging Learning Experience:**
   - Goal: >60% of learners who registered for the program continued and engaged with the program.
     - Result: 80% of learners engaged with the program.

- Goal: >75% of learners completed the course after starting the first module.
  - Result: 72% of learners completed the course after starting the first module.
- Goal: >50% of learners completed the course once they registered on the platform.
  - Result: 58% of learners completed the entire course once they registered on the platform.

Qualitative results reinforced the empowering and engaging learning experience. Many comments highlighted specific aspects of the program, including the interactive discussion boards, gamification of the program, bite-sized videos, and delivery and tone of the course.

7.2 Discussion of Qualitative Results

Results indicated that this program works. The goal of improving financial knowledge and wellness for specific audiences based on best practices in instructional design and user experience mixed with nuanced research of the audiences had merit. Feedback from the surveys also informed the expansion of the content to include more how-to guidance regarding credit and debt management, home ownership, and retirement planning. We simplified some navigation and other user experience components based on the feedback.

As a tool for expanding our impact, the qualitative and quantitative data allowed us to dispel myths about the willingness of consumers to engage with formalized eLearning content around financial matters. We frequently heard from stakeholder partners that people would not engage, did not care, or would not take the time to complete the course. Our data indicated otherwise; the learners are engaged, interested in the content, and invested in learning.

7.3 Quantitative Analysis

The case study used questions adapted from the Consumer Finance Protection Bureau (CFPB), a governmental agency dedicated to ensuring that lenders, banks, and other financial institutions treat families fairly. The study questions included other commonly used financial literacy skills and financial wellness questions. Finally, instead of discussing or using the results of individual questions, the researchers created two instrument measures based on multiple questions to assess the learners' overall financial knowledge (figure 1) and financial wellness (figure 2).

The two aggregate scale measurements, as shown in figures 4 and 5, provide significant advantages over a single-item question measure. This includes the scale instrument's multidimensionality and the measurement's validity, composed of multiple questions assessing the variable. The study questions were administered before the start of the program and after the completion of the program. The responses were analyzed using statistical tests to determine if there was a change following the program in financial skills and behavior.

Financial Wellness Scale Instrument
1. I have too much debt right now
2. Debt and debt payments prevent me from adequately addressing other financial priorities.
3. Thinking about my personal finances can make me feel anxious.
4. If I compare my financial situation to that of my peers, I feel behind.
5. Because of my money situation, I feel like I will never have the things I want in life.
6. I am just getting by financially.
7. I am concerned that the money I have or will save won't last.
8. How present is financial anxiety in your daily life? I think about my personal finance issues...

Figure 4. The Financial Knowledge Scale Instrument

Note. Adapted from the Consumer Finance Protection Bureau (CFPB) https://www.consumerfinance.gov/

Financial Knowledge Scale Instrument
1. Suppose you had $100 in a savings account and the interest rate was 2% per year. After 5 years, how much do you think you would have in the account if you left the money to grow?
2. Imagine that the interest rate on your savings account was 1% per year and inflation was 2% per year. After 1 year, with the money in this account, would you be able to buy...
3. Do you think the following statement is true or false? Buying a single company stock usually provides a safer return than a stock mutual fund.
4. Suppose you owe $1,000 on a loan and the interest rate you are charged is 20% per year compounded annually. If you didn't pay anything off, at this interest rate, how many years would it take for the amount you owe to double?
5. Assume you want the premium payments for your car insurance to be as low as possible. What can you do?

Figure 5. The Financial Wellness Scale Instrument

Note. Adapted from the Consumer Finance Protection Bureau (CFPB) https://www.consumerfinance.gov/

7.4 Variables

The outcome variables, financial knowledge, and financial wellness are described above. The study used four control variables: race, gender, ethnicity, and age (see Tables 1, 2, and 3). Control variables allowed for controlling relevant variables that may extraneously affect the relationships between the variables of interest. By using control variables rather than holding relevant factors constant across learners, we could enhance the internal validity of a study by limiting the influence of confounding and other extraneous variables. Using control variables helped establish a correlational or causal relationship between variables of interest and helped avoid research bias.

7.5 Statistical Measures

The study used a paired-sample t-test, sometimes called the dependent sample t-test. We used the paired sample t-test procedure to determine whether the mean difference between the before and after question responses on financial knowledge and wellness was statistically significant. We used the dependent samples t-test to compare the sample means from two related groups. In this approach, the scores for the compared groups came from the same people. This test aimed to determine whether there was a change from one measurement (group) to another.

7.6 Study Hypotheses

- H1: $\mu 1 < \mu 2$; The mean difference on the financial knowledge scale is higher following the program.
- H2: $\mu 1 < \mu 2$; The mean difference on the financial wellness scale is higher following the program.

7.7 Results

The first section of the results shows the demographic composition of the learners. As the tables below indicate, the learners were majority female, African American, non-Hispanic (93.3%), and between the ages of 15 and 30.

7.8 Descriptive Analysis:

N=866

Table 1. Gender

Gender	Percentage
Female	69.17%
Male	30.14%
Gender Non-Confirming	0.69%
Grand Total	100.00%

Table 2. Race

Race	Percentage
African American	69.17%
White	3.23%
Other	2.42%
Asian American/Pacific Islander	0.58%
Grand Total	100/00%

Table 3. Age

Age	Percentage
15-30	92.3%
46-60	3.81%
30-45	3.70%
65-75	0.46%
Grand Total	100.00%

7.9 Data Analysis Results

In addition to the descriptive analysis above, the study utilized a relational analysis measure, a t-test, to determine any relationship and a change in the outcome variables. The results were as follows shown in Table 4.

Table 4. Paired Samples Test

		Paired Samples Test								
		Paired Differences							Significance	
					95% Confidence Interval of the Difference					
		Mean	Std. Deviation	Std. Error Mean	Lower	Upper	t	df	One-Sided p	Two-Sided p
Pair 1	var1pre - var1post	.03173	1.97994	.06787	-.10149	.16494	.467	850	.320	.640
Pair 2	var2pre - var2post	-1.64943	4.94967	.26533	-2.17128	-1.12757	-6.217	347	<.001	<.001

For the financial knowledge questions, the number of correct responses increased, but the result was not statistically significant; $t(850) = .467$; $p = .640$; $n = 851$, indicating the analysis for this measure had 850 participants, with a *p-value* of *.640 (not significant)*.

There was a statistically significant result for the financial wellness questions; $t(347) = -6.217$; $p < .001$; $n = 348$. This indicates the data analysis for the instrument of financial wellness had 348 participants who completed both the pre and post questionnaire. The results showed the percentage increase in financial knowledge is significant with a *p-value* < *.001*.

Hence, the study fails to reject Hypothesis 1(H1), and reject Hypothesis 2 (H2), and safely conclude the program increased the financial wellness of the participant based on the financial wellness scale instrument shown on Figure 5.

7.10   Discussion of Quantitative Results

The results indicated a statistically significant increase in financial wellness following the program but not in financial knowledge. Based on the study's results, we are looking to add to the knowledge base of the program to increase knowledge retention and transfer to improve learning outcomes. The program and case study outcomes provide meaningful applications to the financial industry, consumer groups, educational institutions, and other governmental and non-governmental organizations. One of the implications includes the recommendation to expand financial literacy education from one solely focused on money to one that leans into the universality of well-being and can make interventions more universally applicable.

8.   How the Initiative was Received by Participants

Qualitative and quantitative results indicated that we achieved the engagement levels and impact on the learning community we set out to accomplish. Our essential measurement for the reception of the course was a net promoter score and qualitative end-of-course survey. The learners positively perceived *KYGYW* based on the Net Promoter Score (NPS). Often used to predict growth of sales, a NPS is a survey-based measure for customer responses to the following question type: *On a scale of 1 to 10, how likely are you to recommend [product] to others?* (Baehre et al., 2021). The responses to the question are grouped into the following categories: promoter (scores 9 or 10) passive (scores 7 or 8), and detractors (scores that are below 7, Baehre et al.; 2021).

Learners were asked in the Program Experience Survey, *"On a scale of 1 to 10 how likely are you to recommend this course to others?"* For the audience the course was created to serve (HBCU students), the NPS during the first semester of delivery reached 75. After the second semester, including an expanded audience, our NPS was 54, which met the industry standard for an excellent e-Learning course. As an online course, we considered this NPS proof of a positive learner experience. The secondary tool for validating the NPS was qualitative survey results, which indicated an overall increase in positive emotional sentiment regarding finances and an overall improvement in willingness to engage with financial matters. Using thematic analysis, we found the most prevalent themes were increased confidence in financial knowledge and decreased stress and anxiety around making financial decisions.

9. Plans to Further Develop the Initiative

The KYGYW program has several strategic growth opportunities in the next 18 to 36 months. The first opportunity is to expand into the workplace benefit and employee learning and development space. The second is to broaden the audience by building a Spanish version of the course to serve more than 62 million Hispanic Americans. The third expansion of the program is to build comparable programs with the same e-Learning format that focus on specific financial decisions or transitions like retirement. These courses will incorporate all the same best practices but allow for a deeper dive into the application and how-to content for a specific topic. Beyond the expansion of the curriculum, the biggest goal is to expand the use of the program to more individuals and use the data to inform continued course improvements and drive impact toward expanded financial health and wellness.

References

Baehre, S., O'Dwyer, M., O'Malley, and Lee, N. (2021) "The use of Net Promoter Score (NPS) to predict sales growth: insights from an empirical investigation," *Journal of the Academy of Marketing Science*, 50(1), pp. 67–84. Available at: https://doi.org/10.1007/s11747-021-00790-2.

Engerman, J.A. and Otto, R.F. (2021) "The shift to digital: designing for learning from a culturally relevant interactive media perspective," *Educational Technology Research and Development*, 69(1), pp. 301–305. Available at: https://doi.org/10.1007/s11423-020-09889-9.

Gidley, J.M., Hampson G.P, Wheeler, L. and Bereded-Samuel, E (2010). "From Access to

Success: An integrated approach to quality higher education informed by social inclusion theory and practice," *Higher Education Policy*, 23(1), pp. 123–147. Available at: https://doi.org/10.1057/hep.2009.24.

Gudmunson, G., and Danes, S. (2011). "Family financial socialization: Theory and critical review," Journal of Family and Economic Issues, 32(4), pp. 644–667. Available at: https://doi.org/10.1007/s10834-011-9275-y.

Jorgensen, T.J. (2020). *Inclusive financial well-being and empowerment: An intersectional analysis.* Doctoral dissertation, University of Georgia.

Jorgensen, T.J. (2022). *KYGYW Impact Report: HBCU and Central Indiana Partners* [PDF file]. The American College of Financial Services https://drive.google.com/file/d/17rFPkW5f9dIwMAxcKQno-_4iA3cMklRz/view

Na, K. and Han, K. (2023) "How leaderboard positions shape our motivation: the impact of competence satisfaction and competence frustration on motivation in a gamified crowdsourcing task," *Internet Research*, 33(7), pp. 1–18. Available at: https://doi.org/10.1108/intr-12-2021-0897.

Remenyi, D. (2013). *Case study research* (2nd ed.). Academic Conferences and Publishing International Limited.

End Notes

1. *Know Yourself, Grow Your Wealth®* is a registered trademark of The American College of Financial Services.
2. eLearnCommerce™ is trademarked by CodeisCode Marketing & Consulting, LLC.

Author Biographies

Valencia L. Gabay is Program Director of Financial Education and Wellbeing, The American College of Financial Services. Mrs. Gabay is an instructional designer, organizational scholar, international speaker, and co-author of *Group Coaching and Mentoring: A Framework for Fostering Organizational Change*. She is currently completing a Ph.D. in Organizational Leadership from Indiana Wesleyan University.

Dr. Timi J. Jorgensen is Assistant Vice President and Assistant Professor of Financial Education and Wellbeing at The American College of Financial Services. Previously, Dr. Jorgensen completed a fellowship with The College. Her research focuses on diversity, equity, and inclusion in financial services and well-being and empowerment.

Valencia L. Gabey et al

Dr. Martha Fulk is Assistant Professor of Financial Planning at The American College of Financial Services. Previously, Dr. Fulk served as a Program Director and Assistant Professor of Financial Education and Wellbeing in the Institute for Learning Innovation and Center for Economic Empowerment and Equality.

Dr. Grady L. Batchelor, Jr. is Senior Vice President, Institute for Learning Innovation, The American College of Financial Services. Previously, Dr. Batchelor served as Assistant Provost, Vice President, Dean, Faculty Director, and Associate Professor of Business Administration at the American Public University System.

The C-4X Protocol for Remote Instructional Support for Physical Classrooms:
An e-Learning Model for the Revitalization of Teacher Education and Classroom Instruction

F. Todd Goodson, Eileen Wertzberger, Debbie Mercer and Tracey Conway
Kansas State University, USA
tgoodson@ksu.edu
ejm7777@ksu.edu

Abstract: As a research university with a large teacher education program, Kansas State University has a long-standing mission of developing new pedagogies to serve the needs of K-12 schools and in preparing the next generation of teachers. Toward that end, we began experimentation with the delivery of remote instruction through telepresence robots as an alternative to the traditional student teaching internship. Extending from that work, we have developed a well-articulated set of protocols for the delivery of remote instruction in multiple formats and contexts, injecting non-local instruction remotely to enhance learning within traditional K-12 classrooms. While we initially turned to the robots to provide a student teaching experience in a single instance when a traditional placement could not be secured, that experience later proved invaluable for teacher education candidates unable to work in face-to-face classrooms during the COVID pandemic. Out of that experience with our "robot student teachers" grew our research into innovations in the use of remote teachers to enhance traditional learning as well as the potential of remote experiences to enrich the teacher education sequence for all candidates. Ultimately, our research led to the C-4X Remote Instructional Support Protocol which focuses on four components unique to distance-mediated instruction:

Keywords: Culture, Co-Teaching, Climate, Construction.

1. Background

When we create remote teaching interactions across distance, we can cause both teachers and students to learn about previously unfamiliar cultures. At

Kansas State University, we are doing that through purposeful experiences for novice teachers across international and regional boundaries. Our research indicates that when we bring remote teachers into an existing physical classroom, we must provide both the remote and the physical teacher advanced practices of the co-teaching model. The C-4X model contains a well-articulated system to prepare both remote and on-site educators to maximize their unique partnership. The establishment of a positive classroom climate is essential to learning, and the C-4X model directly prepares remote teachers in strategies to impact positively remote classrooms. Finally, our model prepares remote teachers to support the construction of new knowledge with methods and methodologies unique to instruction delivered remotely to classroom settings.

2. Introduction

As formal education evolved from an activity limited to the elite social classes to our current understanding of education as a basic human right, one assumption has remained largely unchallenged. That is, the basic unit of instruction is the single classroom controlled by a single teacher. In recent years, the trend toward additional staff to support classroom teachers attempts to reach mainstreamed special needs students has accelerated, but the model of one room/one teacher has persisted as the dominant structure of instructional delivery through the decades. Even as other professions—from physicians to auto mechanics, from attorneys to construction workers—have seen a proliferation of specialization and protocols for advanced teamwork (including the leveraging of non-local expertise to address local practice), education remains stubbornly fixed in its roots which trace to the isolation of individual classrooms. Indeed, as school bells sound to mark the beginning of instructional periods, the ritual closing of the classroom door remains a marker identifying the symbolic closing off of the outside so that the class, the teacher and the students, create learning in private spaces, and while this is both nostalgic and perhaps even romantic in a sense traditionalists can appreciate, our work begins with the assumption that it is past time for K-12 schools to open their physical and symbolic boundaries to the larger world beyond.

Our work connects to two distinct, but interrelated, aspects of professional education. We seek to improve both the way teacher educators prepare teachers for the next generation of classrooms, and we are equally concerned with the quality of learning that occurs withing those classrooms. That is to say, while our work is largely built on research with pre-service teachers, the implications of our work apply to all of K-12 education. We believe our C-4X model holds the potential to enrich the teacher education process and to revolutionize the way face-to-face teachers in physical classrooms can be supported in their work remotely by persons who could be one of several different types of support persons. As a growing teacher shortage threatens education across the globe, we believe our model holds promise for bringing additional resources to K-12 classrooms with remote support for those physical classrooms. Clearly the traditional vision of a single classroom teacher assigned responsibility for all aspects of a single physical classroom must be reexamined in light of current skilled labor shortages. Schools of all types are being forced to rely on individuals who, during previous eras, would not have met minimum standards for professional licensure as educators to serve the needs of students. The profession is moving in the direction of a tiered structure of levels of educator expertise in which the fully prepared master teacher has less direct contact with a few students and more oversight responsibility for less well-prepared professionals who work at the classroom level with small groups of students.

We believe the C-4X model is one uniquely well-suited to these times, as it provides a structure through which highly qualified outside sources (e.g., fully licensed teachers, content experts, professional practitioners, pre-service teachers) can add value to large numbers of remote physical locations synchronously by way of any number of appropriate technologies.

3. The Infrastructure

Our experiences that led to the development of the C-4X Protocol were guided by a series of three opportunities, each building on that which came before. It began when we were unable to secure a student teaching placement for an out-of-state student in our online graduate-level teacher licensure program. It is always a challenge to work across state lines in the United States with K-12 teacher licensure programs, and this particular situation was a worst-case scenario. The student was exceptionally well-prepared and motivated, but the political and logistical challenges in negotiating a placement in a local (for the student) school proved insurmountable. In desperation, we decided to attempt a virtual student teaching experience. In those pre-COVID days, the very idea of a remote student teaching experience was neither established as a professional practice nor widely supported by practitioners and policy makers. Nevertheless, we identified a local elementary school with a bold and creative principal and an innovative classroom teacher and together we agreed to attempt what was then an unspeakably bold proposition. In short, we purchased a telepresence robot, and our graduate student conducted her student teaching virtually in an elementary school in Kansas from her home in another state.

We knew what we were doing was controversial, so rather than attempting to do it without calling attention to ourselves, we did the opposite. We publicized what we were doing to all who would listen. We sent a videographer to the elementary school to film a very short documentary about the experience, and our Director of Field Experiences did a research study documenting the experience (Wertzberger, 2019). What we took from the experience was the idea of *co-teaching* (e.g., Friend, Reising, and Cook; 1993). We had long considered ourselves authorities on the co-teaching model through our traditional residential student teaching protocols (Yahnke and Shroyer, 2014), but the virtual student teacher taught us that co-teaching is a very different proposition when one of the co-teachers is not physically in the classroom. We learned that the depth of communication between a physically present teacher and a remote teacher is exponentially deeper and more substantive, and we brought those insights forward toward the development of the C-4X Protocol. We know from years of professional experience that virtually all student teachers and cooperating teachers say they engage in co-teaching. Our first robotic student teacher taught us that co-teaching is not an either/or proposition. Rather, it is layered and we would learn potentially much deeper than we realized. When one professional is not physically present in the room, the relationship between that professional and the one present requires an entirely new level of communication and planning. Where a traditional student teacher and cooperating teacher might spend an hour and the end of the day planning out lessons, and that is certainly an important part of the mentoring process for the novice teacher. However, professional planning across physical distance adds dimensions that, we now believe, enhance the depth of the planning process.

The second opportunity was one we neither anticipated nor desired, but the global COVID-19 pandemic upended the assumptions that governed teacher education. From the perspective of the pandemic, the objections to our previous work with the remote student teacher seemed quaint. When the governor of our state closed all public schools in her jurisdiction without warning, the schools found themselves scrambling to become adept at remote instruction in a matter of days. At the same time, we had over 200 student teachers in the field who instantly became remote student teachers, and all of objections we confronted to our robotic experimentation that student teaching simply couldn't happen without a physical placement in a physical classroom became moot.

From the two years we were enmeshed in the pandemic, we came forward with the notion of *climate*. In K-12 education we have for many years stressed the importance of classroom climate (e.g., Fraser, 1989). We have stressed to pre-service and in-service teachers the value of establishing a warm inviting environment in which students can achieve without distraction. The trauma inflicted on K-12 schools and teacher education units by the pandemic not only reinforced for us the importance of climate, but we became painfully aware of how much different is the challenge to create a positive climate in a virtual space (especially one in which no one, neither teacher nor students, is participating voluntarily). The pandemic forced us to grow in uncomfortable ways toward creating comfortable non-physical spaces for learners. Looking back at the kinds of advice we traditionally gave pre-service and practicing teachers about classroom climate—truisms about establishing trust, building relationships, setting boundaries, communication—all had to be adapted to the remote contexts imposed by COVID. Moving forward toward our evolving protocol, we came to understand that some of the approaches we use in physical proximity to our students must be adapted when we are teaching remotely. Taking it one more step, when we are bringing an outside presence in remotely to a physical environment, we are forced to consider how to move beyond the initial distraction provided by the non-local teacher, how to move beyond novelty toward a purpose and positive classroom climate that is more than that which could be established either remotely or physically (Wertzberger, 2023; Wertzberger; In Press). We came to understand the remote voice could transform the local climate in uniquely positive ways.

The third formative event was an innovative international service-learning project we developed to take advantage of what we had learned to that point. Based on a long history of engagement with teachers and university faculty in Ecuador, we sent four telepresence robots to four middle schools in Ecuador, and several students in an honors section of our instructional technology class provided remote support for English language teachers on site at the schools there through literature circles (Daniels, 2002). Our research pertaining to this field experience suggests that remote field experiences are a viable way to build the intercultural competencies of educators (Goodson, Clark, Wertzberger, Ellner, Palacios, Under Review).

It was certainly nice to be past the COVID experience of forced innovation and into the more comfortable space of new initiatives driven by faculty experience and expertise. The Ecuador service-learning project took full advantage of what we had learned about co-teaching and climate, but the cross-cultural, international aspects challenged us in new ways. We were forced to consider the importance of *culture* in ways we previously had not. Higher education generally and teacher education specifically has long championed the importance of diversity and multiculturalism. Nevertheless, the United States K-12 teaching force continues to be dominated by white females. Of course, those teachers have all dutifully taken courses in multiculturalism and diversity, and teacher education institutions have been held accountable for providing field experiences that require engagement with diverse populations of American students. However, we have long known we need to do much more to recruit diverse teacher candidates and to better prepare all educators to reach all students.

Our undergraduates working in the Ecuador telepresence service-learning project took away powerful insights about culture that far exceeded what we could have provided with our existing domestic coursework and practicum experiences in local schools. The project also helped us develop the cultural component of the C-4X Protocol as an essential quality necessary for remote support for local physical classrooms. Field experiences that cross national and linguistic boundaries force pre-service teachers to confront their own socio-linguistic heritage and their biases in powerful ways, and this project helped us sharpen our tools for remote support for local classrooms.

As we combined all we have learned from the three foundational experiences, we came to the element of *construction* as the unifying component. The construction of new knowledge, skills, and dispositions that serve as the reason for existence of the classrooms. The remote student teacher was constructing her skills as an elementary teacher as she assisted her students in their construction of the critical skills in literacy, numeracy, citizenship, and so on. Our collective COVID trauma and the accompanying pivot to remote instruction caused us to construct entirely new skillsets with regard to remote schooling in ways we did not previously imagine to be possible. Our Ecuadorian service-learning project forced us to confront communication across cultural boundaries and how remote teachers must construct cultural knowledge to interact with new communities just as the new communities benefit from exposure to the culture the remote teacher brings to the classroom. Remote teachers who would support local teachers must interact, must co-teach, in ways that make the student experience more robust because of the way the local and the non-local cooperate toward a common purpose. It is this complex interaction across the four areas—culture, co-teaching, climate, and construction—that serves as the framework for delivery of remote support for local, physical classrooms.

4. The Challenges

The C-4X Protocol is a powerful framework for a new structure critically needed at this time in education, the bringing of outside expertise to enhance the learning in physical classrooms. The challenges break down into four general areas: technological, interpersonal, cultural/linguistic, institutional/political.

Technological issues are always in the forefront, yet once resolved, they are the least important factors. In each of the three institutional experiences described above, we worked through significant technological challenges (e.g., getting a telepresence robot through the correct ports in a highly secure K-12 district firewall). When the technical challenges are present, they are the most important issues of all because until resolved, the entire enterprise is at risk. We accept at a given that any technologically mediated intervention in local sites will involve initially technical challenges as well as occasional challenges following. It is essential to have the resources in place to respond forcefully and immediately to the initial challenges in order to avoid the entire project losing credibility with both teachers and learners before it can effectively begin.

Whenever we bring personalities from outside into a confined local space such as a classroom, the interactions of the remote person first with the local teacher and then with the local students becomes a critical challenge to confront. The co-teaching area of emphasis is a reflection of the importance of creating a solid bond between the inside and the outside, as the student experience will be enhanced or constrained by the quality of that relationship. It is essential that the instruction leaders, local and non-local, are committed to the process. This is a dish best serve voluntarily. In our experience, nothing stalls the process more than when we discover once the process is underway that a teacher, usually a local site teacher, was mandated to participate. Above we discussed the longstanding culture in education of a single teacher in control of a single classroom. That model not only persists, but anything that opens the classroom to outside voices is potentially intimidating to some classroom teachers. We believe the C-4X model is best approached initially with those local teachers who are, if not eager, at least curious about the process. We further believe our model reflects inevitable trends in education globally, but again, the process of progress moves more quickly with initial participants who are enthusiastic.

Cultural differences provide challenges, and linguistic boundaries, when present, complicate those challenges. It is critical to confront those challenges directly and openly with a common goal of enhanced student learning. We believe that every challenge is an opportunity, and cultural and linguistic boundaries are very powerful opportunities to leverage learning and to expand the worldviews and positionalities of all parties, both teachers and students, if the challenge is met purposefully with a wise understanding of the nature of *difference* and a plan to celebrate cultural differences and integrate them into the overall learning plan.

The final challenge which we have labeled "political" is invisible, yet it is the most serious of all. Institutions such as a school have long functioned as an insular, self-contained phenomenon, and schools have little history of bringing outsiders into their local structures. As mentioned above, the labor shortage in the market for licensed teachers has created a crisis that calls out for additions resources and new structures. The political histories of schools that are largely self-sufficient will not endure through the present time. We believe the C-4X Protocol provides a framework to help break down those barriers to bring outside resources to benefit local students.

5. How the Initiative was Received

As mentioned above, our initial experience with the remote student teacher was challenged, both internally and externally. At the same time, our research into the experience was well-received as a provocative study, but when COVID changed the conversation in unalterable ways, we were positioned (briefly) as experts in the challenge of remote student teaching (although the entire teacher education world would quickly catch up). Our Ecuadorian service-learning work, we believe, addresses critical cultural issues that enrich the experience of prospective teachers (e.g., Phillion,

Malewski, Sharma, and Wang, 2009). One interesting observation that we did not entirely expect that became apparent early on in the Ecuadorian service-learning experience was the fascination on the part of the Ecuadorian middle school students with all things American. We discovered that we needed to help our American pre-service teachers understand what was happening and coach them toward a stance that engaged the students' culture as well. When someone is intensely interested in us, it is flattering and tempting to stay in that warm glow of appreciation and interest. However, that is not ultimately where we want to be. We want to recognize all cultures as inherently valuable and interesting, and we want all parties to emerge from the classroom enriched from each other.

To return to the previous distinction made above between teacher education and K-12 education. Our work focuses on both, but it is also important to unpack those differences and recognize that both areas of focus might not be relevant for all situations. We need to better integrate technology and culture in both teacher education and education in the field. Collectively, we believe our work highlights the potential of technologies to enhance teaching, learning, and teacher education (Johannessen, Rasmussen & Haldar, 2023).

6. The Learning Outcomes

We believe our initiatives advanced learning on several levels, and we believe the C-4X Protocol holds tremendous potential to transform K-12 education in ways we probably cannot predict today with certainty. On the professional level, the in-service and pre-service teachers learned pedagogical skills in terms of the integration of technology, the ability to function effectively within a co-teaching model, the discovery of previously unfamiliar cultures, and the ability to collaborate across space. While it is more difficult to define student learning through the initiatives, it is reasonable to suggest the students gained access to knowledge and expertise they would not otherwise have experienced, and they had the opportunity to participate in the construction of new frameworks for learning as they evolved in response to global events.

Looking at the impact across each of our initiatives, we moved to develop fully our protocols for non-local support for local classrooms. The first point we must acknowledge is the degree and form the non-local support takes. This naturally includes the technology used to bring the non-local support into the classroom. If a remote resource is simply serving as a non-synchronous resource, for example, responding by email to student questions, that is a very different thing than a non-local resource who participates in real time through a telepresence robot. In the first instance, the non-local resource might well be providing an important service, that that engagement is non-physical and non-synchronous. In the second instance, we have a full physical presence in the classroom synchronously. The most likely third scenario would be a non-local resource participating synchronously through a product such as zoom. This led us to develop our understanding along a continuum reflecting both locality and synchronousness.

Non-Synchronous	Synchronous	Synchronous
Non-Physical Presence	Non-Physical Presence	Physical Presence

Next we developed a descriptive framework of the key elements of each component of our C4X model.

Co-Teaching	Climate
• Integrated Planning • Content • Instructional Methods/Activities • Instructional Delivery • Assessments	• Positive Climate Plans • Climate Redirection Plans • On-Going Monitoring/Assessment of Climate • On-Going Climate Enhancement Strategies
Culture	Construction
• Mapping Primary Cultures Present • Planning to Acknowledge and Validate Primary Cultures Present. • Planning to Leverage Cultures Present for Learning • On-Going Evaluation and Revision	• Clearly Defining Intended Learning Outcomes • Mapping Actual Learning Outcomes • On-Going Instructional Revisions • On-Going Programmatic Revisions

Co-Teaching: Co-teaching is a critical component of establishing the professional dynamics of a virtual educational setting. In the realm of teacher preparation, co-teaching requires that the cooperating teacher and preservice teacher engage in ongoing collaboration and planning to ensure that the content, instructional methods, instructional delivery, and assessments are conducive to the locality of the classroom (i.e. virtual or in-person), as well as the level of synchronousness of the learning interactions. In this model, co-teaching positions both the cooperating teacher and the pre-service teacher as learners, as they problem-solve and adapt to the demands of the virtual and physical space.

Climate: In this model, climate refers to both the environment (i.e. virtual and in-person), as well as the inclusive nature of space. For in-service and pre-service teachers, this means that they must intentionally design an environment that affirms students' identities and cultures, makes space for learning differences, and integrates student-centered approaches that are adaptable to the demands and logistics of e-learning settings. They must also redirect and adapt these environments to be responsive to the needs of their learners, as needed. Thus, climate includes both the spatial components, as well as the socio-emotional and cultural realities of their students.

Culture: This framework centers the cultural and linguistic richness of the communities and families that comprise each classroom. This requires that educators learn the cultural identities of their students and communities, and that they actively embed these components into their lessons and pedagogical approaches. It also requires that they prioritize and honor the cultural and linguistic identity of their students in the design of their virtual and in-person environments.

Construction: As a foundational component, construction, and more specifically, co-construction, of learning opportunities and outcomes is essential. Specifically, it is important that teacher preparation programs and educational institutions seek ways to leverage technologies to build intercultural and multicultural experiences that enrich the learning of all participants. This requires extensive engagement of stakeholders, including pre-service and in-service teachers, K-12 administrators, and teacher preparation programs to design, implement, and revise their learning experiences so that they leverage the strengths of various cultures to improve learning outcomes for students.

Each of the four components of the model is the subject of acknowledgment, planning, on-going evaluation, and revision. Collectively, this process ensures both local and non-local instructional resources are fully engaged and aware of the uniqueness of both themselves as individuals as well as the students they are attempting to instruct. Plans are developed, enacted, and constantly revised to maximize both the moment-to-moment climate in the physical classroom as well the contrast between our intended learning outcomes and that which the students are actually learning.

7. Plans to Further Develop the Initiative

As previously indicated, we believe the C-4X Protocol is a framework that can support the transformation of K-12 teaching globally. Schools cannot continue to rely on a single expert teacher solely responsible for learning within physical classrooms. The classroom needs to open to the world, and we simply must find a way to bring outside knowledge and culture to the experiences of students sitting in their local physical classrooms.

To achieve this, we have developed this set of protocols to assist the development of co-teaching skills across time and space. We have processes to bring outside teachers and other sources of knowledge to local classrooms in ways to enhance, rather than destabilize, the classroom climate. We have learned to work with remote and local teachers on leveraging culture in ways that enrich all parties involved, and we suggest that all of this take place within the context of the construction of powerful new knowledge, skills, and dispositions. Our intention is to continue to implement the C-4X Protocol within new contexts, contexts that cross regional, social, national, economic, and linguistic boundaries. We are prepared to assist professional educators in all contexts to develop alternative pedagogical structures that can mitigate the teacher shortage while bringing new voices to classrooms to the benefit of students.

Our first effort toward these ends is our Virtual STEAM Camp project now planning for its third year. Initially a response to the COVID pandemic, this project uses local instructors (mostly current K-12 teachers) to provide a summer enrichment program planned and delivered for remote sites around the world. To date, we have developed partnerships with schools in Ecuador, Colombia, and Nigeria. Plans are underway to expand to additional nations in Latin America, Asia, and the Middle East. Targeting middle school aged students and organized around thematic STEAM topics, these short courses last one week each, so that the local sites can select from our menu four different courses lasting through the month of June (although we are beginning plans to expand this program to a yearlong set of opportunities). The project is a slight adaptation from what we have discussed above in that the primary responsibility for instruction is with the remote, non-local resource (in this case, our teachers hired to deliver the STEAM Camps), but this process involves planning and collaboration as outlined in the C-4X model with the local teachers leading the students in the physical locations. Our ultimate goal is to move toward dynamically connecting those global sites in order to leverage more powerful learning through those connections. It is also our intent to use our Virtual STEAM Camp as a working site to continue our on-going research toward further developing the C-4X model with an initial focus on building out the specific points describing articulating strategies and approaches specific to each of the four components. We look forward to a book manuscript fully elaborating the model for a global audience.

8. Conclusion

Just as is the case with many complicated things, it sounds simple to bring someone in remotely to a physical classroom to assist student learning. The challenges and barriers outlined above are, however, very real. As we have noted, teachers are not accustomed to opening their classrooms to outsiders. Schools lack structures to cross traditional systemic boundaries. As human beings, our conditioned biases all too often make us suspicious of outsiders rather than seeing someone different as an opportunity to expand our personal fields of vision. And before we can get to any of that, we have to be able to make the technology work seamlessly. The truth is, it is very hard. What the C-4X Protocol does is profound in its simplicity. It offers a framework to do something that seems simple but is virtually impossible. With support, the C-4X Protocol can allow willing schools and teachers to break free from existing structures and transform the nature of the experience of receiving a K-12 education. That we believe is important.

References

Aronson, B. A. (2016). From teacher education to practicing teacher: What does culturally relevant praxis look like? *Urban Education*, 55(8-9), 1115–1141. https://doi.org/10.1177/0042085916672288

Baumgartner, L. M. (2001). An update on Transformational learning. *New Directions for Adult and Continuing Education*, 2001(89), 15–24. https://doi.org/10.1002/ace.4

Daniels, H. (2002). Literature circles: Voice and choice in book clubs and reading groups (2nd edition). Pembroke Publishers.

Fraser, Barry J. (1989) Twenty years of classroom climate work: progress and prospect, Journal of Curriculum Studies, 21:4, 307-327, DOI: 10.1080/0022027890210402

Friend, Marilyn, Monica Reising & Lynne Cook (1993) Co-Teaching: An Overview of the Past, a glimpse at the Present, and Considerations for the Future,Preventing School Failure:
Alternative Education for Children and Youth, 37:4, 6-10, DOI: 10.1080/1045988X.1993.9944611Goodson, F. Todd, Clark, Spencer, Wertzberger, Eileen, Ellner, Mark, and Palacios, Eder Intriago. Cross-Cultural Remote Field Experiences: Building Multicultural Competencies in Preservice Teachers through the Use of Telepresence Technology. Under Review.

Johannessen, L. E. F., Rasmussen, E. B., & Haldar, M. (2023). Student at a distance: Exploring the potential and prerequisites of using telepresence robots in schools. *Oxford Review of Education*, *49*(2), 153–170.
https://doi.org/10.1080/03054985.2022.2034610

Phillion, J. A., Malewski, E., Sharma, S., & Wang, Y. (2009). Reimagining the curriculum: Future teachers and study abroad. *The Interdisciplinary Journal of Study Abroad*, *18*, 323–339. Retrieved February 1, 2022, from https://eric.ed.gov/?id=EJ883706.

Sharma, S., Phillion, J. A., & Erik, M. (2011). Examining the Practice of Critical Reflection for Developing Pre-Service Teachers' Multicultural Competencies: Findings from a Study Abroad Program in Honduras. *Issues in Teacher Education*, *20*(2), 9–22. Retrieved February 1, 2022.

Wertzberger, E. (2019). The Future of Field Experiences in Distance Education: A Case Study of Co-Teaching Practices in a Telepresence-Facilitated Field Placement. *Theory & Practice in Rural Education*, *9*(2), 35–46.
https://doi.org/10.3776/tpre.2019.v9n2p35-46

Wertzberger, E. (2023). Critical Spatial Theory: Analysis of the Effect of the COVID-19 Pandemic on First-Year Teacher Practices and Efficacy in Physical and Virtual Spaces. In E. Langran, P. Christensen & J. Sanson (Eds.), Proceedings of Society for Information Technology & Teacher Education International Conference (pp. 1410-1419). New Orleans, LA, United States: Association for the Advancement of Computing in Education (AACE). Retrieved September 21, 2023 from https://www.learntechlib.org/primary/p/222011/.

Wertzberger, E. (In Press). Critical Spatial Theory: Analysis of the Effect of the COVID-19 Pandemic on First-Year Teacher Practices and Efficacy. In *Research Highlights in Technology and Teacher Education*. United States: Society for Information Technology and Teacher Education

Yahnke, S., & Shroyer, M. (2014). Theory into Practice: The KSU PDS Model. *Educational Considerations*, *42*(1). https://doi.org/10.4148/0146-9282.1040

Author Biographies

F. Todd Goodson is Associate Dean for Teacher Education in the College of Education at Kansas State University.

Eileen Wertzberger is an Assistant Professor and Director of Field Experiences in the College of Education at Kansas State University.

Debbie Mercer is Dean of the College of Education at Kansas State University.

Tracey Conway is a Professor of Practice in the College of Education at Kansas State University.

Diagnosis Zombie:
An Interactive Lesson on Brain and Behaviour

Jane Guiller, Alex Oliver, Ken Rice, Emma Gibson and Jordyn McNally,
Glasgow Caledonian University, Scotland, UK
J.Guiller@gcu.ac.uk

Abstract: Diagnosis Zombie is an innovative blended learning experience to enhance learning about brain and behaviour. It consists of a 45-minute online, live and interactive lesson and follow-up, in-person, one-hour small-group collaborative task. The objective is to enhance student learning of complex brain structure and function through an immersive and fun experience. Participants play the role of lab assistants granted access to a secret zombie research facility. Green screen technology situates the 'lead research scientist' in an atmospheric tunnel. Two zombies have recently escaped from this facility. Learners are shown 'recovered footage' of the zombies undergoing experiments before their escape. They are questioned on what they witness using polls and chat. The challenge is to identify 7 brain parts that are compromised in each zombie and showcase these in menu creations designed to nutritionally aid the zombies. The infrastructure needed for this initiative were teaching staff, a learning technologist and two students. Video conferencing software was used, alongside green screen technology, OBS studio, Mixamo, Blender and Sketchfab to create the brain and zombie videos. Significant challenges were overcome in creating this initiative. Initially, a platform was to be used with the instructor wearing a VR headset and manipulating 3D models live and broadcasting online. Animated zombies were imported successfully, but this platform did not allow for audio. Diagnosis Zombie moved to a more stable format of prerecorded video resources using 3D models and zombie animations shown as 'recovered footage', damaged and grainy to fit with the atmospheric backdrop in the live broadcast. Our future plans include a follow-up video call with the zombies using MetaHuman – AI that enables high-fidelity digital humans through the Unreal engine. The initiative was very well received. It had a positive impact on student engagement as shown by behavioural, cognitive and affective indicators, and 90% rated it as an excellent or very good learning experience.

1. Introduction

Diagnosis Zombie is an innovative blended learning experience to enhance learning about brain and behaviour. It was developed as part of a wider 'Co-Creating Immersive Learning Experiences' project, funded as part of an internal university teaching and learning innovation scheme. These projects are aligned with university strategic vision and the goals of transformative education and learning and teaching excellence. A key component of such projects is the collaborative approach between students and staff and across subject areas. Diagnosis Zombie was Phase 1 of the wider project to co-design engaging lessons for first year students using virtual reality (VR) and immersive learning environments.

Figure 1: Diagnosis Zombie title screen

Educators across the world are tasked with providing engaging online and blended learning. Technology has advanced, along with attitudes towards the use of technology for teaching including immersive learning technologies such as Virtual Reality (VR). VR can be defined as a complex media system that enables sensory immersion through specific technology and a sophisticated means to represent content (Makransky & Peterson, 2021). Research supports the use of VR to enhance the student learning experience in a wide range of pedagogical applications (e.g., Allcoat & von Muhlenen, 2018; Dyer et al., 2018; Hamilton et al., 2020; Herrera et al., 2018; Markowitz et al., 2018).

However, it is currently not feasible with large student numbers for learners to simultaneously learn 'in-headset'. Although we have access to VR lab facilities and offer around 150 Applied Psychology undergraduate students first-hand, in-headset experiences per year, we currently cannot send out a headset to every student. VR-by-Proxy (McDonnell, 2022) was proposed as a way to harness the potential of immersive technologies to improve the student experience – a sort of 'middle ground' between traditional methods and virtual reality. One pedagogical advantage is the improved online learning environment in terms of increased use of 3D models for visualisation.

Immersive learning design is a dynamic educational approach that typically falls into one of four types, according to Maas & Hughes (2020). These are simulation, game-based learning, reality technologies and 360-degree videos. However, immersive learning design can also involve other non-technological elements and strategies including storylines, narratives and role play. For example, immersive pedagogy places learners within a narrative. The narrative can be based around real world or fictional scenarios and learners positioned within this. The goal may not be to replicate reality but to get learners to suspend their disbelief and buy into their assigned role. Chirico & Gaggioli (2023, p. 227) describe the positive impact of immersive experiences on learning as 'memorable, meaningful and emotionally engaging'.

The aim of Diagnosis Zombie was to improve the experience of learning introductory neuroscience. Peck et al. (2006, p. 167) notes 'some topics in introductory psychology are more difficult for students than others'. Out of 16 introductory psychology topics, they found students had the second lowest exam scores for biopsychology (neuroscience and biological foundations), even though it typically gets more extensive coverage in introductory textbooks (Griggs et al., 1999). Peck et al. suggest that instructors need to do more to promote students' motivation for, and learning of, biopsychology and neuroscience. As Armellini (2021) argued, student engagement is a two-way process, so we aimed to improve student engagement by creating an engaging blended learning experience to teach a complex and often daunting topic for first year psychology students.

Traditionally, biopsychology is taught using 2D diagrams and images in textbooks. Sahiti and Stamp (2022) argued that certain subtopics in psychology, such as psychobiology and neuroscience, are advised to make more frequent use of visual stimuli (e.g., neuroanatomy) in teaching that may benefit particularly from 3D displays. We wanted to move from 2D images to 3D models and animations to teach brain structure and function.

We wished to move to a more hands-on, interactive and collaborative learning approach to teaching neuroscience to first year psychology students. Capturing students' attention particularly in the online environment was deemed to be a crucial first step in enhancing learner engagement. Finding a way for students to get to grips with the complex terminology involved in neuroscience was also a priority so we wanted to create a memorable learning experience to facilitate retention of knowledge and understanding of the human brain. We needed to create a multimodal experience involving a variety of media formats to capture attention and memory.

Zombies were selected as a vehicle through which complex brain anatomy and function could be taught. Zombies feature in popular culture through film, TV and video games so they are familiar and relatable for learners. They exhibit distinct behavioural patterns such as rage and aggression, impaired cognition and compromised motor skills. Two zombie characters were created, Doug and Eartha. These zombie creations showed complementary behaviours based on the depictions in popular culture of a traditional slow-moving, uncoordinated reanimation (Doug) and the fast and rage-filled zombie (Eartha). Learners were introduced to a storyline involving captured zombies in a secret research facility who undergo experiments designed to test their sensory and motor functions.

This took place during a 45-minute online lesson followed by a 1-hour in-person group task designed to consolidate learning through a word play task (creating a 3-course nutritional rehabilitation menu for the zombies based on their identification of the relevant brain parts in each zombie).

2. Infrastructure

The infrastructure needed to create and run the Diagnosis Zombie initiative involved a team of two lecturers, a learning technologist and two students. Tutors were involved in facilitating the smaller in-person group task. We created and embedded a 'Students-as-Digital Scholars' approach as a key element of the wider project. This entails 'lived learner experience' reflection to inform design of future learner experiences, co-conduct scholarly work and co-create lessons and resources.

Two second-year students were employed in September 2022 to reflect on their experience of learning introductory neuropsychology with a view to enhancing the learning experience of the future cohort starting in October 2022. This involved reviewing current brain structure and function resources used on the introductory psychology module and exploring digital resources including 3D assets freely available from Sketchfab.

Our learning technologist created zombie models using Blender and the face rig functionality. Two zombies were created called Doug and Eartha. The project team created 13 experimental scenarios designed to test the zombie's sensory and motor functions relating to vision, smell, touch, hunger, thirst, movement, balance, facial recognition, pain reaction and aggression, as a way to illustrate brain structure and function and highlight the compromised brain areas in each zombie. Each zombie had 7 dysfunctional brain parts relevant to the exhibited behaviours. We reviewed the freely available zombie animations in Mixamo (e.g., 'zombie vomits', 'zombie falls over') and extracted these for use in the zombie experimental scenarios. The learning technologist and one of our Student Digital Scholars recorded the zombie audio to give Doug and Eartha their voices.

These videos were then used in a 45-minute live, online session broadcast via the university Virtual Learning Environment, Blackboard. This live session was set in a fictional secret underground zombie research facility using green screen technology. The learning technologist created a backdrop for the fictional facility (see Figure 3). The lecturer as 'lead zombie scientist' broadcasted live from this setting using OBS Studio, free and open source software for video recording and live streaming. One of the Student Digital Scholars managed the live polls during the session. Seven poll questions were launched during the session to test learner knowledge and understanding of the 'brain training' (i.e., the 4 short brain structure and function videos using 3D models) and facilitate their application of this knowledge to figuring out the which parts of Doug and Eartha's brains had been affected by this apparent new strain of zombie virus.

140 students were invited to join the session as trainee lab assistants to help diagnose the zombies and were emailed a (virtual) access lanyard prior to the event. A total of 109 students joined the live session via the Collaborate Ultra video conferencing tool in the Blackboard Virtual Learning Environment. They were introduced to the zombie narrative by the 'GRR Lab Lead Zombie Scientist' who was their Lecturer wearing a lab coat and broadcasting live from the GRR zombie research facility. Learners were introduced to the captured zombie narrative then underwent their 'brain training' in introductory neuroscience and watched a series of short videos introducing them to brain structure and function using 3D models of the human brain.

Students attended a smaller seminar class the following week in which they were given materials such as paper, pens, play dough and clay, formed teams and challenged to design a 3-course nutritional menu for each zombie using the 7 dysfunctional brain parts they had identified during the online session. They were given a set of structured lab notes and access to a recording of the live session to aid them in this task. Each team posted their menu creations to a Diagnosis Zombie Nutritional Rehabilitation Padlet wall and from this, the Diagnosis Zombie team selected a winning team based on the number of correctly identified brain parts and creativity of the menu design and presentation.

3. Challenges

Technical barriers were encountered through use of the VR-by-Proxy platform Edify. We were drawn to this platform initially due to the potential to overcome the challenge of creating digital content for immersive learning and VR platforms. VR-by-Proxy (McDonnell, 2022) is argued to hold educational value as an approximation of a fully immersive experience via a Head-Mounted Display (HMD). There may be advantages for learners in engaging with virtual experiences, even when done indirectly. For example, it may capture learner's attention, boost motivation, and enhance engagement, leading to successful achievement of the learning outcomes. Additionally, there is value for all learners in visualising the brain in 3D and understanding its structural components compared to merely examining 2D diagrams. VR-by-Proxy is not a passive learning experience, as learners can collaborate and remotely guide the instructor within the virtual environment, in an interactive session.

Edify provided a number of pre-existing, virtual-world like environments and digital avatars, along with the ability to obtain and import free 3D content from Sketchfab without the need for coding expertise. This meant we could potentially import the brain and zombie models to Edify and then broadcast this to our students via Microsoft Teams (see Figure 2). Figure 2 shows a zombie imported into the Edify virtual lecture theatre environment.

Figure 2: Zombie model successfully imported in the Edify software

After successfully importing 3D brain models to Edify, we tested the manipulation of these in a live context via the university WiFi and encountered problems with the user experience from both educator and user perspectives. We were also aware that some users would potentially have poor WiFi/broadband connections. Another problem was identified with the beta version of the Edify software as we had difficultly importing audio and we needed to be able to talk to our zombies and have them respond to us in order to illustrate some aspects of their dysfunctional brains.

Our learning technologist came up with a solution to use the more stable format of short, high-quality videos for both the 3D brain and zombie animations interspersed with the live broadcast from the secret underground research facility. To do this, our learning technologist created an atmospheric graphic (see Figure 3) and this was used as the background in a live broadcast via green screen technology and OBS Studio.

We revised the zombie storyline to incorporate a narrative of 'recovered footage' and made this grainy to fit with the storyline of the footage being damaged when the zombies mysteriously disappeared after the experiments were conducted. This had the advantage of creating reusable resources in the form of the 13 short zombie experiment videos and 4 brain structure and function videos while also setting up the narrative for a follow-up to teach the next set of learning objectives.

Figure 3: Glasgow Reanimation Research (GRR) Lab

4. How the initiative was received by users or participants

Diagnosis Zombie was very well received by the users. We polled the 98/109 students remaining at the end of the live, online 45-minute session and asked the question 'how would you rate this as a learning experience?'. Ninety per cent rated it as an Excellent (42%) or Very Good (48%) learning experience. We also received many positive comments via the chat function at the end of the live session. A selection of these are below.

"Different way of learning and funny to watch at times!"

"Something new and different and fun"

"Loved it (heart emoji)"

"It was a great way to learn something different!"

"Much easier to digest the information this way"

"So good!!!!!!!!"

"Fun way to learn"

"Really enjoyed it"

"Had a great time, slay Doug slay"

"Fun way of learning the brain and itss (sic) impacts"

"Was something different and funny at times too"

"Fabbb"

"Loved it"

"Superb like"

"Really enjoyed this way of learning"

Eight weeks later students were sent their standard Module Evaluation Questionnaire and Diagnosis Zombie was consistently highlighted as a positive aspect of their course, as shown in the comments below:

"The Zombie thing was really good and really fun and enjoyable which was memorable."

"I thoroughly enjoyed the zombie part of the module - I feel I learned a lot and it was very engaging."

"The zombie interactive diagnosis class was awesome. Personally I enjoyed the brain menu task too."

"The zombie lectures were really well presented, and were very interactive."

"It was extremely fun and made the content stand out in a much different way which helped me to better remember what we were learning."

"The zombie lecture was very engaging and enjoyable. It was a good execution of seeing how brain defects can affect an individual."

Our Student Digital Scholars ran an online focus group via the Line chat app with a small group of participants (N = 5). This let us interpret the positive ratings and comments further, using the framework for student engagement by Bond & Bedenlier (2019) and Bond et al. (2020). Student engagement is defined as 'the energy and effort that students employ within their learning community, observable via any number of behavioural, cognitive or affective indicators across a continuum' (Bond et al., 2020, p. 3). Evaluation data was analysed for the behavioural, affective and cognitive indicators of student engagement and mapped to aspects of the Diagnosis Zombie blended learning design.

+ *Behavioural indicators*

Behavioural indicators are concerned with how learners display learning-oriented behaviour. For example, observational data of the live session showed that students were 'behaviourally engaged' in that they attended the session, took notes and 90% of attendees were still responding to the polls and chat questions at the end of the 45-minute session. The focus group data showed that student engagement was facilitated by making them part of the narrative and capturing and sustaining their attention through the interactive elements of the session such as the live polls. The multimodal elements of text, audio, video and interactive elements helped engage students. They reported feeling immersed in the zombie narrative and appreciated elements such as the access lanyard, the lab coat and the use of green screen technology. One focus group participant made a fascinating comment in relation to the session, showing their ability to temporarily accept fiction as reality. Their statement that "the use of the green screen and that Jane (Lecturer) was in a uniform made it seem more real and it was really effective". The learner's use of the word 'real' is interesting here as it appears the realistic elements (lab coat, research facility backdrop) blended with the fantasy elements worked to capture learners' attention and facilitate understanding.

+ *Affective indicators*

Affective indicators are to do with how a learner feels before, during and after a learning event. It was noted beforehand that students expressed disappointment at being told they were going online for their lectures for one week due to previous dissatisfaction with online learning before coming to university. However, Diagnosis Zombie had more than exceeded their expectations of what online learning could be. Focus group data revealed that students felt they were engaged before, during and after the session as they felt 'excited' and 'motivated to attend' when they received the lanyard granting them access to the GRR Lab as a lab assistant. This piqued their curiosity and excitement about the nature of the session.

Evaluation and focus group data frequently featured the words 'fun' and 'enjoyable' when participants described their experience of Diagnosis Zombie. Learners consistently experienced positive emotions throughout the live session. Humour was also stated as facilitating engagement. Learners said it made a difficult topic more approachable and one focus group participant commented 'it made me want to learn more about the brain' suggesting that it sparked intrinsic motivation for engaging more deeply with the neuroscience topic.

+ *Cognitive indicators*

Cognitive indicators are the strategies that are in place to facilitate learning. It was interesting to observe the aspects of the immersive learning experience that students highlighted as useful to their learning and compare this to our intentions as instructors. The interactivity was consistently highlighted through the evaluation and focus group data as a design aspect that students found very useful for their learning. Participants highlighted that the experience was 'very interactive' and felt this added to their learning. Students appreciated the structured lab notes, which helped them record their observations and remember complex terms and names of brain areas. The design of the session in terms of observing zombie behaviours and relating these to brain function appeared to work for students as they stated 'exploring the brain and observing reactions helped my understanding'. Students reported that this tested their understanding as they had to 'apply their knowledge in a new way' and it made it 'easier to remember brain parts and understand what they do'. Focus group participants also highlighted that the '3D models were very useful'.

Participants also made some useful suggestions for improvements to the design of the session to positively impact learning, e.g. providing the captioned videos before the live session for them to adequately prepare notes and get to grips with the complex terminology, rather than showing them in the live session. This is essential feedback to reduce the cognitive load of notetaking and learning complex terminology during the interactive session.

Focus group participants were also positive about the cognitive value of the follow-up seminar in which they created the zombie menus as this creative task reinforced their learning of the complex neuroscientific terminology through the 'word play' task of inventing dishes composed of brain parts. However, a very small number of students reported in a student-staff consultative group that they did not enjoy working with play dough or clay.

5. The learning outcomes

Student achievement of the learning outcomes was evidenced in a number of ways. First, student performance in the live polls during the online session was recorded. These polls allowed us to capture student learning in the moment and whether or not students were picking up on the clues in the videos. The performance in these multiple-choice poll questions was, on the whole, very good. The dynamic and interactive nature of the session meant that it was possible to replay a video and go over aspects of the learning that the users appeared to be struggling with, as a formative assessment strategy.

We were also able to observe achievement of the learning outcomes relating to knowledge and understanding of brain structure and function through the lab notes completion and zombie nutritional menus in the follow-up on-campus groupwork. We have not formally assessed the work produced for the number of correct answers, although this is planned for the next running of Diagnosis Zombie.

6. Plans to further develop the initiative

Our takeaway messages are that embedding affective, cognitive and behavioural engagement indicators may help facilitate student engagement and learning. This initiative has provided some evidence and future work will look to evidence the learning taking place through student performance in the formative assessments.

Our initiative shows that immersive learning technologies can be used creatively to enhance user engagement. The success of Diagnosis Zombie has been recognised internally through a collaborative teaching commendation in the Teaching Impact Awards 2023 and a successful infrastructure bid to upgrade the VR lab facility. This lab has now been renovated opened up as a multimedia studio to grow cross-university collaborations in immersive learning experience design.

We are currently working with colleagues in Applied Computer Games on the next instalment of Diagnosis Zombie to launch in October 2023. This will see a rerun of the original Diagnosis Zombie with enhancements based on the evaluation data and then a new session in which we finally track down our zombies Doug and Eartha, one year on from their mysterious disappearance and have a live video call with them.

We are exploring use of digital avatars as realistic digital human representations of Doug and Eartha to chat with them (either online or on-campus). We will have our participants generate questions and present some new symptoms to teach the next section of the course and facilitate achievement of the learning outcomes relating to aphasias and neurological abnormalities of the right and left hemispheres of the human brain. Currently, we are exploring MetaHuman and working on an Epic MetaGrant for Education application for this work. Zombies are a popular cultural phenomenon that are iconic and relatable for students. They can serve as a springboard for discussions across psychology, biology and ethics.

Diagnosis Zombie 2 will address the next set of course learning objectives through reconnecting with the zombies who, as it will be revealed, were taken by a zombie activist group. This lets us teach ethics around the nature of the experiments in DZ1 and also introduce related interdisciplinary and contemporary material, e.g. the concept of 'psychobiome' – the link between the composition of the gut microbiome and CNS functions such as mood, cognition and mental health.

References

Allcoat, D. & von Muhlenen, A. (2018). Learning in virtual reality: Effects on performance, emotion and engagement. *Research in Learning Technology*, 26. https://doi.org/10.25304/rlt.v26.2140

Bond, M. & Bedenlier, S. (2019). Facilitating Student Engagement Through Educational Technology: Towards a Conceptual Framework. *Journal of Interactive Media in Education*, 11. https://doi.org/10.5334/jime.528

Bond, M., Buntins, K., Bedenlier, S., Zawacki-Richter, O. & Kerres, M. (2020). Mapping research in student engagement and educational technology in higher education: a systematic evidence map. *International Journal of Educational Technology in Higher Education, 17*(2). https://doi.org/10.1186/s41239-019-0176-8

Chirico, A. & Gaggioli, A. (2023). How real are virtual emotions? *Cyberpsychology, Behavior and Social Networking, 26*(4). https://doi.org/10.1089/cyber.2023.29272.editorial

Dyer, E., Swartzlander, B. J. & Gugliucci, M. R. (2018). Using virtual reality in medical education to teach empathy. *Journal of Medical Library Association*. https://doi.org/10.5195/jmla.2018.518

Griggs, R. A., Jackson, S. L., Christopher, A. N., & Marek, P. (1999). Introductory psychology textbooks: An objective analysis and up-date. *Teaching of Psychology, 26*, 182–189.

Hamilton, D., McKechnie, J., Edgerton, E. & Wilson, C. (2020). Immersive virtual reality as a pedagogical tool in education: a systematic literature review of quantitative learning outcomes and experimental design. *Journal of Computers in Education, 8*(1). https://10.1007/s40692-020-00169-2

Herrera, F., Bailenson, J., Weisz, E. Ogle, E. & Zaki, J. (2018). Building long-term empathy: A large-scale comparison of traditional and virtual reality perspective-taking. *PLoS ONE, 13*(10). https://doi.org/10.1371/journal.pone.0204494

Maas, M. J., and Hughes, J. M. (2020). Virtual, augmented and mixed reality in K–12 education: A review of the literature. *Technology, Pedagogy and Education, 29*, 231–249. https://10.1080/1475939X.2020.1737210

Makransky, G. & Peterson, G. B. (2021) The Cognitive Affective Model of Immersive Learning (CAMIL): A Theoretical Research-Based Model of Learning in Immersive Virtual Reality. *Educational Psychology Review, 33*, 937–958. https://doi.org/10.1007/s10648-020-09586-2

Markowitz, D. M., Laha, R., Perone, B. P., Pea, R. D. & Bailenson, J. N. (2018). Immersive virtual reality field trips facilitate learning about climate change. *Frontiers in Psychology, 9*. https://doi.org/10.3389/fpsyg.2018.02364

McDonnell, N. (2022). Virtual reality without a VR headset? It can be done! https://www.edify.ac/blog/vr-by-proxy-a-step-change-for-esg-training

Peck, A. C., Ali, R. S. & Levine, M. E. & Matchock, R. L. (2006). Introductory psychology topics and student performance: Where's the Challenge? *Teaching of Psychology, 33*(3), p. 167-170.

Sahiti, Q. & Stamp, J. A. (2022). The use of visuals in undergraduate neuroscience education: Recommendations for educators. *Teaching of Psychology, 49*(3), 276-283. https://doi.org/10.1177/00986283211000326

Author Biographies

We are an interdisciplinary team co-creating immersive learning experiences for undergraduate students, based at Glasgow Caledonian University in Scotland. In our project team are academics Dr Jane Guiller and Dr Alex Oliver, Learning Technologist Mr Ken Rice and Student Digital Scholars Emma Gibson and Jordyn McNally.

Jane Guiller et al

Digital Presentations in Higher Education:
An Australian Perspective

Tomayess Issa and Dr Mahnaz Hall
Curtin University, Australia

Tomayess.Issa@cbs.curtin.edu.au
mahnaz.hall@curtin.edu.au

Abstract: The usage of digital presentation assessment tasks in postgraduate units, namely ISYS6004[1] – Green Information Technology and Sustainability and ISYS6014[2] – Knowledge Management and Intelligent Systems at an Australian university will be investigated in this study. A digital presentation task has been included in higher education units as it has become increasingly evident from industry feedback that graduates lack fundamental skills, both personal and professional, that are required for their studies and future careers. Students should acquire and/or improve these abilities to be prepared for both their studies and employment, since businesses throughout the world need their employees to have specific talents and attributes. By completing a digital presentation task as part of their overall academic assessment, students will develop various skills, engage in independent learning, and learn to access new, cutting-edge information as it becomes available nationally and internationally. The inclusion of a digital presentation assessment in the ISYS6004 unit is intended to encourage students to share their understanding of the course content by discussing the new sustainability model that will be implemented by an actual company to become more sustainable. In the ISYS6014 unit, students are expected to create and present an ontology for an actual company to seek the classification and explanation of entities in a logical way. Before the final submission, the lecturers' formative assessment including academic integrity principles is conducted, aiming to act with honesty, trust, fairness, respect, and responsibility. This formative feedback is intended to help students improve their work

---

[1] ISYS6004: This unit examines, and analyses issues related to green information technology, sustainability, models, and developing and establishing a new Information Technology (IT) sustainable strategy.

2 ISYS6014: This unit introduces knowledge management from an Information Systems perspective. It includes Knowledge discovery, Knowledge Management Processes, Knowledge Capture, Knowledge Management Strategy and Planning, Knowledge Management Models and Tools and Knowledge continuity management, Artificial Intelligence (AI) systems, expert systems, ontologies, semantic web, and Organisational Learning and Organisational Memory.

before the final submission, and to give them the knowledge they require to prepare and present a digital presentation that meets the assessment criteria in terms of content, layout, and delivery. The adoption of these techniques by lecturers will help to ensure that generative AI tools like ChatGPT and Bard are used less frequently (Dwivedi et al., 2023; Volante et al., 2023).

Digital presentations in higher education can present challenges for lecturers and students. 1) Students' assessment tasks are graded according to specific criteria, with rubrics related to language, delivery of supporting material, central message, sources and evidence, conclusion, and/or recommendations; 2) students need constant encouragement and motivation by their lecturers and fellow students so that they are able to deliver oral presentations confidently and without hesitation. In this study, the completion of the digital presentation assessment was inspiring for the students and lecturers, as students learned new concepts and benefited from the lecturers' formative feedback on how to prepare the PowerPoint slides' content and layout and how to present in a professional way. The design of the digital presentation assessment task had several aims: 1) to improve students' oral communication, time management, self-confidence, motivation, and English-speaking skills; 2) to increase students' interest in learning; and 3) to help students collect, organise, and construct relevant information. These skills were improved through specific activities undertaken in class by individuals or teams. The students were motivated to complete tasks on time while seeking and obtaining cutting-edge information to support their work. In the future, digital presentation assessment tasks will be part of other units from different disciplines in the same faculty and other faculties in the University as a means of strengthening research goals and purposes.

1. Introduction

Currently, a job profile requires employees to be equipped with advanced personal, professional, and technological skills that will enable them to contribute to economic and social growth. Therefore, higher education institutions should take some responsibility for ensuring that students are adequately equipped with the skills required by future employers. To this end, lecturers have begun to use digital presentations as one of the assessment tasks designed to impart and improve students' personal and professional skills, particularly those sought by organisations and businesses. Additionally, a number of studies (Goulart et al., 2022; Ramos et al., 2023) have shown that using technology, such as digital presentations, will motivate students to become autonomous learners and strengthen their academic and interpersonal skills, particularly because it gives them ready access to their lecturers' comments.

The main objectives of including digital presentation assessment tasks in higher education courses is to allow students to demonstrate how they organize and apply information and principles in their presentations. This approach encourages students to engage in independent learning, while also improving their personal and professional skills and knowledge. The digital presentation task in the two units required students to conduct a real-world case study of a company and present their sustainability model with a focus on the application of information technology (IT). Furthermore, the digital presentation had several objectives: to persuade the audience, to meet the assessment criteria, and to show the level of organisation demonstrated by the students. Furthermore, there are two main reasons for utilising this assessment approach: 1) today's students are lacking several necessary professional and personal skills required for their studies and future workplace; and 2) it is important that academic integrity be maintained, especially in an era when AI tools can be used as a means of generating assessment-related work.

2. The infrastructure

In this study, 138 students from ISYS6004 (from 2018 to 2023) and 89 students from ISYS6014 (from 2018 to 2022) participated. Our students are part of the postgraduate level, completing their Master of Commerce in Information Technology and Information Systems, and their age ranges from 25 to 45 years. The nations represented by our students are Australia, Asia (including India), the Middle East, North and South America, Russia, Mauritius, and various parts of Africa. A diversity of different cultures and nations is a significant aspect of these units, since during their engagement in class activities, all students are obliged to interact with and share their knowledge and skills, experience, and cultural opinions with other students. Students can learn from one another and through their interactions, they develop a sense of self-worth, communication skills, and confidence by exchanging knowledge and cultural views. To achieve the project objectives, a digital presentation model was used in both units (see Figure 1).

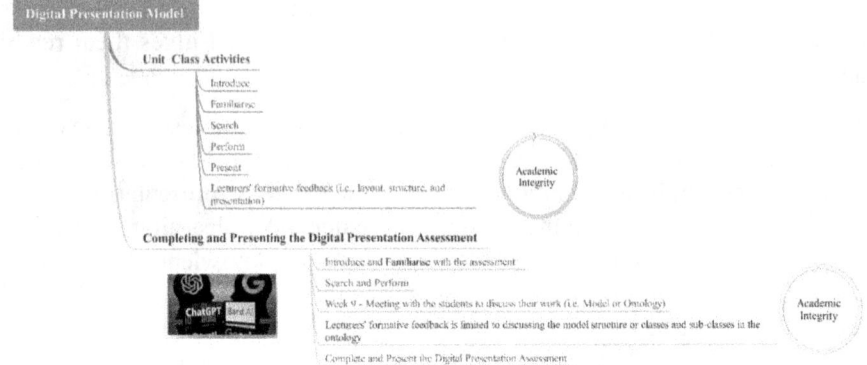

Figure 1: Digital presentation model – prepared by the lecturers.

The digital presentation model is divided into two phases: 1) unit class activities, and 2) completing and presenting the digital presentation assessment. In the first phase, the unit class activities are introduced in the first week of the semester, and the lecturers introduce the activities, explaining their aims and providing accurate guidelines for completing them. Students familiarise themselves with the activities by searching for the appropriate answers using the library databases to perform and present them based on the activity guidelines. During the class, the students present their activity findings to their colleagues using PowerPoint or a concept plan individually or in teams. Formative feedback is essential in our teaching, as we provide advice to students in order for them to improve their learning, achieve high-quality academic outcomes, sustain results, learn from their mistakes, and acquire new knowledge. Furthermore, this type of feedback gives students an indication of what they are doing well and where they may need to focus to better succeed. In addition, the formative feedback in the first phase encourages, motivates, and guides students to the correct path and provides instructions to help them perform well in the digital presentation assessment. After the presentation, the lecturers provide their formative feedback on the students' presentations based on the layout, structure, and delivery, taking into consideration the integration of academic integrity principles. The major impact of this experience is that the students' professional and personal skills, motivation, and confidence gradually improved.

As for the second phase, in week nine, a virtual 30-minute meeting is conducted with each student to discuss and provide formative feedback toward the IT sustainable model structure for ISYS6004 and the classes and subclasses in the ontology for ISYS6014. These tasks are critical to the digital presentation because unless students understand them, they will be unable to fulfil the objectives of the digital presentation. During the meeting, the lecturer asks each student whether his or her contribution is original and to acknowledge the factors that motivated them to complete the assessment task. Based on the digital presentation model in ISYS6004 and ISYS6014, the number of referrals for academic misconduct and requests for extensions have decreased dramatically, while the assessment's average mark has increased by 28.5% for ISYS6004 and by 17.6% for ISYS6014 (see Table 1). These percentages determine that our study outcomes are reliable and valid.

Table 1. ISYS6004 and ISYS6014 Digital Presentation Average - Prepared by the Authors.

ISYS6004 unit Digital Presentation average 10%	
2018	6.4%
2019	6.8%
2020	7.3%
2022	7.5%
2023	8%
ISYS6014 Unit Digital Presentation average 15%	
2018	8.8%
2019	9.3%
2020	9.8%
2021	10%
2022	10.5

Adopting and implementing the digital presentation model in both units, especially the lecturers' feedback, prevented students from repeating the same mistakes, and improving their learning approach and independent thinking skills. In addition, integrating academic integrity into the digital presentation assessment motivated students to complete their work with their team based on the detailed assessment guidelines and lecturers' formative feedback. This, in fact, minimised the use of generative AI tools such as ChatGPT and Bard as both assessments for ISYS6004 and ISYS6014 are based on actual companies in Australia and overseas, and students are required to share the company websites with the lecturers to confirm their availability.

For ISYS6004, besides the digital presentation, students were required to complete a report for a real company, identifying its current IT problems and, based on examining several models that focus on sustainability and green information technology, they developed a sustainable IT model that will be used in the future to make the company more sustainable. Based on the report's findings, the students presented a 25-minute digital presentation in MP4 format, discussing the problems, model, and recommendations. For ISYS6014, students developed an ontology for an actual company by describing the classes, sub-classes, domains, and relationships between them to obtain the necessary knowledge required for top-management decision-making.

3. The challenges

Digital presentation marking and motivating students can be challenging. A rubric (see Appendix 1) with the following criteria was utilised to assess each student's digital presentation: language, delivery, supporting material, central message, sources of evidence, conclusion, and/or recommendations. The practical assessment is worth 55% for ISYS6004 and 45% for ISYS6014, and digital presentation is worth 10% in ISYS6004 and 15% in ISYS6014. The use of formative assessment and clear assessment rubrics encouraged students to have a learning experience that was engaging, inspiring, and memorable.

Considering motivation, the lecturers urged their students to participate fully in class activities initially by completing certain activities individually or in groups. The lecturers played a positive role in class as they examined every student's input and discussed this during the planning stage, offering timely formative comments to improve the student's involvement before the submission. Following this, the students were required to submit their results based on their research and activities and discuss them with their peers. All students, especially the more reserved ones, were encouraged and inspired by this activity to complete their assignments on time with high quality.

In terms of measuring and evaluating the learning outcomes of our study; ISYS6004 students are required to complete three assessments namely, wiki collaborative writing (25%); reflective journal (20%), and practical assessment including digital presentation (55%). For ISYS6014, the assessments are reflective journal (30%), blog assessment (25%) and practical assessment including digital presentation (45%). The reflective journal assessment is an individual assessment intended to provide students with valuable experience when reviewing and recording the main points in materials from textbooks, journal articles, and the Internet critically, creatively, and reflectively.

In addition, this assessment encourages students to keep up with their reading and their ongoing search of WWW sites for information relevant to the unit. The reflective journal not only requires a summary of materials; it is also intended to indicate students' reactions to and opinions about the material provided by various sources. Each journal must include comments from the textbook(s), e-journals, WWW Internet sites, TV programmes, and other media regarding ISYS6004 and ISYS6014 materials. This assessment developed the following skills: research, writing, technology, information search, critical thinking, reading, and use of Endnote.

As for the practical assessment, students are required to individually present their ISYS6004 (i.e., IT sustainable model) or ISYS6014 (i.e., ontology) assessment outcomes as a digital presentation. The presentation (duration: 25 minutes) must be recorded in MP4 format and uploaded with the PowerPoint slides to Blackboard. Following this presentation, ISYS6004 students submit a written report based on the digital presentation. This report should be approximately 2,000 to 4,000 words (maximum) in length, including diagrams, appendices, and references. The report should examine an actual IT department in an Australian or overseas organization. As for ISYS6014, students submit a PowerPoint presentation based on their application and creation of a knowledge management ontology for a real project using Protégé 5.5.0 software. This assessment task is intended to develop the following skills: research, oral presentation, technical skills, writing, critical thinking, decision-making, and Endnote software.

Finally, the wiki and blog assessments allow students to add, update, and modify contents on a website. The main purpose of this assessment task is to encourage students' independent learning, collaboration, and interaction. Students need to undertake several challenging exercises that require using the Wiki or Blog Tool (as individuals or in teams) to analyse and evaluate practical real-life case studies and subsequent uploading of the results to the Wiki or Blog to be evaluated by the lecturers and student peers based on the quality (not quantity) of the discussion questions submitted each week. The lecturers check the discussion board at least twice a week, on Monday and Thursday afternoons. This assessment task developed communication skills: writing, reading, debating, written presentation, oral skills, and concept map design.

4. How the initiative was received by the users or participants

Both informal and formal feedback was gathered during the semester to show the students' perceptions of their university learning experience, and this feedback included comments about the unit and the lecturers' teaching methods. In our university, we collect two types of evaluation feedback to determine whether or not the educational goals are being met. Informal feedback is a teaching and learning innovation that allows students to anonymously comment on the unit's structure, layout, the lecturers' instructions, assessments, and how the learning experience could be improved during the semester. This feedback is intended to help lecturers improve their approach before the end of the semester and in the future.

Another method is formal feedback (eVALUate), which is collected through the University's formal evaluation process at the end of the semester. It is intended to gather and evaluate student feedback about their educational experience and gives them an opportunity to provide anonymous assessments of the units and teaching style. Students additionally communicate their opinions on their learning using the reflective process, which increases their level of involvement with the subject. During the fourth week of the semester, students' opinions are gathered through informal feedback while they remain anonymous. While the informal student feedback is only comprised of qualitative comments, the official (eVALUate) evaluation includes both quantitative and qualitative replies.

Based on the formal and informal feedback, the students confirmed that completing a digital presentation promoted their personal and professional skills and it was very interesting, motivating, and exciting.

ISYS6004 and ISYS6014 students provided the following comments regarding the digital presentation assessment task:

- The digital presentation was the best experience in this class. It was my first time to do a presentation about something I'm interested in, so I was enjoying it while I was doing the slides and searching for powerful content as well as editing it after each feedback.
- Interactive seminar with in-depth knowledge about green IT and sustainability. Gave a clear view of the term sustainability. The assessments were unit related and showed us ways in which green IT can be implemented in all sectors of the environment.
- The digital presentation assessment is very helpful in this unit. I learned many things from this unit and the assessments, especially how to give professional presentations and how to create an ontology for a real company.
- It was an amazing experience to have "knowledge management" and an intelligent system. I learned a lot from this unit.
- The practical assessment (including the digital presentation) was the most important part, which I liked very much. It helped me understand the core points of the subject matter. Moreover, it also provided the opportunity to develop new ideas, which was the most awesome thing.

5. The learning outcomes

The use of assessment tasks requiring digital presentations in the ISYS6004 and ISYS6014 units encouraged students to strengthen a wide range of personal and professional skills, as well as improving their motivation and confidence. Importantly, in week nine, a meeting was held with each student to ensure that their work was original and to determine the factors that motivated them to complete the assessment on time. The course content of ISYS6004 unit materials were related to sustainability and Green IT. On the other hand, the ISYS6014 students learned about various topics related to unit materials, such as KM tools and processes, and Artificial Intelligence (AI).

The formal feedback (eVALUate) for the ISYS6001 and ISYS6014 units from 2023 to 2018 is displayed in Table 2. The quantitative results for the ISY6004 and ISYS6014 units range from 90% to 100%, which is deemed exceptional in relation to the overall satisfaction. Students were happy and satisfied with the learning outcomes, assessment tasks, motivation, and overall satisfaction. The quantitative results for the best learning item range from 90% to 100%, which indicates that students were also very satisfied and pleased with the lecturers' effective teaching and presentation style. Many students also confirmed that their lecturers' teaching approach is exceptional and unique at Curtin University. According to student feedback, the lecturers are very approachable, encourage students to submit their assessments on time, and offer formative feedback to help them fully comprehend the assessment requirements and develop the necessary skills from completing each assessment task.

Table 2. ISYS6004 and ISYS6014 formal feedback (eVALUate)

Year	Students enrolled	Response rate	Unit	Item 1 Learning Outcomes University Average	Unit	Item 4 Assessment University Average	Unit	Item 8 Motivation University Average	Unit	Item 9 Best Learning University Average	Unit	Item 11 Overall satisfaction University Average
ISYS6004 unit												
2023	12	25%	100		100		100		100		100	
2022	24	57%	100	90	100	86	100	85	100	88	100	88
2020	10	30%	100	91	100	86	100	86	100	88	100	85
2019	22	68%	100	90	100	87	100	86	100	88	100	84
2018	23	57%	92	90	100	86	100	86	100	87	100	84
ISYS6014 Unit												
2022	25	28%	100		100		100		100		100	
2021	24	37.5%	100	91	100	86	100	86	100	88	100	88
2020	12	33.3%	100	91	100	86	100	86	100	87	100	88
2019	12	83%	100	90	70	86	80	86	90	88	90	84
2018	16	69%	100	90	100	86	100	86	100	88	100	84

ISYS6004 2023 and ISYS6014 2022: the university average is unavailable.

The students shared the following comments about the lecturers' teaching style and class activities and assessments:

- To be honest, I have never been taught by a lecturer(s) so welcomed in their office like them. The other thing which I was so excited about is the fast way of replying to the emails.
- I really like their way of teaching by providing examples and activities in the class. Just perfect knowledge and a nice presentation. Their biggest strength is their communication with each student separately and altogether via email. They stayed connected and kept reminding us of every little detail.
- The class was very interactive and engaging. I was a little sceptical doing the unit online, but the lecturer(s) was very supportive and addressed every query I had. Appreciate having her as my lecturer(s) this semester.
- The interaction and feedback I received on my tasks helped me considerably to know my weaknesses, thereby identifying where I need to put more focus in overcoming them and possibly making them into strengths in the future.
- The lecturer(s) has done excellent work, providing students with interesting, impressive lectures in a consistently professional way. Large amounts of

excellent sustainability development techniques have been presented to the classes. The arrangement of group in-class assessments provides students with valuable opportunities to learn from others; discussing with other students regarding the sustainability issue, particularly when some of the group mates are from different cultural backgrounds, is a very impressive and interesting experience. Due to the fact that each student has a stressful study load, the lecturer(s) has been very kind to postpone the deadline for assessments.

- I would like to thank the lecturer(s) for my being so welcomed at their office for me and my classmates. These enquiry hours helped me a lot to understand what is required in the journals, the presentation, and the report. The lecturer […] was helpful enough to ease the understanding of this unit for all students. Again, thanks a lot and a lot for that knowledge.
- The lecturer(s) very enthusiastic and willing to go the extra length to make sure we have the support we needed for our academic progress regardless of whether it is about the unit or not.
- There is a lot of interaction in the class which is really good. You speak with a lot of knowledge in class, you are very energetic and enthusiastic about the course, which makes the class enjoyable to be in. Very hard working and highly organized when it comes to giving feedback on assignments, exercises, and journal. There are no delays.
- The other areas of knowledge I have obtained from this unit is improving my English and research skills. That is, the task of writing approximately 3000 words from a variety of articles improved my skills in understanding complex writing as well as analysing the written text.
- Their (the lecturers') biggest strength is their communication to each student separately and altogether via email. They stay connected and keep reminding us of every little detail.
- The ISYS6014 unit provides a clear introduction to what knowledge is and what to do with it. The assigned assessments not only encourage us to use knowledge management skill, but also enhance the sharing and learning process through teamwork. Individual assessment provides a complete picture of learning outcomes.
- The ISYS6004 unit was great with such an engaging lecturer! Tomayess is very passionate about this subject; she managed to transfer her knowledge to us and engage the whole group. The topics were well presented and explained with a lot of up-to-date information and statistics, especially in sustainability and green IT. The assessment tasks were thoroughly explained, and appropriate and constructive feedback was given for making improvements in our work. There was a diverse range of learning resources and tasks, e.g., videos, wikis, group presentations, concept maps digital presentation, etc., which broadened our experience.

- The ISYS6004 unit helped me understand the importance of sustainability and green IT and the need to take the subject further to make a change in the world for the better. Furthermore, I learned how to be creative and strategic in my thinking to help society make a change regarding sustainability. Lastly, this unit helped me develop my communication and teamwork skills, which were enhanced through the various assessments.
- I think the class activities in ISYS6004 unit were really helpful. Additionally, the final assessment (including the digital presentation), even though comprehensive and time-consuming and sometimes overwhelming, helped a lot in enhancing the knowledge and awareness required to reach the goals of the unit and improved other skills, including researching, writing, etc. Not to miss out, the outstanding interaction method delivered by Dr. Tomayess and quick response to any enquiries were other factors that contributed to enhancing the knowledge. Her dedication to the unit and the class was really appreciated.
- The lecturer's biggest strength is her enthusiastic, energetic, and active communication with each student separately and altogether via email. She stays connected and keeps reminding us of every little detail.
- I love Tomayess passion for this unit and how she shared it with us. Sustainability is important and must be addressed across all fields and disciplines, especially in businesses. The unit helped me understand ICT's impacts and what actions we can take to mitigate these impacts. The class was always interactive and enjoyable to attend and participate in. The videos she shared with us were eye-opening and very interesting. Additionally, I really appreciate Tomayess's willingness to provide specific guidelines, feedback, and support with assignments.
- From my experience, the three assessments are designed in a constructive way, and by doing them with the help of the learning materials provided by the professor, I have achieved the learning outcome. Three assessments are very comprehensive; sometimes I feel it is a bit much, but by accomplishing them, it is helpful to achieve the learning outcome.
- Every assignment and lecture were well defined. I enjoyed studying the unit. It has changed my lifestyle and way of thinking.
- Two things: 1) The lecturer was helping us and accepting drafts of our assignments; she was listening to all our questions and happy to help. 2) The unit content gives us a good idea of the future of technology.
- The class was very interactive and engaging. I was a little sceptical about doing the ISYS6014 unit, but the lecturer was very supportive and addressed every query I had. I appreciate having her as my lecturer this semester. The most helpful aspect was the ontology, which makes the work easier and more interesting.

- The ISYS6004 unit is interesting. And the assessments were also good for helping me understand the unit much better. Even though the assignments were a bit hard, I think they really helped me a lot to improve my personal skills in writing, presenting an idea, and more.

In conclusion, based on the formal feedback (see Table 2) and several students' comments, the digital presentation task required by ISYS6005 and ISYS601 allowed students to obtain the necessary cutting-edge knowledge and skills and developed their ability to learn independently. They acquired and strengthened the skills required for their current studies and the workforce in the future. Currently, universities are faced with a huge challenge as generative AI tools like ChatGPT and Bard are being used by students for their assessment tasks. Therefore, one of our responsibilities as educators is to minimise the use of such AI tools. One way to achieve this is to meet with students and confirm that any assessment tasks that are submitted are their own. Furthermore, the digital presentation of their work will allow the assessors (lecturers) to gauge each student's level of understanding and the extent to which the completed task meets the assessment criteria. Finally, as academics we have the responsibility to present course content that enriches students' knowledge and improves their professional and personal skills. The activities and assessment tasks within each unit are aligned with the University's objectives, one of which is to ensure that graduates have the necessary skills and knowledge required by the employment market.

6. Plans to further develop the initiative

This study confirmed that using digital presentation in postgraduate units at an Australian university enhances students' independent learning, motivation, and confidence. Completing the assessment task will minimise the use of generative AI tools, as, during week nine, we asked students to submit drafts for feedback to detect plagiarism and improve their work before the final submission. Based on using formative feedback, requests for extensions and academic misconduct have dropped dramatically, and students have learned to prevent repeating the same mistakes and improve their learning behaviour and technical skills. Furthermore, by presenting their work in MP4 format, students can share their learning and new knowledge, which is an important component of this assessment task. This exercise was an interesting and outstanding achievement for both units, as the digital presentation average increased by 28.5% for the ISYS6004 and by 22.5% for the ISYS6014. Although the scope of the study is limited to ISYS6004 and ISYS6014 units, to increase the reliability of the initiative, in 2024 the same assessment approach will be employed in other postgraduate units in various faculties at Curtin University, with a future rollout in other universities to compare how students perceive digital presentation assessment, strengthen the research outcome, and add real-world case studies to motivate postgraduate students.

References

Dwivedi, Y. K., Kshetri, N., Hughes, L., Slade, E. L., Jeyaraj, A., Kar, A. K., . . . Ahuja, M. (2023). "So what if ChatGPT wrote it?" Multidisciplinary perspectives on opportunities, challenges and implications of generative conversational AI for research, practice and policy. International Journal of Information Management, 71, 102642.

Goulart, V. G., Liboni, L. B., & Cezarino, L. O. (2022). Balancing skills in the digital transformation era: The future of jobs and the role of higher education. Industry and Higher Education, 36(2), 118-127.

Ramos, R., Ferrittu, G., & Goulart, P. (2023). Technological change and the future of work Global Labour in Distress, Volume I: Globalization, Technology and Labour Resilience (pp. 203-212): Springer.

Volante, L., DeLuca, C., & Klinger, D. (2023). ChatGPT and cheating: 5 ways to change how students are graded. The Conversation 15 May 2023. Retrieved from https://theconversation.com/chatgpt-and-cheating-5-ways-to-change-how-students-are-graded-200248

Students' digital presentation (Sample):

- https://www.dropbox.com/scl/fo/eypfq476dz4rz9ypm8an8/h?dl=0&rlkey=2yhbo050fient8z1551ghmift
- https://drive.google.com/file/d/1us_6OHJ0xz-wgrrjeBd1d9FaTOQKC3eN/view
- https://drive.google.com/file/d/15ItAssXKMfsgcWRDmmKUDxFzjjxhDE0B/view

Appendix 1: Digital Presentation Rubric

Standards / Criteria	Below Expectations (Fail) 0-49	Meets Expectations (Pass) 50-59	Meets Expectations (Credit) 60-69	Exceeds Expectations (Distinction) 70-79	Exceeds Expectations (High Distinction) 80-100
Language (OC)	Language choices are unclear and minimally support the effectiveness of the presentation. Language in presentation is not appropriate to audience.	Language choices are appropriate for the discipline and the task. Grammar is sufficiently correct for audience understanding.	Language choices generally support the effectiveness of the presentation. Language in presentation is appropriate to audience. Evidence of some grammatical errors that cause some difficulty for audience understanding.	Language choices are appropriate and effectively used for the discipline and the task. Evidence of minor grammatical errors that rarely cause difficulty for the audience.	Language choices are imaginative, memorable and compelling, and create a riveting presentation. Language in presentation is appropriate to audience. Grammar is correct for audience understanding.
Delivery (OC)	The presenter's delivery techniques detract from the presentation. The presenter did not achieve adequate audience engagement (varied eye contact).	The presenter's delivery techniques adequately convey information. The presenter's delivery techniques achieve sufficient audience engagement.	The presenter adequately conveys relevant information through good presentation skills.	The presenter's delivery techniques strongly convey relevant information. The presenter's delivery techniques achieve strong audience engagement.	The presenter successfully conveys information effectively and maintains audience engagement through exceptional presentation skills.
Supporting Material (OC)	The overhead transparencies make insufficient reference to information and minimally supports the presentation or establishes the presenter's credibility/authority on the topic.	Supporting materials make sufficient reference to information and/or analysis, and generally support the presentation or establish the presenter's credibility/authority on the topic.	Supporting materials make appropriate reference to information and/or analysis that generally supports the presentation or establishes the presenter's credibility/authority on the topic.	A range of supporting materials is used to enhance information and/or analysis and strongly supports the presentation and establish the presenter's credibility/authority on the topic.	Significant supporting materials make clear, appropriate reference to information and/or analysis that significantly supports the presentation or establishes the presenter's credibility/authority on the topic.
Central Message (OC)	Central message is vague and is not explicitly stated in the presentation.	Central message is sufficiently clear and is stated in the presentation.	Central message is clear and consistent with the supporting material.	Central message is substantially clear and effectively stated; it is reinforced with the supporting material.	Central message is compelling. It is precisely stated, reinforced, memorable, and strongly supported.
Sources and Evidence (WC)	Incomplete and inadequate use of credible relevant sources, and Chicago referencing style was not used. Less than 15 academic journal references and textbooks, which are dated 2010 or later.	She demonstrates some use of credible, relevant sources and/or data to support ideas that are situated within the discipline and genre of the writing. Problems with Chicago reference style presentation.	She demonstrates consistent use of credible, relevant sources and/or data to support ideas that are situated within the discipline and genre of the writing. Less than 15 academic journal references and textbooks, dated 2010 or later. Minor problem with Chicago reference style.	She demonstrates the consistent use of a range of credible, relevant sources and/or data to support key ideas that are sentient to the discipline and genre of the writing. Slight errors with Chicago reference style presentation. Still less than 15 academic journal references and textbooks dated 2010 or later.	She demonstrates the skilful use of high-quality, credible, relevant sources and/or data to develop in-depth ideas that are appropriate for the discipline and genre of the writing. Excellent work under the references, using Chicago reference style correctly. Using 15 academic journal references and textbooks dated 2010 or later.
Conclusions and/or recommendations (OC)	The conclusions and/or recommendations are vague. Conclusions are not logically supported by the evidence and/or process of analysis. Assumptions are inadequately described.	The conclusion and/or recommendations are clear and relevant. Conclusions are generally supported by the process of analysis. Important assumptions are stated.	The conclusions and/or recommendations are sound, clear and relevant. Some conclusions are generally supported by the evidence and/or process of analysis. Assumptions are stated and described adequately.	The conclusions and/or recommendations are relevant, significant and organised. Most conclusions are logically supported by the evidence and/or the process of analysis. Assumptions are stated and comprehensively described.	The conclusions and/or recommendations are robust, comprehensive, relevant, significant and organised. All conclusions are logically supported by the evidence and/or the process of analysis. Assumptions are stated, comprehensively described and justification for their use is provided.

Author Biographies

Dr. Tomayess Issa is a senior lecturer, completed her doctoral in web development and human factors. She supervised PhD, MPhil, and Master's dissertations, and three of her PhD students were awarded a Letter of Commendation from the Chancellor of the University. She received local and global awards for teaching and supervision.

Dr Mahnaz Hall is a lecturer and a member of the Academic Capability Development team in the Faculty of Business and Law at Curtin University, Australia. She provides capability-building and practical guidance on innovative and effective approaches to academic skills development, assessment and curriculum design, as well as teaching practices.

uQualio Video4Learning

Hatla Færch Johnsen, Christian Bjerre Nielsen, John Gage
uQualio, USA
HJ@uqualio.com
CBN@uqualio.com
John@uqualio.com

1. Introduction to the objectives of the e-Learning initiative

The UN's Sustainable Development Goal No. 4 is Quality Education and is meant to ensure all people with inclusive and equitable quality education and promote lifelong learning opportunities for all.

The reason why this is so important is that education increases wealth & reduces poverty, leads to better health, prevents inequality & injustice, drives sustainable growth, and helps us protect the planet.

Our mission is to democratize learning by providing an affordable means for learners everywhere to gain access to the knowledge and skills that will help them to improve their lives, and their communities through education. So uQualio was founded to create and support fundamental changes in the way education and training is delivered, accessed, and maintained worldwide.

While remote learning offers people an opportunity to participate in programs far from where they live, to date, most Learning Management Systems (LMS) have been both expensive and complex, and only available to wealthy people and organizations in developed nations.

Enter uQualio, a low-cost, high-utility video eLearning SaaS solution, that offers an all-in-one package for users of all backgrounds. uQualio is a cloud-based video learning platform that is based on democratic Nordic learning principles according to which learning should be available for anyone, free, or nearly free. At uQualio, we strive to make training and learning easy and affordable for everyone.

uQualio is a profit-with-a-purpose company. We sell the online video training platform to companies and schools that pay for it, then offer it to startups at a reduced price, and donate the platform to NGOs. We passionately believe that making training accessible to everyone is a tangible way to affect positive change.

The platform itself is a video microlearning platform with built in gamification that we have developed to make it easy for subject matter experts in any area to share knowledge no matter whether for private, public, or e-commerce purposes. It is built on known technologies but put together in a new innovative way that makes it very easy to learn, and to retain knowledge in many different areas, so we can spread knowledge to improve the world for us all.

2. The Infrastructure

2.1 People

In November 2017 Christian Bjerre Nielsen (engineer, 30+ years of software development experience) as CPO & and Hatla Færch Johnsen (master in business and psychology and 20 years' experience) as CEO started developing uQualio, a video training software platform to democratize learning through easy spreading of knowledge, know-how, and innovative ideas. We believe that knowledge sharing and learning should be simple and accessible. Our mission is to make a highly effective, easy-to-use, and affordable online video training platform with self-service onboarding, to disrupt traditional cumbersome HR LMS learning systems.

uQualio' s vision is clear; to provide an online video learning platform that makes it easy and affordable for anyone to create and distribute highly effective video learning whether for private, public, and/or e-commerce purposes. With a gamified bite-size video microlearning methodology that makes it easy and fun to educate people in any size companies, start-ups, schools, or NGOs worldwide.

With headquarters in Veksø, Denmark, and an office in Ann Arbor, Michigan U.S.A., uQualio serves customers in Europe, the Americas, the Middle East, Africa, and Asia. To date, there are more than 10,500 users globally in areas as diverse as General Data Protection Regulation (GDPR) consulting, traffic control systems, medical equipment suppliers, municipal government entities, airports, hospitality, manufacturing, software, extended enterprises, charitable organizations, NGOs, schools, as well as other educational and service programs. Several NGOs are using the platform to improve the world.

uQualio's business model is straightforward:

- Companies buy our bite sized training platform for ecommerce, private, protected, or public purposes (low price for public training to spread more knowledge.)
- We donate the platform to NGOs with a good purpose.
- Start-ups get 50% discount in the first year.
1.

2.2 Software solution

uQualio is a SaaS browser-based app that does not require a download from the app store. This makes it simple to distribute courses as no download is needed to their computer or device prior to commencing training. The threshold to get users to start is much lower when they simply click the link and the big start button.

Secondly the platform is built with video at the core – the rationale is simple… We all go to YouTube to learn new things in the moment of need. The uQualio format makes it possible for schools and companies to get their own white-label video learning platform where they own the content and the data.

Interactive video-based eLearning is a highly engaging format that helps learners to focus and stay engaged. With video, learners can see and hear information presented in a dynamic and entertaining way, making it easier to understand and retain the key learning content. Video eLearning further provides a multisensory experience that engages learners on multiple levels, making it more effective for retaining information and improving learning outcomes.

In the system, you can turn any long video or webinar into bite-sized microlearning. Without any additional video editing software or video trimming tools, you can turn your videos into smaller, bite-sized micro-eLearning video clips directly with uQualio. Repurposing webinar content can therefore be done in a few clicks.

You can add titles and descriptions to each video to make it simpler for learners to find exactly what they are looking for without having to go through the entire video.

As an admin we have built the system so that it is easy to create and distribute learning. You brand the platform, build a distribution channel, and make the video content that you want available to your learners. The standardized video learning platform for education makes it easy to be consistent across your organization, while making sure everyone is getting and understanding the same topics.

You can add questions to each video to ensure that your learners understood the key messages correctly and add badges to gauge each learner's understanding level.

A video eLearning platform makes it easy to train anytime and anywhere. Log in from any device or browser and complete courses. Courses are digitally accessible online 24/7 on any device.

With uQualio you can create courses and share them in one or multiple channels targeted at different users, whether they be customers, partners, or students with different access rights.

Students are engaged by adding gamification as part of the training. People love quizzes, badges, and certifications and that makes it easy to make learning fun.

Communication and invitations on the platform are made by either sending emails and text messages to users individually or in groups. Having the ability to communicate via text messages is effective as users check their text messages frequently and almost as soon as they receive the message– 90% of text messages are read within 3 minutes (Source: https://www.cloudcontactai.com/sms-vs-email/). Emails are not checked as eagerly. Furthermore, the students can use the built-in feedback system to send back document assignments or video messages as part of their communication with the teacher.

> i. *The system has built-in reporting so you can track and measure your student's progress across the board with our customizable reporting tool.*

Anyone can sign up for a free trial account with self-service video guides, available for any step. Making it extra easy to use the secure, fully customizable online video learning platform for videos, supporting documents, interactive quizzes, built-in communication to and from users, gamification, reporting & analytics, multi-language options, and digital multilevel passing badges that can be shared on social media if relevant.

At uQualio, we aim to give power to the people by creating a horizontal structure where employees have control over their time, tasks, and approach, which helps all team members to engage, invest, and own processes. Video eLearning is an ideal tool for implementing a self-managed training program as users train where and when they need, and work in a self-paced way, a model that often brings increased satisfaction.

The uQualio platform is based on known technology but put together in a new and innovative way. The camera in smartphones makes it possible for any 'teacher' to record a video, and with the fast internet streaming the new possibility has emerged that makes it possible for people to view and get training and information in bite-sized format on their own device, computer, tablet, and smartphone, no matter where they are. So, this in combination has made it possible for almost anyone to create highly efficient learning to share with almost any target group through QR codes and links, or with invitations through SMS or email.

In this way we are giving the customers the tools they need to create, publish, and administer content in-house resulting in significantly reduced content development costs for many smaller businesses, groups, and organizations. Furthermore, the platform has no upfront costs, so getting started is free, and as it is a self-service onboarding platform there are no start-up costs or upfront investments to get a platform.

3. The challenges

3.1 Beating the forgetting curve.

One of the major obstacles in any learning environment is "the forgetting curve" by Ebbinghaus (Ebbinghaus, H. (1964). Memory: A contribution to experimental psychology). If some time has spanned between learning and using the material, it's only natural to forget all about it. So, one of the problems we have tried to solve is how do we ensure that this doesn't happen.

There are no guarantees in life, but a proven, and very successful learning methods are Spaced Learning (https://elearningindustry.com/spaced-learning-neuroscience-based-approach-to-foster-knowledge-retention), 'Microlearning' (https://scholar.google.dk/scholar_url?url=https://www.brain.edusoft.ro/index.php/brain/article/download/582/627&hl=en&sa=X&ei=p_2mZLSaJ8r2mgH68LmoAg&scisig=ABFrs3xAqDXL_HAOX1yK6fb8hi8h&oi=scholarr), and last but not least 'Lean Learning' (https://hbr.org/2019/10/where-companies-go-wrong-with-learning-and-development).

Basically, Spaced Learning relies on the power of repetition. If a certain amount of information is repeated repeatedly, in a wide variety of ways, it will be embedded into the mind.

In uQualio you see a video, you answer quiz questions, then you take a final test. This means the new knowledge is presented to a learner 3 times in a course.

The key in spaced learning is to RE-visit information to turn it into knowledge. In revisiting information, our brain inspects it and encrypts it – making it into something the brain can identify. The next step is to consolidate it.

Consolidating is essentially entering the data into long-term memory. Every day, every second, we consume a lot of information (intentional as well as unintentional). Initially, our brain stores these memories in short-term memory compartments with like or similar content. It is only when memories are consolidated that they can be recalled when needed. As data is repeated the brain can more easily imprint the information, consolidate it, and store it long-term.

Modern brain research shows that to make effective education, learning must be divided into small chunks - microlearning. It is most effective when it is delivered in chunks of a maximum of two to five minutes in length. Researchers have often discussed the maximum number of things we can remember at a time in our working memory, and the most recent studies set the limit at 3-4 pieces of information. Working memory is the memory used to temporarily store information while it is being processed before it is stored in short-term memory. This means that if you want to support the brain's natural ability to remember, new knowledge must be divided into small chunks of max. 2-5 minutes that only contain 3 things to remember at a time. This is bite-sized microlearning.

3.2 Lean Learning

Lean learning is about making knowledge available in the moment of need – learning the overall before the need arises, but getting the details in the moment of need, so like in lean manufacturing and the lean startup before it, lean learning supports the adaptability that gives organizations a competitive advantage in today's market. It's about learning the core of what you need to learn, applying it to real-world situations immediately, receiving immediate feedback and refining your understanding, and then repeating the cycle. To begin practicing lean learning, organizations need to move from measuring credits earned to measuring business outcomes created. Lean learning ensures that employees not only learn the right thing, at the right time, and for the right reasons, but that they retain what they have learned.

The uQualio interactive video eLearning platform makes it easy to create and share spaced learning programs. Simply upload your microlearning videos to make courses, use the intuitive administrators' control module to select how often the learners view the content – hourly, daily, monthly, or whatever schedule best meets your needs, publish, and everyone is on their way. And the learners can repeat the knowledge as often as they need it until they remember it.

With uQualio, learners can expect an interactive experience that keeps them engaged and focused. Features like quizzes, tests, and interactive videos enhance the learning process and ensure that information is retained. Plus, our platform is user-friendly and easy to navigate, making it simple for both trainers and learners to use.

3.3 Further challenges solved by using uQualio

Lower Training Costs: Overall, video eLearning provides a more efficient and effective way of delivering educational content compared to traditional eLearning methods. No matter whether to upskill, gain new knowledge, or simply explore interests, video eLearning provides a convenient, flexible, and cost-effective solution. You lower training costs by eliminating travel, venues, and instructor-led courses. Bringing your training online allows students to train at will and for courses to be updated when needed.

Save Time on Training: Video learning is a time-efficient way of learning, as it allows learners to consume information quickly and easily. With video learning, learners can pause, rewind, and replay content as needed, ensuring they fully understand the material before moving on. So overall uQualio helps students learn online, on-demand, and at their own pace. Ensure maximum knowledge retention and understanding by implementing quizzes and tests.

A secure and private learning environment, making uQualio a better option for organizations that need to ensure the security and privacy of their training material. There are two options for sharing content: public or private. Content published on a public channel can be viewed by anyone, while content shared on a private channel can be viewed only by invitation sent via email or SMS.

Increase impacts of workshops & classroom training: Help participants to perform better by making material available on the uQualio platform for review after the session has ended. That way, everyone has access to the key knowledge or lessons anytime and anywhere on any device.

4. How uQualio has been received by the users or participants

The learning system has been really well received by an increasing number of customers and their users – in many different use cases already: General Data Protection Regulation (GDPR) training, traffic control systems onboarding, medical equipment suppliers sales partner training, municipal government entities onboarding of new employees, airports security compliance courses, hospitality, manufacturing onboarding training, software & hardware end-user training for extended enterprises, charitable organizations, **NGO adult literacy programs**, as well as other educational and service programs.

uQualio is also being used for financial training of underbanked refugees, technical end-user training, school programs in developing countries, training municipal workers, and more.

Since our founding in 2017, nearly all our customers have reported significantly positive gains in a variety of matrices.

Specific examples include the ease of incorporating the platform into existing structures, the low subscription cost, enabling businesses to transition from document-based training to video eLearning, enhanced learner engagement, the ability to create a unified training experience for in-person as well as remote applications. Overall reduced costs, both in terms of money and time spent onboarding, upskilling, retraining, and update training.

4.1 Awards

uQualio has received several awards for its innovative design and usefulness.

- NextGen Learning system 2023 and nr. 13 worldwide by Craig Weiss.
- Global Excellence Awards winner 2023
- uQualio is Nordic Winner of Tech Rocketship Awards 2022
- uQualio is the Best End-to-End Video eLearning Platform 2022
- Global Business Awards 2021 – Best Video e-Learning Software
- INNOVATION & EXCELLENCE AWARDS 2021 AWARD WINNER
- CMO Leadership Awards EU-2021

5. The learning outcomes

Our customer testimonials are filled with positive feedback, stories of how the platform has transformed their training programs, customer interaction, and most importantly, enhanced their ability to deliver information about their goods and services.

Here are some customer testimonials and quotes about what the learning outcomes have been for their different use cases.

5.1 Manufacturing training

In 2022, uQualio participated in a comparative study by MADE – the Manufacturing Academy of Denmark - who tested uQualio's video learning solution on their Learning Factory, as one of several learning solutions to make it easy to learn to operate an industry robot.

The study was designed to discover which learning technologies are best suited for training employees in production companies. Five categories of assistive technology were included in the study:

- uQualio video eLearning platform,
- Virtual Reality
- Augmented reality (Hololens),
- Assisted Reality (RealWear)

"When digital training replaces peer-to-peer training, the workflow improves as employees are able to perform their core tasks rather than training peers." Says Camilla Nellemann, Senior Consultant, Ph.D. from MADE.DK

Hatla Faerch Johnsen, Christian Bjerre Nielsen and John Gage

The chart below contains a brief explanation of the study results that showed that video turned out to be the most efficient way of training.

Method	Test result	Cost	Advantages	Dis-advantages	Recommendations
Paper	5/12 completed the task within 25 minutes	- Work time for development of paper manual. - We used PowerPoint, which most people have installed on their computer	- Easy and cheap to develop yourself - Easy to flip through a paper manual	- Difficult to formulate a written instruction that everyone can understand - At least one hand is used to hold manuals during task solving	Suitable for organizations without a desire to digitize training
Video on mobile	7/12 completed the task within 25 minutes	- Work hours for the development of videos, as well as subscription to a learning platform. - We used uQualio.	- Easy to develop and maintain the videos - Easy to access and watch the videos on the platform via QR code	- One hand is used to hold the mobile phone while solving the problem - Notifications on the phone can be disturbing	Suitable in a training environment where mobile/tablets are allowed
VR (Virtual reality)	7/12 completed the task within 25 minutes. NB! the test subjects were given the videos as help during task solving after their VR training	- Work time to learn how to use VR as well as collaborate with external developer on content. - We used an Oculus Quest VR headset and software from SynergyXR.	- Training is possible without access to physical facilities/equipment - Risk-free to fail	- Expensive to have interactive content for VR developed and maintained by a consultant - New technology must be learned - VR discomfort may occur - The functionality of VR depends on the type of software.	Suitable for cases where virtual exercise is not possible
RealWear (Assisted reality)	3/12 completed the task within 25 minutes	- Work time to learn how to use RealWear and develop content for RealWear, as well as purchase of RealWear	- Easy to develop and maintain content yourself - Easy to navigate with voice control	- New technology must be learned - The call function reduces initiative and independence. - Difficult to see the screen clearly due to ergonomic challenge	More suitable as distance assistance than distance learning
Hololens (Argumented reality)	1/12 completed the task within 25 minutes	- Work time to learn how to use HoloLens and develop content, as well as purchase HoloLens and software for HoloLens. - We used software from SynergyXR.	- Easy to develop and maintain content yourself - AR elements are intuitive - Comfortable to wear the Hololens	- New technology must be learned - The functionality of the Hololens depends on the type of software	Suitable when the task requires the hands to be free

(Read more about the research here: https://uqualio.com/post/best-learning-solution-for-industry-4-0-video-ar-vr-realwear-and-which-learning-technologies-work-for-what)

This study has been replicated by DAMRC (Danish Advanced Manufacturing Research Center), a research institution, which focuses on performing many different projects to help the machining industry become even better. DAMRC has used uQualio to train random employees in one of their member companies. The challenge they were exploring was how to bridge the lack of TAP testing engineers. TAP testing involves understanding how a machine performs – and this technology is something that requires a lot of skill. The study found that video learning with the UQualio platform allowed the company to train a 16-year-old to become a TAP testing engineer.

> *"Initially, we were curious if we could make someone, who is not a TAP test engineer, learn how to use this technology. That's the reason why we figured out that uQualio would perhaps be the way for us to*

teach them – where the system operator could learn it in their own way and at their own pace – and we wanted to do it remotely because we are located in the heart of Jutland.

I witnessed a 16-year-old boy, who didn't know anything about machines, but tried a video instruction in uQualio, and he was really fast at learning it. Likewise, a 35-year-old operator was also quite fast in getting to know how to use it. " Mikkel Steen Meldgaard, Innovation Manager, DAMRC.

5.2   Compliance training

Kapi – Video2learn, is a course vendor that sells video eLearning courses based on Personal Data Regulation (GDPR), competition law, IT security, and marketing and they needed an easy-to-use, yet comprehensive platform for distributing their video content.

"The key benefit of uQualio is that you can jump to whatever question in a video segment, that you've answered incorrectly, and learn the right answer. The client can generate an employer certificate upon completion... but we do tell the client, 'It's not about just completing the course, it's about understanding it.' And uQualio makes it possible to see just how much the client's employees have understood the course. Which is critical in sensitive areas such as GDPR." Says Karina Juul Jensen, CEO of Kapi

5.3   Product end-user training

Fremco, an International Machinery Manufacturer, making internet fiber blowing machines needed an efficient means to remotely train users of their machines.

"Fremco's revenue normally rises by 25% annually. In 2020 we achieved a revenue increase of 34% - much higher than previous years. This was only possible with the use of uQualio." Says Kenneth Filipsen, After Sales Manager, Fremco, Denmark

5.4   NGO training of illiterates in the USA

CBREE Research, Community-Based Research for Engagement and Education, needed a way to connect with individuals, communities, and businesses to support various initiatives designed to build healthy and vibrant communities.

"We use the platform to educate adults on topics to increase their social abilities – e.g., to teach parents about media literacy so that they guide their children in the responsible, ethical, and safe use of the Internet, and to instruct people what the rules of house renting are and what to be aware of when signing a lease on a house." He continues *"We chose uQualio because it is the best platform on the market for video-based education course design and distribution."* Says Ramo Lordeni, Ph.D. Chief Executive Officer, CBREE Research

5.5 Training of municipality caretakers & senior citizens

DIGI Rehab offers a unique digital exercise solution for seniors to maintain their health and needed a way to efficiently train the municipality caretakers to support the seniors.

"The social and health care assistants ... often lack IT skills. They work under strict timelines. That's why we needed an efficient way of teaching them those skills, and it has to happen fast, so they can focus their effort on care, their important task." Says Buster Skyum, IT & Development Consultant DigiRehab, Denmark

5.6 Sales partner training in Africa & the Middle East

FUJIFILM needed a unified means of training, communicating, and monitoring the results of its programs for its employees and external partners across two continents: Africa and the Middle East.

"I need a system where I can take users on and off according to need and where I was not bound for many months. Having a user assigned to a license is a waste of money for my company. An expensive solution I couldn't bring to the board which is why I choose uQualio and at the same time it offered the flexibility, security, and support – which is essential to us!" Says Christiane Hunold, Strategic Innovations Manager, FUJIFILM Medical Imaging and IT Solutions

5.7 Software & Hardware training

APPLIED INFORMATION connects intersection controllers, preemption systems, school beacons, road signage, and more, in the United States. The Preemption system enables green waves in the intersection to ensure that emergency vehicles can arrive on average 62 seconds earlier than without the system.

Applied Information uses the uQualio platform to train its own employees, customers and end-users in an innovative way across the U.S. So far Applied Information has leveraged uQualio to craft 76 comprehensive courses, featuring over 350 educational videos that have collectively garnered an impressive 17,000 views. Furthermore, they have issued an outstanding 3,000 certificates, helping learners earn IMSA continued education credits.

The company publishes all its training video courses publicly, the content can be viewed freely by anyone, and viewers who complete the sessions are automatically enrolled as 'users'. The certifications are very often taken by ambulance drivers and police officers, as they need to be able to operate the system correctly to ensure the effects of the system.

Peter Ashley, the VP of Business Development at Applied Information explains that the main benefits he has gotten is:

"The main benefit is security and control. In other video training platforms, I cannot be 100% sure that my data isn't shared with a third-party. Or on YouTube, for instance, I cannot be sure that an ad from our competitor won't show up at the beginning of our training video. Well, the fact that we can "convert" our user manuals into video-based courses was the main one. But also, that we control the flow of information, so we could tailor it to our needs was a major benefit. That means, we can convey knowledge and expertise in our eLearning."

Furthermore, he has told us that this marketing approach was a game-changer, easing onboarding, saving time and money, while increasing sales and simplifying customer account management.

5.8 Retail training of shop floor staff

Hamelin is a major French Corporation, represented in Denmark by a subsidiary responsible for seven countries. The broad product line includes high-margin items with higher complexity that makes training sales reps difficult, expensive, and time-consuming.

180-200 sales reps at 25 – 30 locations were trained online in DK and afterwards in all Scandinavia. The campaigns featured competition for prizes between sales reps at different locations. Throughout the training period, the competitors, both individuals and teams, competed to complete sessions first and achieve the highest scores. The winners received various prizes like dinner for two, tickets to the movie theater, and so on.

While sales of low-margin products remained unchanged, the sales of high-margin products increased 70 – 80%. Participants of the training program cited product details 'being top-of-mind', as the primary reason for increased sales numbers.

5.9   STEM School Education

Thai School Online makes it possible for children from kindergarten to high-school level to study in Thai no matter where in the world they are – for this they use uQualio as their delivery platform.

On uQualio they have comprehensive microlearning courses for all topics and as kids like watching educational videos, they are seeing quite some success.

5.10   Is the initiative transferrable to other settings incl. validity and reliability.

As shown above the current customer base come from all over the world incl. USA, Canda, Europe, South Africa, Dubai and Thailand, and the platform is used for many different kinds of training in many different disciplines, across age groups and learning types, and in different countries and cultures, so our conclusion is that uQualio is transferrable to many different settings.

Our customers test our platform's validity every day, monitoring the results, and determining if it is benefiting them. Our customer retention rates speak for themselves, to date, our average customer has remained on the platform for 22 months.

As for academic testing of video eLearning's validity and reliability, we have been able to find little data on this subject, possibly because of the immaturity of the industry.

6.   Plans to further develop the initiative

At uQualio, we listen to our users, and use their input to develop the platform. We like to call it 'kaizen[3] – Scandinavian style'. Kaizen is a compound of two Japanese words that together translate as 'continuous improvement'. While core Scandinavian values include equality, teamwork, progressive social action, careful planning, and fair play.

Hatla Faerch Johnsen, Christian Bjerre Nielsen and John Gage

Our development process is ongoing and includes acting on customer requests and suggestions, adding and refining features such as built-in video editing capacity, expanding customer branding options, simplifying, and enhancing the UI (user interface) and UX (user experience), ensuring the platform is reliable, customer data is safe, and monitoring developments in the world of video eLearning in order to provide the best service possible.

Our development roadmap is published on our website (https://uqualio.com/post/uqualio-development-roadmap/) and is continually updated to give our customers an overview of our pipeline.

Our aim is to become the top-ranked learning platform and recognize that we will achieve that goal most readily with the help of our entire community. Being top-ranked means that we can achieve our mission: To ensure all people with inclusive and equitable quality education and promote lifelong learning opportunities for all!

Author Biographies

Hatla Færch Johnsen is CEO & Co-founder of uQualio. She has a Master of Social Science from Roskilde University, Denmark in Business & Psychology. She has 20+ years' experience with communication, business development, and strategy in IT, pharma, and consulting.

Christian Bjerre Nielsen is CPO & Co-founder of uQualio. He has a Master of Science in Electronic Engineering and 30+ years international experience in management, leadership, and quality in software industries.

John Barry Gage is Sales Associate Americas for uQualio. He has a Bachelor of Arts, School of Education and 30+ years international experience in education, leadership, and business.

Blended Learning UK (James Paget University Hospital NHS FT)

Tom King[1], James Pereira[1], S.J. Leinister[2], Sue Down[1] and A.D. Simpson[2]
[1]James Paget/BLUK
[2]University of East Anglia, UK

tom.king@jpaget.nhs.uk
jerome.pereira@jpaget.nhs.uk
s.leinster@uea.ac.uk
Sue.Down@jpaget.nhs.uk
andieroid@gmail.com)

Abstract: The primary objective of the course was to provide cutting edge medical education to post-graduate students in a cost effective and internationally applicable manner. This is with an overarching goal of improving patient outcomes and tackling global healthcare challenges. The Blended Learning team consists of different professionals who are the directors, marketers, technologists and administrative staff. There is a long history of working with the University of East Anglia, currently standing at more than 20 years. There is further collaboration with other professionals, such as members of the NHS consultant faculty, clinicians and educators, supervisors, and regional convenors. There are various types of software used for the different aspects of online course delivery, from video creation and editing, to 360 technology. A main challenge has been to change the mind sets of academics and clinicians as to the effectiveness of our online learning initiatives. This was addressed by our team who collaboratively developed unique and interactive educational packages and a flexible and easily accessible website. Interaction is a frequent problem with distance learning, however, the technologies in place on our courses necessitate engagement, meaning interaction is guaranteed for anyone who wishes to complete the course. The international nature of these courses has also come with certain challenges, however, we have managed to overcome these obstacles. Feedback from three different data sources reported improved clinical decision-making, and critical thinking for blended learning in comparison. Development plans include a range of new courses as well as; expansion of our scholarships, greater utilisation of appropriate and engaging technologies including AI and 3D Video, and spearheading several new initiatives.

1. Introduction

Blended Learning UK provides a suite of on-line and blended learning courses for healthcare workers, ranging from short orientation courses to three-year Masters degree programmes. The aims of the endeavour are to improve patient outcomes and find solutions to global workforce challenges through better education of the workforce. We seek to achieve these aims by developing innovative educational methodologies that optimise user engagement and provide a time-efficient delivery of learning.

Most of the courses are designed for international delivery and we emphasise flexibility and access as core components of the course delivery. The courses are designed to be cost effective, since we aim for them to be as accessible as possible, and we recognise that resources available to students can be a barrier to enrolment. By keeping the costs as low as possible, we aim to continue expanding delivery of distance learning into less economically developed countries, in the hopes of delivering training in countries that have limited access to high quality educational programmes. Ultimately, we aim to ensure that we offer enjoyable and interactive courses, as we believe, the best learning outcomes are achieved when the students enjoy the course.

Our experience is built on the University of East Anglia Master of Surgery and MSc courses that have been running for over ten years and now include students from over 60 countries. The first course to be launched in 2011 was the Masters degree programme in oncoplastic breast surgery. Oncoplastics is a comparatively new discipline within breast surgery which places equal emphasis on the cosmetic outcome of the surgery and the oncological imperative of dealing effectively with the cancer. It is now regarded as best practice in the management of women with breast cancer. There is an established training fellowship for Oncoplastics, but the trainees are based in different breast units around the UK. An online course seemed to be the best way to provide the theoretical underpinning that should underpin their clinical training. Following the successful implementation of the programme, we introduced courses in colorectal surgery and regional anaesthesia. These courses continue to run.

When we entered the international arena, it became apparent that there was a market for stand-alone Continuous Professional Development courses. The individual modules from the Masters programme are offered for this purpose. Students can register for these modules and receive a Certificate of Participation as evidence for their CPD portfolio. They may choose to undertake the summative assessments for the module and gain credits that can contribute to the Masters degree or Postgraduate Diploma should they later choose to study for a formal qualification.

In 2018 we introduced a *Competencies in Emergency Surgery* module that ran for 16 weeks and covered the Emergency Surgery curriculum of the Royal Colleges of Surgeons. The increased need for on-line courses that resulted from the COVID pandemic led us broaden our remit to develop short courses targeted to specific health care settings and skills aimed at a wide range of health professionals and students. The first of these was an *Introduction to ICU* in response to the need for clinicians from other disciplines to be seconded to ICU in response to the pandemic. This was followed by new courses in wound care, and clinical skills, aimed at nurses and medical students. More substantial courses released in the past year include *Saving Babies Lives*, a six-module programme for midwives and obstetricians, which was designed to meet the CPD requirements of the Midwifery Council and the Royal College of Obstetricians and Gynaecologists and aimed at the UK market. *An Introduction to Breast Care Nursing* comprises two six-week modules and has recruited from the UK and Africa. Taken together, these courses are working to improve the skills of those currently within healthcare and attract others to the sector. Going forward, we will continue to expand the portfolio into new specialties such as ultrasound and endoscopy providing ever more comprehensive online medical education.

Our longer courses focus on critical thinking and clinical decision making, delivering an evidence-based approach to practise which is central to the delivery of effective clinical work. They are fully interactive Considering the importance of international delivery of these courses, flexibility and access are also at the core of the programme's objectives. Cost effectiveness is another feature of the courses that we endeavour to maintain, since we aim for the project to be as accessible as possible, and we recognise that resources available to students can be a problem. Hence, we aim to continue expanding delivery of distance learning into less economically developed countries, in the hopes of delivering training in countries that require superior educational programmes. Ultimately, we aim to ensure that we offer enjoyable and interactive courses, as we believe, where there is a joy of learning comes the best learning outcomes.

2. The infrastructure

The Blended Learning team consists of different professionals: medical professionals, educationalists, marketers, technologists and administrative staff and is based within the James Paget University Hospital Trust. The programme is led by Professor Pereira and Professor Leinster who launched the Masters programme at UEA over ten years ago. They continue to be actively involved in the needs assessment for new courses and in the design of courses. They are supported by other clinicians relevant to each course and by the educational technologists in the development of the courses. The technologists are also responsible for the delivery of the courses.

The team collaborate widely with clinicians and educators from the UK and overseas in the needs assessment and in the design of the courses. Many of these collaborators will also act as tutors on the on-line courses as required. We benefit from the input from our regional convenors in North/Sub-Saharan Africa and the Middle East, Southeast Asia and India, and Latin America. Through these connections, we have managed to recruit candidates from over 60 countries. The regional convenors also provide important insights into the clinical environment in their regions, which contributes to ensuring that the programmes are relevant to their region.

There are several different types of software used in both the development and delivery of these blended learning courses. On the advice of our e-technologists, courses are built in Moodle, an open-source learning platform widely used by universities and other educational institution. It has a range of customisable functionalities that enables us to design courses to our requirements. It has proved to be a stable, easily managed platform. Videos are an integral part of all the courses. The team's e-learning technologists use Adobe Premier Pro and Acrobat for video-editing, and once videos are completed, they are then uploaded to Vimeo, which is used as a host. Once all the content is ready, it is uploaded to the Blended Learning website on Moodle. A recent innovation is the use of 360-degree visualisation created on 3D vista, software allowing for more interactive aspects to be included in our educational packages.

Student engagement in the courses is tracked using a progress bar. Each on our courses has a personal progress bar, allowing them to view their progression of the course. They can use this to manage their engagement with the course. The faculty can monitor the students' progress and prompt those who are failing to engage satisfactorily. Those students on credit bearing courses must complete at least 80% of the workload before they are awarded their qualification. The Masters students are required to track their clinical competencies as an intrinsic part of the qualification using the software package, Logitbook. This can be extended to other courses where a record of competency is necessary.

Interactivity is an important feature of online education. A lack of interactivity is a common issue with online courses and has been associated with negative educational outcomes for the participants (Maor & Volet,. 2007).

"The systematic examination of a set of selected, research-based studies on professional online learning revealed that professional online courses under research scrutiny had not been designed explicitly to foster knowledge sharing and the creation of communities of learners."

A community of learners is developed through interactivity and user engagement. We use discussion forums as a central part of our learning strategy. For the Masters programmes, the forums are a form of problem-based learning centred on clinical scenarios. Engagement with the forums is monitored and students who are failing to engage are contacted to discover the reason. In this way, interaction is encouraged. These forums also involve e-tutors guiding students and providing feedback on their input, which provides opportunity for reflection and engagement.

The 3D videos are another interactive tool of the courses which provide for a more stimulating form of learning. The student must actively participate in order to progress through the video and can choose the order in which they address the topics in the video. This interaction is intended to ensure that they remain more engaged than would be the case with a simple linear video.

3. The challenges

A main challenge had been to change the conservative views of academics and clinicians who assume that online learning cannot be as effective as face-to-face learning, especially in clinical disciplines. Overcoming this scepticism has been a slow process of presenting the outcome of the programme in conferences and workshops. A significant number of online tutors were recruited through personal contact and persuasion. As they became enthusiastic for the programme, they helped to persuade their colleagues by word of mouth.

The programme was specifically established to meet the challenge of delivering high quality education in the subspeciality of oncoplastic breast surgery to a dispersed group of senior surgical trainees. There was no centre in the UK that had enough trainees to form a functioning learning community. An online approach seemed to be the logical answer, but the challenge was finding a time that was suitable for all the trainees as they were on different duty rotas. The asynchronous discussion forum allowed the trainees to engage with the learning at a time convenient to them. The educationists on the team were experienced in the design and delivery of problem-based learning in a face-to-face format and adapted this approach to the online environment in keeping with theories of adult learning. Each module comprised seven case-based scenarios followed by a revision period prior to the summative assessment required for the award of university credits contributing to the award of a degree or postgraduate diploma. An important element of the courses was the formative assessment which was provided at the end of each topic within the modules, which allowed the students to monitor their learning. The formative assessment included knowledge tests and a *Script Concordance Test (SCT)*. The latter test format assesses a student's decision-making and so emphasised importance of this aspect of the learning. In the initial iterations of the programme the online learning was supported by face-to-face study days at the beginning and end of each module. Since the pandemic, these have been replaced by live Zoom conferences which fulfil the same function of encouraging networking between the students and faculty and allowing for more in-depth discussion of contentious topics.

An important feature of the programme is the recruitment of senior clinicians with relevant specialist expertise from across the UK as e-tutors to facilitate the forums. The geographical dispersion of the faculty raises challenges to maintaining the quality and consistency of the approach. To address this, regular training days are held for the tutors during which they share their experiences and have input into the ongoing updating and modification of the courses.

While the original focus of the course was on the clinical competencies of the students, we were aware that the role of a consultant surgeon required leadership and management skills together with an understanding of research and its applications in the clinic. To meet these challenges, we added a research module and a module in healthcare leadership and management. The format for these was modified but followed the same educational principles. The outcome was a unique and interactive educational package and a flexible and easily accessible website. Feedback from students at the end of each 16-week module has helped us to refine the content and method of online delivery. The success of the oncoplastic breast surgery course encouraged us to develop other courses based on the same format.

As noted above, interaction is a frequent challenge in distance learning. This is particularly an issue when the courses are credit-bearing and lead to a validated qualification. In response, we monitor learner engagement carefully through a progress bar built into our online courses. Our students can track their level of engagement and aim to meet the 80% participation requirement for each of the two-week topics for all the modules. Student engagement is monitored by the admin team and students who are falling behind are sent email reminders. Participation levels are checked at exam board meetings and candidates who did not meet the criteria for engagement would not be successful in completing the module. Because of the emphasis on engagement, it is imperative that the courses provide meaningful opportunities for interaction to ensure that participants will have an increased chance of meeting the ongoing, rigorous standards in medical education and training. Our interactive technologies such as 360-degree videos and forums aid in this objective of making online courses more engaging. Through interactive videos, students are given the opportunity to take a more immersive approach to educational materials, resulting in more contextual, consolidated learning. Forums provide students with the chance to interact with their contemporaries as well as tutors. The ability to discuss case scenarios means that participants can get an insight into different clinical approaches, providing them with a more captivating way of learning.

The success of the courses in the UK led to roll out internationally, facilitated by our regional convenors. The international roll out presented a fresh series of challenges. The standard of English inevitably varies across different regions, making a universal package more complex to deliver. For our degree and diploma course we adopted the rigorous screening approach mandated by the University of East Anglia. This has also influenced the way we recruit onto our non-university courses, ensuring that only students who meet a minimum written potential are accepted. We recognise that it would be unfair to set any student up to fail due to language issues, so they are encouraged to re-apply once they can meet a base-level of written English. Going forward, we are exploring translation of our courses, currently focusing on Latin America.

Another challenge with international courses is that students come from different educational backgrounds with different pedagogical approaches. It is important that the ethos and structure of the courses is accessible to all, regardless of their previous educational background. We have attempted to streamline the design, layout, and structure of our courses so that regardless of which region participants are from, they are guaranteed a user-friendly learning experience. Pricing the courses appropriately in an international market is important, recognising that certain regions will have more resources to invest. Scholarships helped to alleviate this problem for individuals, however, we also introduced some variation in course prices dependent on which country applicants are from.

The final international dynamic issue arises from difference in time zones, as arranging meetings, meeting deadlines, and structuring the course can be difficult. The inherent flexibility of the courses has alleviated this problem, as self-driven learning enables candidates to undertake their study around work and domestic schedules.

4. How the initiative was received by the users or participants

The initial evaluation of user satisfaction was the feedback from the students at the end of each module. This has been consistently positive. For example, the data from 354 of the Masters students who completed the end of module evaluation in 2019 to 2022 showed high levels of satisfaction in the primary aim of the courses, which was positive impact on clinical practise (94%). They also reported 94% positive responses on the quality of e-tutoring, 88% for effectiveness of Problem Based Learning, and Script Concordance Tests, 79% for website access and usability and 72% for impact on decision making skills. Free text feedback identified some areas where improvement was needed. These were considered by the team and the wider faculty and, where appropriate, adjustments were made. While student satisfaction is the lowest level of course evaluation, this demonstrates that the various components of the Blended Learning UK site and courses are successfully delivered, and users frequently found that in their opinion the courses effectively met the objectives of the programme.

A pilot study for a new online course *Competencies in Emergency Surgery* gave an opportunity for a more rigorous evaluation of our approach. The course is aimed at 1st and 2nd year trainees in surgery. The outcomes were based on the Intercollegiate Surgical Curriculum Programme of the Royal Colleges of Surgeons which defines the requirements for surgical training in the UK. In 2018, all the 1st and 2nd year surgical trainees in the

UK were sent an invitation to participate in the pilot study. Sixty-four trainees responded and were randomised into two groups. Both groups sat a Script Concordance Test that tested their knowledge and decision making in a series of emergency surgery scenarios that they could expect to encounter in their routine clinical practice. Group A then took part in an 8-week module that had a similar format to our Masters courses with the addition of a flipped learning component. Each week the students were given learning materials on day 1, which included a reading list and instructional videos. On day 3, they were presented with a clinical scenario and expected to engage with the online, asynchronous forum to discuss the management of the case with their peers, facilitated by an e-tutor. The weekend with a formative quiz to allow the students to assess their learning for that week. Group B continued with their usual learning in their hospital setting.

After eight weeks, both groups of students re-sat the original SCT. The pre-test scores for both groups were the same: (A 6.45; B 6.59 p=0.78). At 8 weeks Group A's scores had improved significantly (7.96 p<0.001) while Group B's remained unchanged (6.54). The difference between the groups was highly significant (p=0.005). Both groups then took part in a further 8-week module in the same format as previously based on eight different clinical problems. In addition, Group B were allowed reading rights on the previous discussion forums but were not able to contribute to them. They were able to access the learning materials for these weeks. At the end of week sixteen, both groups sat a new SCT which concentrated on the material taught in the second eight-week period. The scores on this test showed no difference between the groups (A 7.13; B 7.18 p=0.87).

The students also completed a questionnaire assessing their confidence in managing a range of common surgical emergency. This was scored on a Likert scale ranging from 1 very underconfident to 5 totally confident for each scenario. The mean score for all eight conditions was then calculated. There was no difference between the scores for the pre-test (A 3.49; B 3.54 p=0.13). At week eight there was a marked improvement in confidence ratings by Group A but no change in Group B (A 3.88 p<0.001; B 3.54 p=0.94). By week sixteen, the ratings for Group A had further improved (4.07 p,0.001) but Group B now had a similar level of confidence (4.02; p A v B=0.85). Engagement with the online learning improved the students self-rating of confidence. The catch up displayed by Group B may reflect their engagement with the Group A materials from the first week.

The pilot study produced evidence that our online course could provide additional benefit for trainees undergoing routine, in-person clinical training as well as being highly rated for student satisfaction.

The critical question is whether these findings translate into an impact in day-to-day performance in the workplace. The ultimate measure is the impact on patient outcomes. The knowledge and skill level of the clinician is only one of a variety of factors that affect patient outcomes. As a result, there are no simple criteria that can be applied to measure the effect of an educational intervention. We opted to carry out a qualitative study of the perceptions of graduates from the Oncoplastic Breast Surgery course of the benefits that they had gained from the course.

We approached graduates from the past decade whose contact details were available through the UEA Alumni Office. Twenty-five of the alumni, now all practicing consultant breast surgeons, responded. All the respondents perceived that the course had had a positive impact on their clinical practise. Twenty-four considered that it had assisted in their career progression and reported that participation in the course had resulted in a significant increase in the number of cancer patients they treated annually. This suggests that we are impacting clinical practise and meeting stakeholder expectations. The alumni of the programme also said that their confidence in their clinical practise had been improved by the courses, giving them the necessary skills to follow a career in oncoplastic breast surgery. The respondents also reported that they engaged in research and quality improvement projects after graduation. The clinical leadership and management module has enabled several of our graduates to start new services, such as introducing breast units, family history clinics, lymphoedema services, and others into their local institutions. All the participants also agreed that the course had prepared them to be effective trainers.

5. The learning outcomes

One of the core achievements of these innovative courses is the positive impact on women diagnosed with breast cancer over the last 12 years of successful course delivery. Since the commencement of the Oncoplastic Breast Surgery programme, a low estimate would be that participating surgeons have treated over 150,000 cancers and reviewed at least 2 million female outpatients globally. We anticipate a similar impact of the courses in Regional Anaesthesia and Coloproctology. Furthermore, prior to COVID, our courses recruited candidates from 30 countries, which now has candidates registered from 60 countries, which demonstrates that our programmes are highly effective. According to the World |Health Organisation (WHO) *"the chronic under-investment in education and training of health workers in some countries and the mismatch between education and employment strategies in relation to health systems and population needs are contributing to continuous shortages."* Given this challenge that currently faces the global health service, the courses run by this programme are effective at helping to tackle this problem. Since starting over a decade ago, there have been hundreds of participants who have completed the blended learning courses. It is hard to place an exact figure on the number of graduates due to the collaborative nature of the programme with the University of East Anglia, however, across the different specialities catered for there has been a large number of professionals go through the course. This in mind, there is no doubt that the Blended Learning UK project has successfully worked to tackle the problem of training and education in the medical community. This is especially true considering the previously mentioned estimates on the patient outcomes, which will be multiplied across our portfolio of different courses. *Care* Nursing and 10 free places for our *Breast Ultrasound* course. This strategy will facilitate healthcare professionals to impart their knowledge and skills to their colleagues, helping to improve the care of women with breast cancer in Kenya, Zimbabwe, Nigeria, and Uganda. Another core achievement of the programme is that we have been able to offer a full scholarship to undertake our Masters in oncoplastic breast surgery for deserving surgeons from the sub-Saharan region of Africa. We have also provided 20 free places for nurses from these regions to undertake our *Introduction to Breast Care Nursing* and ten free places for our *Breast Ultrasound* course. This strategy will facilitate healthcare professionals to impart their knowledge and skills to their colleagues, helping to improve the care of women with breast cancer in Kenya, Zimbabwe, Nigeria and Uganda.

6. Plans to further develop the initiative

In previous years, the courses have provided qualifications for breast surgeons, coloproctologists, and anaesthetists. However, based on the success from our university blended learning programmes, we have expanded the project's educational portfolio to a wider range of healthcare professions in the NHS. The James Paget University Hospital have funded further innovation by establishing Blended Learning UK, which is an NHS organisation, and now an acknowledged centre of excellence for online health education by Healthcare UK. Obviously, new courses are the focal point of the development of the initiative. Courses are currently in development in; diabetes, endoscopy, orthopaedics – hip and ankle surgery, and organ transplant. These will help to upskill an increased number of specialities across the field of healthcare education, furthering the claim to be made that Blended Learning is revolutionary to medical teaching. The programme also hopes to continue with the expansion of scholarships to serve under-resourced health settings. Recently, the courses have seen interest from Vietnam, who have requested further development of our course in wound care, which will be at the forefront of medical education in their country. This is a perfect example of how our blended learning courses have led innovation, and will continue to do so in the future, not only in the UK, but internationally.

There are also plans to utilize more modern technologies, such as more advanced 360-degree interactive videos and designated apps. While there is already some 3D in use by the project, more cutting-edge software will be used going forward to provide the most modern and up to date experience of the interactive features of the course. The team have recently purchased 2 virtual reality headsets, which will allow better design and therefore delivery of the 360 elements of the courses, which are currently only used in a few different procedures and tours. Through this development, the courses will become more interactive and engaging.

The Blended Learning Programme is also spearheading a new initiative called the Schools project. This involves children from 16-18 working together in a team who will represent their school. They will be tasked with creating an innovative way of delivering a set curriculum of information. This is aim of working with young minds of the future to bring in innovation, gaming, and immersive technology skills, with potential to unlock new ways of delivering training and blended learning. Rocks & Rachet-Jacquet (2022) state that *"to deliver pre-pandemic rates of care for patients in a similar way could therefore require a substantial increase in the number of hospital beds. Under our central projections, in which time spent in hospital continues to fall but at a slowing rate, an additional 23,000 to 39,000 general and acute hospital beds would be required."* To help tackle this problem, Blended Learning UK is leading the Homes from Homes project, which aims to address the demonstrated national hospital bed crisis. By freeing up beds in hospitals across the trial region, there will be more available for those who are in greater need. This will be achieved by moving patients who are well enough to leave hospital into residential beds in the homes of volunteers. These projects indicate the development and evolution of the Blended Learning UK project, and how the courses are successful in achieving the programme's goals.

References

Maor, D., & Volet, S. (2007). Interactivity in professional online learning: A review of research-based studies. *Australasian journal of educational technology, 23*(2). Available at: View of Interactivity in professional online learning: A review of research based studies (ajet.org.au) (Accessed: 5th July 2023).

Rocks, S. and Rachet-Jacquet, L. (2022) How many hospital beds will the NHS need over the coming decade?, The Health Foundation. Available at: https://www.health.org.uk/publications/reports/how-many-beds-will-the-nhs-need-over-the-coming-decade (Accessed: 05 July 2023).

World Health Organisation (2023) Health Workforce. Available at: https://www.who.int/health-topics/health-workforce#tab=tab_1 (Accessed: 05 July 2023

Biographies

Professor Jerome Pereira is Executive Director/Programme Director for Blended Learning (JPUH/UEA). He is a Consultant Oncoplastic Breast Surgeon at James Paget University Hospitals NHS Foundation Trust and Honorary Professor of Surgery. Professor Pereira is Programme Director for multiple Specialist e-Learning Mastership Programmes at the UEA, Norwich, currently recruiting candidates from over 60 countries and Programme Director for multiple NHS blended learning courses in nursing, midwifery, specialist nursing, and endoscopy commissioned by Health Education England.

Professor Sam Leinster is Joint Programme Director & Educational Consultant for Blended Learning. He is Emeritus Professor of Medical Education. And has a clinical background in General Surgery and Surgical Oncology. Former Inaugural Dean at Norwich Medical School University of East Anglia, UK, and Director of Medical Studies at the University of Liverpool where he led the introduction of a new undergraduate curriculum.

Tom King et al

Associate Professor Sue Down is Honorary Associate Processor – University of East Anglia. She is Associate Professor at the University of East Anglia and Consultant Oncoplastic Breast Surgeon and Clinical Lead for Breast surgery at the James Paget University Hospital. She completed initial surgical training in Manchester, and a PhD in Cancer Studies at the University of Birmingham.

Andrew Simpson is an E-Learning Consultant and until recently was the E-Learning manager for the UEA's Specialist Masters Programme, having worked on specialist education projects since qualifying as a teacher early in his educational career. He has been working with the James Paget team for over a decade, on health education projects particularly around the technical development but also on the educational aspects.

Tom King is a Blended Learning Research Officer. Until recently Tom undertook a 12-month contract with Blended Learning UK to analyse student feedback questionnaires, which will concluded with a published paper. This aim was to provide clear evidence that the UEA and Blended Learning UK programmes are indispensable to education for Healthcare Professionals

Towards building a sustainable community through social platforms

[1]Sweta Patnaik and [2]Nadine Sonnenberg
[1]Department of Clothing and Textile Technology & Technology Station Clothing and Textiles, Cape Peninsula University of Technology, Cape Town, South Africa.

[2]Department of Consumer and Food Sciences, Faculty of Natural and Agricultural Sciences, University of Pretoria, Pretoria, South Africa.

patnaiks@cput.ac.za
nadine.sonnenberg@up.ac.za

Abstract: Textile waste is a major concern in the global textile and fashion supply chain, but also more specifically in the local South African clothing industry. With excessive volumes of donated post-consumer textile waste passed on from developed countries to African communities in addition to textile waste generated locally, the pursuit of sustainable textile waste management strategies is sorely needed. When such strategies involve the creation of entrepreneurial opportunities and employment for, amongst other, disadvantaged communities and/ or individuals with disabilities the resulting outputs offer substantial social, economic, and environmental gains. With these goals in mind, the efforts of students and lecturers at two tertiary institutions were combined to create a digital platform that shares information and ideas on textile waste management strategies. For their part, final-year Clothing Retail Management students at the University of Pretoria collaborated with "Clothes To Good" community members to generate and streamline upcycling, downcycling, and reselling solutions for post-consumer textile waste collected in the Gauteng region. Clothes To Good is a non-profit organisation, that in association with major clothing brands, has created inspiring entrepreneurial opportunities for mothers of children with disabilities and also canvassed the support of major firms to employ adults with autism and other mental disabilities. Students created presentations of their ideas that were easy to follow and that could be digitally shared on the communal platform. The same was done at CPUT, Cape Town where students created products from offcut waste to make creative artefacts in various forms. There were multilingual digital storytelling videos on the most commonly spoken regional language of South Africa. The videos were compressed and images were sourced for low-tech accessibility. They were made available via YouTube and WhatsApp keeping the data constraint and ease of access in mind. The project currently has no cost involved to any party, yet earns new skill sets and provides a source of income during these difficult times. The goal is to transform the primary idea that people have; a unidimensional understanding of what sustainability comprises and not how it could have a multidimensional impact on the society, and environment and improve the quality of life. The approach to the impact has been multimodal with pre and post-surveys, and focus group interviews with entrepreneurs and small businesses. Further research will include establishing an entrepreneurial hub to ensure access to stakeholders.

1. Introduction

In adopting a triple-bottom-line approach, it is important to focus on the environmental, social, and economic dimensions of sustainability. In recent years, much critique has been directed toward the environmental repercussions of the clothing and textiles industries, specifically the excessive waste it creates from initial raw material extraction to the eventual disposal of unwanted garments (McKinsey & Company, 2023). Yet, notably, while industry stakeholders have devoted increased attention to curbing further environmental harm, the social and economic dimensions do not always feature as prominently in the fashion agenda. The social and economic dimensions are often pivotal for achieving sustainable development goals in emerging economies such as South Africa that are in dire need of initiatives to stimulate growth and entrepreneurship against the backdrop of high levels of unemployment. In this regard, the opportunity presents itself to explore entrepreneurial avenues through which textile waste can be utilised for economic and social benefit, whilst simultaneously reducing the environmental repercussions of the clothing and textile industry.

COVID-19 had a significant impact on entrepreneurship and more specifically SMMEs (Kuckertz & Brandle, 2021; Syriopoulos, 2020; Gregurec et al., 2021). The pandemic caused unforeseen transitions in various entrepreneurial aspects, including market patterns, consumer demand, and the implementation of new policies. Technological experts viewed COVID-19 as a global disruption that either created opportunities or posed challenges to existing business models through the adoption of new technologies (Kuckertz & Brandle, 2021; Gregurec et al., 2021). SMMEs, for example, started embracing digital technologies to prevent closure, which was not widely observed before. Entrepreneurial ecosystems, consisting of networks, infrastructure, culture, and intermediaries, play a vital role in supporting SMMEs (Ratten, 2020 (1&2); Scott et al., 2021; Spigel & Harrison, 2018; Fubah & Moos, 2021). However, there is no consensus on the definition of entrepreneurial ecosystems among scholars. To date, research on the impact of COVID-19 on SMMEs has primarily focused on Western countries, neglecting developing countries like South Africa, despite their significant challenges (Stam & van de Ven, 2021; Isenberg, 2010). South Africa, a country that was heavily affected by the pandemic, lacks research and support for entrepreneurs, especially regarding job losses and high unemployment rates. Relying solely on the government is not a sustainable option, given the unstable global economies. There is a crucial need for research on the impact of COVID-19 aftermath on entrepreneurship to provide a better understanding of the crisis. In addition, textile waste is a significant issue both globally and in the local context, yet offers the ideal platform for entrepreneurial opportunities. This case study highlights the importance of entrepreneurship in the clothing and textiles industry to reduce waste and emphasizes the need to assist the unemployed through accessible e-learning platforms. Current educational programs may have limitations such as cost and geographic location, hindering entrepreneurs' access. To address this, a low-tech, easy-access e-learning mode was developed to reach rural communities with limited knowledge and awareness. COVID-19 has increased access to technology, enabling individuals to generate innovative ideas and work independently to create income sources. Web-based interventions have been proven effective in engaging viewers and fostering interest in learning. A Google Sites website was created as an e-learning intervention to educate stakeholders and provide innovative ways to make products from waste materials.

2. The infrastructure

The case study involves an amalgamation of initiatives of two departments across two different universities in South Africa, one being a traditional university (University of Pretoria) and the other being a university of technology (CPUT). The B. Consumer Science Clothing Retail Management degree is based in the Department of Consumer and Food Sciences at the University of Pretoria (UP). The department combines expertise from various disciplines, which allows for novel interdisciplinary approaches in the pursuit of sustainable development goals while addressing the current digital trends. The Clothing Retail Management programme exposes students to various courses during their four years of study, but among these, Textiles 411 (TKS 411) is a core module and is specifically focused on new developments and issues surrounding sustainability in the textile and apparel industry. A hybrid approach is followed whereby part of the module is presented in face-to-face encounters and the online component is facilitated via UP's Blackboard Collaborate platform. As pointed out earlier, textile waste is a critical issue in the global and African context, and for these reasons, much attention is devoted to the topic in the TKS 411 module, as well as innovative technologies and practices that students may employ in their future career paths to reduce the amount of waste generated in this industry. Led by Dr. Nadine Sonnenberg, senior lecturer, and TKS module coordinator, students embark on a community engagement project with members of the Clothes To Good (CTG) non-profit organisation to gain in-depth insight into the methodologies, benefits, and challenges associated with post-consumer textile waste accumulation, sorting, and redistribution from a local community perspective. CTG draws together a broad community base consisting of 108 micro-businesses (56 owned by mothers of children with disabilities), other non-profit organisations, as well as major retail brands such as H&M and Levi's, that have partnered with CTG in driving meaningful, sustainable positive social impact in enterprise development, inclusion (especially people with disabilities), and caring for the environment. Through this community base, CTG has over the past decade set up the infrastructure to process and recycle hundreds of tons of post-consumer textile waste annually. More information can be derived from their website: https://clothestogood.com/

Site visits to the CTG premises in Centurion, Gauteng form part of the TKS 411 students' practical training. During these visits, they are engaged in textile waste sorting exercises (based on European Union Waste Hierarchy principles) and various upcycling, downcycling, and reselling initiatives.

Figure 1. Clothes To Good community members guiding UP students on how to sort post-consumer textile waste into various categories based on waste hierarchy principles.

Equipped with the exposure they have acquired on-site and the background they have gained through their online course material, students are challenged to develop innovative solutions that could potentially streamline and/ or expand CTG's current upcycling, downcycling, and/or reselling operations through technology, media, or other resources. These solutions are formally presented (online/ face-to-face) to CTG community members and academic moderators. Solutions are judged based on various criteria compiled by the TKS 411 lecturer in collaboration with CTG management.

Based at CPUT, Dr. Sweta Patnaik specifically focuses on creating entrepreneurial opportunities through textile waste reduction strategies. The synergies between the two institutional offerings provided the ideal platform for collaboration and the co-creation of this project. The initial ideas came together along with Mr. Shamil Isaacs, Manager of Technology Station Clothing and Textiles at CPUT in Cape Town. He is an industry expert who supports the clothing and textile sector in enhancing innovation and competitiveness. His expertise lies in design, innovation, product performance, entrepreneurship, and understanding consumer needs. Through workshops, short courses, and custom interventions, he provides support to the industry. Dr. Sweta Patnaik, a senior lecturer in the Department of Clothing and Textile Technology at the Faculty of Engineering and the Built Environment, utilizes e-learning in her teaching, learning, and research. She is passionate about her work and has received institutional teaching excellence awards for her contributions to e-learning at the institutional level. The project also involves students, lab staff, and members of the community, particularly those associated with the Bambanani for Social Development organization, including the team leader and the women who work there.

The project was conceived with multiple perspectives in mind. Firstly, the aim was to create awareness among students about sustainable approaches, environmental consciousness, community service, and waste reduction. As the students began working on their products and witnessed their ideas coming to life, the idea emerged to extend this concept to create an online platform for the community and explore how it could help address the high unemployment rates in South Africa. Additionally, feedback was collected by posting images of the students' work on the department's Instagram page, using polls to gauge consumer preferences, which received positive responses. The website is accessible free of charge and is designed to be user-friendly and data-savvy. It shares ideas and operations through publicly available images, allowing easy access for anyone interested. In addition, lab experts are available to provide additional support when needed. Moreover, individuals with a sewing background who are eager to learn and create such products can receive offcuts of raw materials to make wonderful products. Post-consumer textile waste and offcut fabrics can be widely sourced, including companies and manufacturing units that are willing to provide fabrics to support entrepreneurs or community-run organizations. Comparing similar platforms, it is safe to say that there is no other platform in South Africa specifically created by experts from the education, clothing, or textile industry that offers such easy creative ideas for anyone to earn a living. All that is required is a sewing machine and some stitching experience, which can go a long way. The images uploaded on the website serve as a guide to help individuals create environmentally friendly, cost-saving, and trendy products.

To support learning, asynchronous lessons are available through the Technology Station Clothing and Textiles, and WhatsApp is used as a simple and effective means of communication across all age groups. As for the market for these products, there are numerous platforms and consumers willing to purchase them. For example, market days can be conducted within institutions, inviting staff and students from various departments. Products can also be sold to shop owners in urban markets or exchanged among community members to meet their needs.

Both departments collaborated to ensure they use various social media platforms that collectively assist students to learn, explore, collaborate, and gain knowledge from diverse sources. This mix of digital social platforms not only contributed to knowledge creation within the departments but also enabled skill sharing with SMMEs. They include – Instagram, Facebook, Institutional web pages, Google sites, and YouTube. Google sites, in particular, serve as a prominent and collaborative platform for students and newly partnered SMMEs. These platforms can be used to showcase evidence of student work, engagement with communities and are a source of open learning for all. It was therefore deemed ideal to combine and stage initiatives from both institutions in the pursuit of textile waste reduction and assisting SMMEs in broadening their entrepreneurial efforts.

The videos on the Google website include narrations that stakeholders can listen to in their preferred language. Stakeholders can contact us through the "Contact Us" section to express their needs, and we will strive to assign the appropriate staff to assist them. Examples of work done by students are shared on the website, serving as references for others to recreate designs or styles based on their preferences. Interested individuals can fill out a Google form linked on the website to reach us directly for support and assistance. Each product type is accompanied by a set of images and brief explanations on how to create that particular product. The website also provides a means for visitors to contact us through a Google form, allowing them to provide feedback, suggest changes, or raise concerns regarding the webpage. We are open to incorporating any updates or enhancements that would improve the learning experience. The webpage follows Clark and Meyer's multimedia principle and best practices for e-learning, leveraging graphics, words, and video clip narration to effectively communicate content.

The website's design and development process involved extensive stakeholder involvement, including community members, staff, students, and industry peers. Expert suggestions and feedback were carefully considered for each section, and input was gathered from potential consumers through social media platforms. Community members with sewing backgrounds were invited to learn and understand the process, finding the information helpful, trendy, and creative. The website's design, colour scheme, wording, and images were appealing to them.

Evaluation and feedback forms were created on the website to gather stakeholders' opinions on how the website contributed to their learning. Overall, the responses were positive, highlighting the effectiveness and quality of the learning experience. While there were areas for improvement, the website received favourable feedback. The technology used for the website is kept simple to ensure ease of use, and if the website is handed over to other department colleagues in the future, the transition will be smooth. Web analytics will be conducted using Google Analytics. New videos will be periodically created to align with emerging trends, and initially, images will be uploaded followed by a series of events explaining the product-making process.

The following images below provide evidence of student learning, and allow students to see themselves as future entrepreneurs by creating their own business pages online.

Figure 2. Pictures of offcut fabrics to make removeable and reversible couch covers

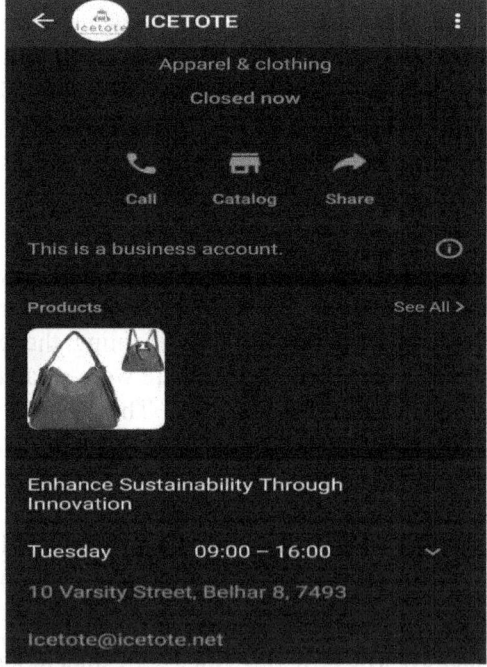

Figure 3. Evidence of students creating their own business account

Figure 4. Collecting leftover fabrics from the department

3. The challenges

When adopting hybrid teaching approaches, and incorporating community engagement into course curricula, there are bound to be certain challenges that need to be overcome. With regard to face-to-face community engagement and contact, it is important to prepare students well in advance to ensure they get the most from site visits, yet simultaneously work toward the benefit of the community and also respect community members' principles, values, and beliefs. This is also important for an online social community platform. To ensure that community engagement remains aligned with the institution's teaching and learning objectives, there are Institutional Units for Community Engagement that have developed tools to assist in preparing students for community engagement. This includes, among others, orientation video clips (addressing various issues ranging from dress code, and respectful communication with community members to safety guidelines), which were shared with students via Blackboard Collaborate and WhatsApp platforms prior to face-to-face site visits. In addition, various clips relating to SMMEs operations, their mission, values, and collaboration with other major stakeholders were shared with students to ensure they are well informed and prepared to participate in activities. Students were further briefed regarding the constraints under which work is conducted onsite and otherwise and what to expect, especially when interacting with disabled members of the SMMEs team. A major challenge presented itself in coordinating site visits to fit in with students' timetables and subject module contact time. Moreover, spatial constraints and the limited availability of staff/ volunteers made it impossible for an entire class to be accommodated on-site at the community projects simultaneously. This was overcome by dividing the students into smaller groups at the beginning of the semester, allowing each group to visit sites a set number of times, which was then carefully planned into their timetables, and thereafter, confirmed on a weekly basis with the management to ensure that site visits could still be facilitated as planned and cause minimum disruption to SMMEs daily operations. It should be noted that even though dates and times were planned in advance, changes in schedules had to be accommodated. Quick responsiveness was made possible via WhatsApp communication and Blackboard announcements. Open, timely, and clear communication channels between staff, lecturers, teaching assistants, and students allowed for all groups to be given equal exposure to onsite activities and experiences throughout the semester. Transport also presented somewhat of a challenge, but funding was made available by the institution for rental vehicles to transport all student groups to the community project site and back to campus within the given timeframes.

4. How the initiative was received by the users or participants

The idea for this initiative originated and was finalized in November 2019 for CPUT and 2022 for UP when students were tasked with creating products and/or entrepreneurial business solutions that ultimately drive the pursuit of textile waste reduction. A market day was organized to raise awareness and engage with the community. The work was also presented at an international conference in Pretoria. However, with the onset of the pandemic in early 2020, it became challenging to progress further. Similar circumstances persisted in 2021. 2022 was the year when the initial stage of this case study was presented. Therefore, this year, we made an effort to revive the initiative in full force. We began by reaching out to entrepreneurs and sharing our ideas and students' work through videos and images. Currently, external funding is not required, so we haven't sought financial support from external sources.

When we shared this initiative with students and staff, it was well-received and welcomed. Similarly, when we presented it to the community, we were pleasantly surprised by the positive response from skilled workers. They appreciated the concept and ideas, expressing their interest in using them to create products that could generate extra income. Although the feedback were predominantly vocal there were a few comments which we received via the feedback form from them as follows:

Sweta Patnaik and Nadine Sonnenberg

What was your reaction after going through our page?

48 responses

It was interesting, however it would be nice if you had an "about" page with a description of what the purpose is and who is involved and how this has positive impacts as all the visuals are already there. It would just make the page more interesting and interactive

I believe this is an excellent initiative that is being implemented. However, I was a bit disoriented on the site as there is not a lot of information about who you are, what you are doing and what the site is about. After figuring out what it is about I loved it.

Somewhat insightful but needs more info on the project and aim. Images a big blurry and without captions makes it hard to understand what is shown. Steps on how to make items are very educational and interesting !

It's a very cool initiative and idea, just lacking in information and presentation on the Web page.

I felt it was an interesting concept, making products out of waste. However, the (mobile) page is difficult to navigate and lacks precise descriptions of the project/endeavour

Very interesting website. Loved the innovative designs as well as the concept as a whole.

What was the most liked and least liked page or subpage?

48 responses

Most liked: Student products, great and inspiring products, just lacking some more in depth information on each one. Definitely encourages one to learn more overall.

Least liked: Home page, as it doesn't immediately give context or information on what it is I'm browsing which is slightly disorientating.

I mostly liked the possibility to get instructions on the process subpage - it is well described and each item is well highlighted
I also liked that the pages load very quickly.
I mostly disliked the home page (design, information and functionality is not optimal)

I liked that they gave steps on how to make a bag from waste. I feel that so many people would love that idea and would love the fact that they own a bag that no one else has.

Most liked = students projects. Least liked= quality of the pictures

Most liked: Steps with processes on how to make items and items
Least liked: Home page- It lacks some interesting information and pictures

Lastly, any suggestions or feedback for changes or improvements in order to make learning better.
48 responses

I think it's important that there are descriptions as well as written steps of the processes that take place, the videos could also be more holistic instead of just separate steps as that would be more interesting

I would make an "about us" or "our mission" page that goes with the home page. Where you describe what the page is about and what it can be used for and why you started it. Make it a bit more personal.

Give a short description on what the project is about.
Give captions under items with more info for example who made it, from what it it made and material and pricing if to be sold.
Add more colour to the website.

The home page needs a tonne of information on what the Web page is about and what you can expect on the different pages/sub-pages.

The site can have a built in video player or display YouTube content with a plug-in rather than having links to Google drive as this can be inconvenient.

Some pages need to be removed or reworked, as the "student work" page can be accessed but has no

This feedback serves as important qualitative data to assess the broader interest in our webpage. Quite a few stakeholders appreciated and showed willingness in learning more. They felt the processes were simple and could be easily learned and made by anyone willing to learn and earn a source of income.

In addition to online feedback, community members warmly received students into their midst during face-to-face site visits and went to great lengths to explain and demonstrate their current operations and how they deal with textile waste. Following the site visits, students were asked to submit reflections surrounding their experiences at the site via the Blackboard Collaborate platform. Students were in awe and reported that they would never have comprehended the complexities of the community projects without seeing it for themselves. The following represent a few examples of verbatim text drawn from the students' online reflections:

"It was an incredible learning opportunity as I was able to discover more about the fashion industry and the different spheres one can go into other than just the traditional avenues. I also learned a lot about the waste and negative impacts of the fashion industry and that there are ways in which we can reduce this." "I learned how much textile waste there actually is. Seeing how much clothing was donated to

Clothes to Good was shocking to me as it was so much more than I expected..." "I gained a volume of knowledge and skills about sustainability throughout the process. I learned a lot of knowledge about waste management. CTG allows one to understand the importance of prolonging the lifespan of items and eliminating waste. It really educates one on the skills and practices of reducing, reusing, and recycling. I also learned what circular economy is and how through the transformation of second-hand clothing into new products, an individual can close the loop. Not only does this reduce waste but also the reliance on raw materials. In terms of sustainable fashion practices, one learns the skills of ethical sourcing, eco-friendly materials, fair trade, and the social and environmental consequences of textile waste and fast fashion."

Figure 5. CTG community members collaborate with UP students to assess post-consumer textile waste for reselling, upcycling, and downcycling purposes.

Yet, community engagement should never solely focus on what students can derive from the experience, but, instead, should also revolve around what the community members can gain from it. Feedback received from management and community members has been consistently positive with some of the initiatives suggested by the students already implemented since the project's inception.

An external moderator of students' proposals and ideas shared the following in her feedback:

"Their coverage of the range of issues across different disciplines in the business was also phenomenal for students without work experience. They showed a practical understanding of these business aspects and more importantly demonstrated the ability to scope practical application which came from a strong business theoretical foundation. I wish there is a way that we can easily capture such a moment to share

with HR personnel in the industry. I have worked with consultants and employees alike that are incapable of doing this. Well done to these students. They have a bright future."

5. The learning outcomes

Integrating the community engagement project into the various departments' module outcomes underscores some main drivers for curriculum transformation including responsiveness to social context, diverse epistemologies, inclusive pedagogies, classroom practices, building entrepreneurs, as well as openness and critical reflection. Students engaged in critical thinking and reasoned debate, whereby they analysed, reflected, evaluated, and conceptualised arguments and solutions surrounding contemporary textile issues in the clothing and textiles domain. In particular, recognition was given to textile issues and developments that are unique to the African context and how it impacts the larger socio-economic and natural environments. These outcomes were evident in students' reflections and could be evaluated based on the recommendations and solutions they delivered to the community participants. Beyond the scope of the community engagement project, students' perspectives on sustainability were broadly impacted as exemplified in the following reflection:

"I have gained a more sustainable-orientated mindset regarding my actions and link it to my daily lifestyle. I am thinking more about the amount of waste I as an individual and in my household, we as a family generate. I am thinking of new methods and ways of how to dispose of my waste and also save things like electricity and other resources necessary. I have started thinking more about problem-solving and long-term solutions and lastly, I feel I've learned a lot about collaborating with others, for example in a team, with bigger companies and being more open and listening to what others have to say and how they feel, than just enforcing my way of thinking and my feelings. This project has taught me the importance of forward thinking and effective communication as it is the key driver in building relationships and finding solutions for our problems. The knowledge I have gained was related to thinking more locally and traditionally, as sometimes the most simple and traditional of ideas can be more effective."

Ultimately, all stakeholders in the fashion supply chain have a role to play in the pursuit of sustainability and fashion circularity, necessitating the new generation of fashion designers, manufacturers, and retailers to exercise greater caution in the choices they make. Much can be done to positively impact students' mindsets through projects of this nature and ensure that they form part of this new generation.

6. Plans to further develop the initiative

The initiative aims to spark students' interest in developing similar concepts and ideas that can be shared with the community. The first step was to bring in more educational institutions together to take this forward on a broader scale. Further to this with broad acceptance, the goal is to secure funds either through the institution or external sources to create a more professional, paid website specifically tailored to the target demographics of stakeholders. We plan to conduct further research in this area and present our work at national and international platforms. Recognizing the steady progress and potential, the department at CPUT, in collaboration with the Technology Station, and SMMEs envisions the creation of an "Technopreneurial Hub." This hub would establish a lab-based unit to provide a platform for unemployed individuals and alumni from the department who have been impacted by job loss or are now inclined towards entrepreneurship in the thriving realm of sustainability and waste management. The hub will be further supported via collaboration with UP researchers that focus on textile waste reduction initiatives. Given the evident need and stakeholder interest, the platform has the potential to effectively address the educational requirements of the community in an efficient and cost-effective manner.

Since its inception, this project has drawn much attention and positive feedback, which gained further momentum in 2023. The success of this project has inspired other institutions to follow suit for e.g., in 2023 CTG opened its doors to clothing students enrolled at other tertiary institutions based in Gauteng to participate in similar exercises as those offered to UP students and for CPUT students to allow access to their facility to other levels students. In addition, CTG has over the past year received funding from prominent industry stakeholders to enlarge its current facility and to further expand its operations to Cape Town and KwaZulu Natal. On the other hand, for CPUT the project has allowed them to potentially submit the much-applauded and acclaimed Erasmus application partnering with UP. This could positively impact their capability to facilitate similar learning experiences for students at tertiary institutions beyond the scope of a particular region but the whole of South Africa.

References

Fubah, C.N.; Moos, M. Relevant theories in entrepreneurial ecosystems research: An overview. *Acad. Entre. J.* 2021, *27*, 1–18.

Gregurec, I.; Tomičić Furjan, M.; Tomičić-Pupek, K. The impact of COVID-19 on sustainable business models in SMEs. *Sustainability* 2021, *13*, 1098.

Isenberg, D.J. How to start an entrepreneurial revolution. *Harv. Bus. Rev.* 2010, *88*, 40–50.

Kuckertz, A.; Brändle, L. Creative reconstruction: A structured literature review of the early empirical research on the COVID-19 crisis and entrepreneurship. *Manag. Rev. Quart* 2021, 1–27.

McKinsey & Company. The State of Fashion 2023.
   https://www.mckinsey.com/~/media/mckinsey/industries/retail/our%20insights/state%20of%20fashion/2023/the-state-of-fashion-2023-holding-onto-growth-as-global-clouds-gathers-vf.pdf Accessed: 7 September 2023

Ratten, V. Entrepreneurial ecosystems. *Thun. Int. Bus. Rev.* 2020, *62*, 447–455.

Scott, S.; Hughes, M.; Ribeiro-Soriano, D. Towards a network-based view of effective entrepreneurial ecosystems. *Rev. Manag. Sci.* 2021, 1–31.

Spigel, B.; Harrison, R. Toward a process theory of entrepreneurial ecosystems. *Stra. Entre. J.* 2018, *12*, 151–168.

Stam, E.; van de Ven, A. Entrepreneurial ecosystem elements. *Small Bus. Econ.* 2021, *56*, 1–24.

Syriopoulos, K. The impact of COVID-19 on entrepreneurship and SMEs. *J. Int. Acad. C. Stud* 2020, *26*, 1–2.

Author biographies

Dr Sweta Patnaik is a Senior Lecturer, Teaching & Learning coordinator and Curriculum Officer in the Department of Clothing and Textile Technology, Faculty of Engineering and the Built Environment. Her research interests are around waste management, sustainability, e-learning and blended learning which she publishes nationally and internationally. She has won the Nelson Mandela University Alumni Rising Star Award 2020 as well as the first recipient of the prestigious DAAD UNILEAD scholarship 2021. She is the recipient of Institutional Teaching Excellence Award 2022. She is the Editorial Advisory Board Member for the Journal of Applied Research in Higher Education and member of the SABS committee.

Dr. Nadine Sonnenberg is a senior lecturer in the Department of Consumer and Food Sciences at the University of Pretoria. Her research and teaching are focused on sustainable clothing consumption practices for which she obtained funding from various sources, including the National Research Foundation and the Carnegie African Diaspora Fellowship Programme. She actively participates in community engagement projects that involve post-consumer textile waste disposal and recycling. Her research on consumers' sustainable behaviour, which spans a 20-year timeframe, has been broadly published in various scientific journals and presented at both local and international conferences.

Student teachers use of an eportfolio for authentic assessment

Sibongile Simelane-Mnisi
Tshwane University of Technology, South Africa

simelanes@tut.ac.za

1. Introduction

In higher education, authentic assessment can refer to more than just real-world activities or the workplace (McArthur, 2023). This author argued that authentic assessment could also be linked to social justice and is not just about the task itself, but also pertains to the relationship between the persons/students and the assignment, as well as their sense of wellbeing. In other words, authentic assessment requires students to engage through their sense of responsibility, awareness of their possibilities, an understanding of pedagogical relationships, self-reflection, critical reflection, and a critical hope in the learning process (McArthur, 2023). Sakti (2023) indicated that authentic assessment is one of the methods lecturers employ to measure the ability of students to achieve the learning outcomes utilised in learning activities. In this initiative, students applied authentic assessment in online assessments, whereby gathering data about them and their learning processes were used to make assumptions about their social character.

Various types of authentic assessment that are often used relate to cases, exhibitions of performance, portfolios, problem-based inquiries (also known as action research), written assessments, and project-based assessments (Darling-Hammond & Snyder, 2000; Sakti, 2023). The types of authentic assessments that were applied during the course of study as formative and continuous assessment in this initiative were practical cases, demonstrations of performance, discussion forums, written assignments, online tests, and eportfolio. On the discussion forum, for instance, students participated in group discussions about to Technological, Pedagogical and Content Knowledge, where they analysed the case study and indicated their application of Technological, Pedagogical and Content Knowledge (TPACK) as student teachers. In one of the practical tests' students developed a lesson plan created worksheets and examination question paper using MS Word. The tasks that were taken by the students required the integration and application of knowledge and skills as they are used in daily life for the work of teaching.

In 2022, the student teachers at a Study University of Technology in South Africa were registered for a Postgraduate Certificate in Education Information Communication and Technology in Education was one of the modules within this course. The Information Communication and Technology (ICT) in the Education module comprised topics such as an introduction to computer technology, hardware and software for teachers, the learning theories used in technology education, computer ethics and security, an introduction to application software in learning and teaching relating to Microsoft Word and Word Online, Microsoft Excel and Excel online, Microsoft PowerPoint and PowerPoint online, Microsoft Publisher, and Canva. An active learning strategy was employed, which required student teachers to participate in authentic tasks during the course of the year. Active learning requires students to participate actively in their learning rather than passively listening (Patiño, Ramírez-Montoya & Buenestado-Fernández, 2023). I may argue that active learning favours student-centred approach to learning, which is the preferred method of learning and teaching at the study university. It was, therefore, critical that learning activities in this module follow suit.

The summative assessment was completed leveraging integrated assessment with the electronic portfolio. As part of the authentic assessment initiative, student teachers used an electronic portfolio (ePortfolio). A portfolio is a tool for continuing professional development that encourages people to be accountable for their own learning and to show their outcomes (Pospíšilová & Rohlíková). On the other hand, an e-portfolio is the development of a document portfolio that enables students to compile and present the evidence of their work in digital format (Basu, 2015). This implies that an e-portfolio allows the application of multimedia relating to images, animations, audio, and videos, as well as social media networks, which sets it apart from a traditional portfolio. The e-portfolio is regarded as one of the educational strategies that emphasizes constructive learning (Ismael, 2023). This is because an e-portfolio links information to real-world situations, pays attention to the development of all areas of the learner's growth, and encourages students to think critically (Chen & Crook, 2020). e-Portfolio gives students a venue to consider their educational experiences, highlight their accomplishments, and assess their personal development while fostering metacognitive abilities.

In this course, the summative assessment was conducted using integrated assessment. Integrated assessment is the type of assessment that describes how the assessment will be conducted to determine the learner's applied competence and successful completion of the learning requirements for the qualification (Chweu, Simelane-Mnisi & Mji, 2023; SAQA, 2022). The integrated assessment was called the final integrated assessment, and students created an electronic portfolio (ePortfolio) using the Google Site, reflecting on their responsibilities, possibilities, understanding of pedagogical relationships, self-reflection, and critical reflection in the learning process. The e-portfolio was comprised of authentic assessments that were conducted during the course of the year.

In this initiative, the eportfolio offered student teachers an opportunity to demonstrate their ability to compile, arrange, assess, and think critically about materials and information sources, as well as provide self-reflection about the use of ICT in education in the South African context. This evidence is often gathered over time and in various assessments using different ICT tools and application. In the eportfolio, student teachers were expected to select three (3) of their best continuous activities or assessments based on the following themes and assessments:

- Introduction to Computer Technologies, Hardware and Software for Teachers: Theory Assignment and Theory Test
- Software Application in Education
    - Word processing: Lesson plan and worksheet and examination
    - Spreadsheet: Multiplication table, learners' information, test results and infographics.
    - Presentation: Interactive PowerPoint presentation together with a lesson plan
    - Desktop publishing software: [3 x certificates, and event poster]

Student teachers had to evaluate the module in the narrative critically. In their evaluation, they had to indicate how the module had contributed to the development of their knowledge, skills, and values as 21st-century teachers. Furthermore, they had to point the benefits out, the challenges, and the areas for improvement in each assessment or theme. They had to make use of videos and images to enhance the text. They were encouraged to be innovative and creative in their designs. For the final submission, they were required to structure their selected activities on Google Sites (site.google.com) with links to the relevant activities.

Google sites comprised four (4) pages. Page 1 was about the cover page or home page, structured in the following manner:

- Banner (of your choice) with the name of your portfolio
- Your image and detailed information
- Overview of the module for the whole year: The content of the module and the presentation
- Add the footer: Your own slogan (related to technology-enhanced learning and teaching)

Page 2 included the three best continuous activities or assessments. Here, they had to provide the name of the page. This page included

- Link to all three activities of your choice with improvement
- Reflection on assessment/theme with reference to the
    - benefits
    - challenges
    - areas of improvement in each assessment/theme

Page 3 focused on digital learning; the student teachers provided reflections on the use of digital technologies to promote student engagement in a blended approach (online and face-to-face). In each of the identified tools, they reflected on the benefits, challenges, and areas for improvement based on the following:

- Draw and explain the TPACK model (technology, pedagogy, and content knowledge) and discuss the TPACK implications in education. Indicate how you can apply the TPACK model in your field of specialisation.
- Discuss how the learning management system influences your learning, focusing on its advantages and disadvantages as well as areas for improvement.
- Explain how live classes with MS Teams encouraged you to become involved, engaged, and interested in the lesson.
- Identify and illustrate the five interactive technologies we used in classes to foster engagement and participation.

Page 4 comprised module reflection. The student teachers were required to respond to the following questions/instructions:

- How has the module contributed to your development of knowledge, skills, and values as a 21st-century teacher?
- Create a video for the closing statement (1: 30 sec min video)
- Add an educational technology quotation.

All the assessments, including the ePortfolio, were uploaded to the learning management system (LMS). The objective of this initiative was to expose students to authentic assessment and create an ePorfolio as evidence of their academic performance to be future-ready graduates who can establish connections with social justice and increase their employability in the field of education.

2. The infrastructure

The participants in this initiative were 60 student teachers and one lecturer. The purpose of this module was to provide student teachers with the knowledge, skills, and values necessary to employ digital technologies in learning, teaching, and assessment. As a result, it was necessary for student teachers to have access to hardware and software to enhance their digital competencies. Digital competency is the ability to use ICTs, including hardware, websites, and software, to access, process, transmit, and store digital information (Tomczyk et al., 2023). The study by Mangwegape and Mollo (2023) in South Africa discovered that student teachers' ICT competence was still below levels of substitution and augmentation. Tomczyk et al. (2023) argued that currently, in the 21st century, it is critical to equip future student teachers with digital skills, as this is an area of interest in the context of education. This implies that the Study University of Technology also aimed to contribute to the global level of preparation of future teachers to effectively use ICT from an educational and teaching perspective. As part of the module requirements, the hardware and software were mentioned in the study guide.

The hardware technologies that student teachers were required to at least have access to relate to a computer, laptop, or mobile device (smartphone, tablet, or iPad). Mangwegape and Mollo (2023) indicated that most higher learning institutions have been investing in enhancing learning through providing access to various types of computer technology, from personal computers (PCs) in the form of desktops and laptops to the relatively more portable form of tablet PCs, in order to improve learning outcomes for students. This is also observed in this initiative, where the majority of the student teachers relied heavily on the institution's computer laboratory. The contact classes were conducted in the computer laboratory. The computer laboratory had sufficient computers. All the students had access to their computers. There were no students sharing computers. The computer laboratory had a stable internet connection. However, all the students in this initiative had a smartphone. The use of mobile devices for learning is supported by Masilo, Simelane-Mnisi and Mji (2022), who argued that currently, almost all students studying at a higher education institution have mobile devices, and the majority are reported to use a personal smartphone. Furthermore, these authors mentioned that students intend to engage in learning tasks using mobile devices. This notion was observed in this study as student teachers utilised their smartphones during the learning process.

The software applications that were utilised during the course of the study included the internet, Wi-Fi (data from the institution), the LMS and its mobile App, the Microsoft 365 applications: MS Word, Excel, PowerPoint Publisher, and MS Teams, Google applications: Word, Excel, PowerPoint, YouTube channel, Google Site, Canva, and the Proctoring tool. Wang (2021) recommended that student teachers should be taught software programs divided into four different categories: teaching tools (such as drill and practice), constructive tools (such as spreadsheets), communication tools (such as e-mail), and information tools (such as online resources) to enhance pedagogy.

It is worth pointing out that the Study University provided the students with free access to software relating to the LMS and its mobile app, the Microsoft 365 applications: MS Word, Excel, PowerPoint Publisher, MS Teams, and the Proctoring tool. This contributed immensely to their academic performance, as they did not have to focus on purchasing the software licenses. It was found in the study conducted by Tomczyk et al. (2023) in Italy and Poland that both countries employ word processing and multimedia presentation production software on a regular basis. Future teachers will occasionally make use of cloud storage tools. Rarely is software for managing databases, spreadsheets, or specialized multimedia editing used.

To enhance the institution's software, the lecturer made use of third-party software that was available for free to students. The software included Google applications: Word, Excel, PowerPoint, YouTube channel, Google

Site, and Canva. The software requires students to access it with their Gmail account. Most of the students had Gmail accounts, as they all use social media platforms. The use of third-party software was also advocated in the study conducted by Ngao, Sang and Kihwele (2022) in Tanzania. The findings in their study showed that student teachers employ a variety of software and learning platforms, social media, online information gathering, and journal subscriptions to obtain learning resources to improve their teaching and learning practices.

The internet and Wi-Fi (data were obtained from the institution). The institution provided students with internet data according to their smartphone's service provider on a monthly basis. This sentiment was supported by Masilo et al. (2021), who indicated that students had access to hotspots outside of class as well as Wi-Fi in the classroom. This allowed students to access the learning material on the LMS and other technologies while learning off campus.

In this module, students also used third-party interactive tools relating to Mentimetre, Slido, Kahoot, and Jamboard to encourage student engagement, interaction, and participation during online and face-to-face classes. The use of these tools was motivated by study conducted by Simelane-Mnisi and Mngavani (2022) who demonstrated the use of third-party interactive tools while presenting live Microsoft Team classes to promote active learning.

A blended approach to learning was the preferred learning and teaching method of delivery. It was preferred because Westerlaken et al. (2019) advocated the importance of blended learning in academic settings, which has increased over the past few decades, since it not only makes learning more student-centred and less teacher-centred but also has the potential to enhance interaction between students and teachers, which would improve learning. Furthermore, blended learning approaches have shown to significantly increase the efficacy and efficiency of relevant learning experiences for pre-service teachers (Ndlovu, 2023).

The infrastructure, in particular ICT in education, made a significant contribution to improving the digital skills of the student teachers pursuing this course. With these ICTs, teaching took priority over technology. This sentiment is supported by Ngao, Sang and Kihwele (2022), who emphasised that integrating ICT into teacher education is crucial and that student teachers should be supported and encouraged to have a positive learning mindset and use ICT in their teaching strategies. Furthermore, Purwanto and Tawar (2024) argued that when choosing a software and platform for online learning, at least two factors must be taken into consideration: the platform's usability and comprehension, as well as its potential to support the achievement of learning outcomes.

When dealing with infrastructure in this project, it is crucial to bring up the South African electrical issue of load shedding, which causes power outages in various time zones and locations. Load shedding has a significant detrimental influence on ICT integration in learning, teaching, and assessment, especially in the context of education. Simelane-Mnisi (2023) indicated that South Africa's load shedding has a negative effect on the fourth sustainable development goal of 2030 (SDG4), which is to provide high-quality education, as the challenge of digital learning and transformation was noted (UN, 2022). According to Khoza (2023), the main load-shedding challenges in South Africa affected pre-service and in-service teachers who were required to complete their teaching practice online. These student teachers were required to submit YouTube links with their teaching videos, and other in-service teachers were at ease using MS Teams to observe classrooms. In this initiative, load shedding had little impact on contact classes. However, online classes were disrupted because they were conducted in the evenings. In this case, online classes were recorded, and the recordings were made available on the learning management system. However, in order to continue teaching, the lecturer had to use the backup battery and a smartphone network point.

3. The challenges and solutions

The challenges were that students' teachers in this module lacked the knowledge and skills with regard to technology integration in learning and teaching and the use of relevant methods, strategies, and pedagogy. Furthermore, student teachers did not know how to create a lesson plan or storyboard that incorporated technology. In addition, the student teachers were not familiar with the Google Site. The majority of the students did not own a YouTube channel. Some of the students did not give lecturers access to various files in their ePortfolio. These challenges were overcome by exposing the student teachers (TPACK). Furthermore, student teachers were also taught the application of TPACK in their field of specialisation. They were exposed to various learning and teaching methods, strategies, and assessments to apply with technology. During the course of the study, one of the authentic activities required student teachers to establish relationships with the schools where they envisaged doing work-integrated learning. In this school, they had to identify and describe the existing technology. The student teachers attended online MS Teams classes where the lecturer empowered them to create Google Sites and YouTube Channels. By the time they had engaged with the integrated assignment, the students had mastered the functionalities of creating their ePortfolio using Google Sites. The lecturer had to request that students give her access to various files and links on the Google site.

4. Evaluation of learning outcomes

The learning outcomes that were achieved by the majority of the student teachers were that they were able to:

- Create an ePortfolio on Google Site displaying creativity and critical thinking skills on their development in ICT in education.
- Critically evaluate the module in the narrative, indicating how the module contributed to their development of knowledge, skills, and values as 21st-century teachers.
- Reflect on the benefits, challenges, and areas for improvement in each assessment or theme.
- Reflect on the module's contribution to their development of knowledge, skills, and values as 21st-century teachers and create a video for the closing statement.

The majority of the student teachers were able to create an e-portfolio on Google Sites when they evaluated the module critically. These were measured in terms of their development of an ePortfolio, which was evaluated using a rubric on the LMS as well as student feedback. This sentiment was observed in Pospíšilová and Rohlíková (2023), who argued that using an ePortfolio application for assessment has a substantial influence on student autonomy and active learning.

It was found that most students passed the final integrated assessment. The integrated assessment results showed that 40 student teachers passed the ePortfolio with a mark between 50% and 100%. About eight student teachers did not submit the ePortfolio, while some did not give the lecturer access to the ePortfolio even when the link to the ePortfolio had been submitted. Darling-Hammond and Snyder (2000) argued that the evidence that student teachers provide in their portfolios is often used to determine whether or not they are deemed ready to complete the program. It is worth noting that upon submission to the assignment tool on the LMS, the lecturer checked if all the links were accessible and requested that the students give her access.

In terms of student feedback on the assessments conducted, it was found that the student teachers acknowledged their exposure to the ePortfolio. The authentic assessments equipped students with innovative ICT skills, which made them future-ready graduates. This was observed by 96.7% of the students, who indicated that the lecturer always gave relevant assignments and examples. McArthur (2023) emphasises that authentic assessment should shift from task performance to social context, whereby students are able to comprehend themselves individually and their social well-being to be able to solve societal challenges.

The findings revealed that the integrated assessment required students to complete the work conducted during the course of the year. The results showed that 93.3% of the student teachers revealed that the lecturer always created a variety of continuous assessment activities for developing various skills. Most of the student teachers (83.3%) revealed that the integrated assessment was fair as it was based on the work covered. The use of various assessments is emphasised by Darling-Hammond and Snyder (2000), who highlighted that these assessment strategies help address some of the core problems of learning to teach in a society where many factors influence learning. It is for this reason that Sakti (2023) argues that authentic assessments of learning cannot be made instantly.

The results showed that 93.3% of the students revealed that the lecturer always awarded badges to students who achieved outstanding results on assessments on the LMS. Schoeman and Fon (2023). It was indicated that students who had more badges performed better and were motivated to learn more because of their badges. The results showed that 90% of the student teachers indicated that the lecturer always administered the marks faultlessly. The results showed that 80% of the student teachers revealed that the lecturer returned marked tests and other work promptly. Furthermore, the findings revealed that 86.7% of the student teachers indicated that the lecturer clearly indicated how the marks were allocated. Lecturers employ various marking tools to give students more informative feedback about their strengths and weaknesses (Mahmoudi & Bugra, 2020).

It was discovered that 83.3% of the students indicated that the lecturer always used an intelligent agent to monitor and track students at risk for marks achieved below 50% and to monitor student progress on the LMS. Intelligent Agents is an LMS tool that enables lecturers to customise learning and communication with students under a number of various release conditions, and lecturers can send pre-written, individualised emails to students depending on a range of criteria, including quiz or test results, unit placement, course enrolment etc. (Leshinsky, 2022).

The student teachers were asked to add any comments about the lecturers' teaching. It was found that the students appreciated activities that encouraged engagement and made sure they grasped this concept. Student teacher 1 responded, "She engages us in a number of activities. Her lessons are very insightful! Student teacher 2 indicated, *"Our lecturer is a credible teacher who always makes sure that students understand the lesson. Other students expressed appreciation for the lecturer's teaching approach. In this case, the student teacher revealed that her teaching methods allowed them to understand the content, and she made the lesson extremely interesting and fruitful. Student teacher 4 mentioned that the lecturer used different teaching aids to make the content easy to understand and relatable. In turn, student teacher 5 mentioned that "she has completely changed my perspective on how I view ICT in education."*

5. Plans to develop the initiative further

The lecturer plans to expose student teachers to more authentic tasks so that they can learn to develop the interaction for social justice, consider the interaction between the person or student and the assignment, as well as their sense of wellbeing, in addition to the learning tasks. The student teachers should be taught certain technology, such as Education 4.0 tools. Since the release of ChatGPT and the influx of AI-based tools in higher education, lecturers need to rethink the approach, design, and facilitation of learning, teaching, and assessment in the 21st century, and authentic assessments should be explored further. In this case, lecturers might design complex scenarios or problems that will require students to make use of AI tools as part of the analytical process and the demonstration of critical thinking and decision-making skills.

It is imperative that the Study University utilise the strengths and industry-aligned practices of AI use while maintaining the integrity and honesty of academic practices. This implies that lecturers still need to ensure that students grasp the content knowledge, skills, and values and take advantage of AI to personalise and promote adaptive learning. Various authentic assessments, such as students critiquing and improving the text resulting from AI, should be further explored, and other forms of innovative assessments will be explored further in the future. For instance, lecturers can develop authentic project-based assessments that require students to employ AI tools to solve real-world problems or analyse large datasets, demonstrating authentic application and critical analysis.

References

Basu, R., (2015). Use of e-portfolios in higher education: Application of constructivist theory for effective learning. *Advances in Computer Science and Information Technology (ACSIT)*, 2(3), pp.186-190.

Chen, B., & Crook, A. D. (2020). Using e-portfolios to foster self-regulated learning in higher education: A systematic review. *Computers & Education*, 145, 103755.

Chweu, E. M., Simelane-Mnisi, S., & Mji, A. (2023). Exploring Assessment Types, Instruments and Methods of Assessing Knowledge, Skills and Values in Higher Education. In Mafalda Carmo, *Education Applications & Developments VIII Advances in Education and Educational Trends Series*, pp. 218-227.

Darling-Hammond, L., & Snyder, J. (2000). Authentic assessment of teaching in context. *Teaching and Teacher Education*, 16(5-6), 523-545.

Ismail, S. S. (2023). barriers towards the implementation of e-portfolio in education based on the diffusion of innovation theory. *International Journal of Learning, Teaching and Educational Research*, 22(4), pp. 512-540.

Khoza, S. D. (2023). The 'blemishes' of COVID-19 at South Africa's higher education institutions. *Journal of Pedagogical Sociology and Psychology*, 5(2), 62-70.

Leshinsky, A. (2022). Intelligent Agents on the D2l Platform: A qualitative exploration into educator use and understanding of asynchronous course elements to promote course personalization, Doctoral dissertation, North-eastern University.

Mahmoudi, F., & Bugra, C. (2020). The Effects of Using Rubrics and Face to Face Feedback in Teaching Writing Skill in Higher Education. *International Online Journal of Education and Teaching*, 7(1), 150-158.

McArthur, J. (2023). Rethinking authentic assessment: work, wellbeing, and society. *Higher Education*, 85, No. 1, pp. 85-101.

Masilo, G., Simelane-Mnisi, S., Mji, A., & Mokgobu, I. (2021). Students' behavioural intention and challenges to bring your own device (BYOD) in higher education during COVID-19 and beyond. *World Transactions on Engineering and Technology Education*, 19(1), 10-15.

Mangwegape, B. K., & Mollo, P. P. (2023). Exploring the integration level of information and communication technology (ICT) by Setswana student teachers at a university of technology in South Africa. *Education and New Development*, pp.168-171. https://doi.org/10.36315/2023v1end036

Ndlovu, B. N. (2023). Using transformative pedagogies in higher institutions? Narratives of foundation phase pre-service teachers in a rural context. In *Advancing self-directed learning in higher education*. pp. 158-174. IGI Global.

Ngao, A. I., Sang, G., & Kihwele, J. E. (2022). Understanding teacher educators' perceptions and practices about ICT integration in teacher education program. *Education Sciences*, 12(8), 549.

Patiño, A., Ramírez-Montoya, M.S., & Buenestado-Fernández, M. (2023). Active learning and education 4.0 for complex thinking training: analysis of two case studies in open education. *Smart Learning Environments*, 10(1), pp.8.

Pospíšilová, L., & Rohlíková, L. (2023). Reforming higher education with ePortfolio implementation, enhanced by learning analytics. *Computers in Human Behavior*, 138, 107449.

Purwanto, A., & Tawar, T. (2024). Investigating The Role of the use of computer Hardware, software and lecturer involvement on online universities student satisfaction. *UJoST-Universal Journal of Science and Technology*, 3(1), 1-13.

Sakti, B. P. (2023). Types of authentic learning assessment, *Attadib: Journal of Elementary Education*, 6 (2), 342-350.

SAQA, (2022). Policy and criteria for the registration of qualifications and part-qualifications on the National Qualifications Framework. Pretoria: SAQA

Schoeman, H., & Fon, F. (2023). The efficacy of issuing badges as an incentive during emergency remote teaching: A Case Study. In EDULEARN23 Proceedings, pp. 5129-5137, IATED.

Simelane-Mnisi, S. (2022). Evaluating the quality of design and the development of online modules in higher education. *World Transactions on Engineering and Technology Education (WTE&TE)*, 20(4), 264-271.

Simelane-Mnisi, S., & Magavani, C. (2022). Increasing student engagement and interaction in live Microsoft Teams classes. December 2022, DigiTalk2022 International Conference on Teaching, Assessment and Learning in the Digital era. Durban, Umhlanga, South Africa. pp. 24-33.

Tomczyk, Ł., Fedeli, L., Włoch, A., Limone, P., Frania, M., Guarini, P., . & Falkowska, J. (2023). Digital competences of pre-service teachers in Italy and Poland. *Technology, Knowledge and Learning*, 28(2), 651-681.

UN, Sustainable Development Goal 4 (SDG4), 23 September 2009, https://www.sdg4education2030.org/the-goal

UN, SDG4 Education 2030 High-Level Steering Committee Contribution to the 2022 High-Level Political Forum on Sustainable Development: The State of Education-SDG4 Review (2022), 23 September 2009,www.sdg4education2030.org

Wang, Y. M. (2001). Student teachers' perception and practice of the teachers' role when teaching with computers. *Journal of Educational Computing Research*, 24(4), 419-434.

Westerlaken, M., Christiaans-Dingelhoff, I., Filius, R. M., De Vries, B., De Bruijne, M., & Van Dam, M. (2019). Blended learning for postgraduates; an interactive experience. *BMC Medical Education*, 19(1): 1-7.

Sibongile Simelane-Mnisi

Author Biography

Dr. Sibongile Simelane-Mnisi is a senior instructional designer and a part-time lecturer at Tshwane University of Technology. She is a 21st-century teacher who is passionate about research. She supervises postgraduate students. She has authored and co-authored research articles and chapters in books published in South African and international peer-reviewed journals.

ECS1500:
An Economics Module to Accommodate Diverse Learning Needs of Young Adults

Cecilia J. van Zyl
Department of Economics, University of South Africa

vzylcj@unisa.ac.za

1. Introduction

One of the United Nations' sustainable development goals (SDGs) is to ensure inclusive and equitable education and promote lifelong learning opportunities for all. Currently, the world is falling behind in this goal (United Nations, n.d.). Due to its scalability, distance education can contribute greatly to overcoming the lack of education opportunities in developing economies (Daniel, 2022; Ukaoha, Abdullahi & Chiemeke, 2018). This case study provides an overview of the development of an introductory Economics distance education module that is designed to provide students with the largest possible chance to be successful, despite possible characteristics and challenges that may hinder achievement.

1.1 An overview of the module

Economics 1500 (ECS1500) is a 12-credit (120 hours) module that introduces students to basic micro- and macro-economic principles and applies these principles to the South African economic environment. It is presented at the University of South Africa (Unisa), which is the largest open distance learning university in Africa. The student numbers are high, between 3 000 and 6 000 students per semester.

Students enrolled for ECS1500 are expected to be able to apply economic principles and tools to analyse basic economic situations. When studying Economics, students have to ensure that they have mastered certain concepts before they can proceed to the next step.

Most of the students enrolled for this module are enrolled for a Higher Certificate in Economics and Management Sciences. They are doing this course to obtain access to study for a B.Com Degree and also to prepare them for such study. This qualification should also prepare students to become independent, self-assured learners who take responsibility for their own learning. Most students who enrol for this module are engaging with both higher education and distance education for the first time. Therefore it is important that clear guidance is provided so that students understand what is expected from them.

To inform our module design, we had to determine who our students are, what motivates them and what challenges they experience.

1.2   Who are our students?

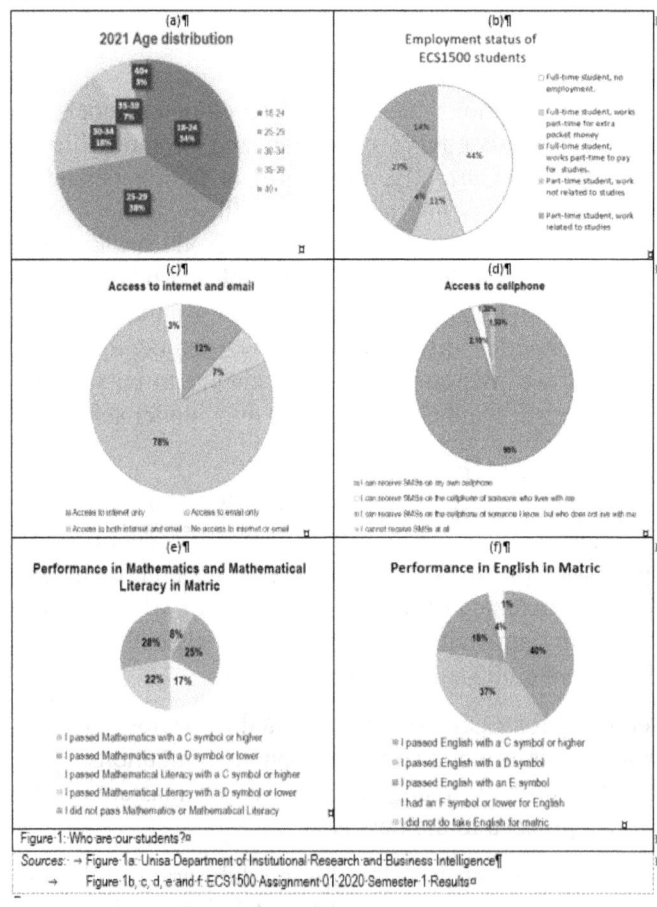

Figure 1: Who are our students?
Sources: → Figure 1a: Unisa Department of Institutional Research and Business Intelligence
→ Figure 1b, c, d, e and f: ECS1500 Assignment 01 2020 Semester 1 Results

Our students are mostly young adults as 72% are younger than 30 and 38% are between 25 and 29 (Figure 1a). Despite the fact that Unisa is a distance education institution, our students are mainly full-time students who do not work or only work for pocket money (Figure 1b). They have access to the internet, email and cell phones (Figures 1c and 1d). Our students are proficient in English, but not in Mathematics (Figures 1e and 1f).

1.3 What motivates our students?
Based on the fact that our students are young and unemployed and that they did not perform well in Mathematics at school, we can assume that they are studying at Unisa because they do not have any other option. However, just the fact that they are registered with Unisa indicates that they wish to succeed and make progress in life.

1.4 What challenges do our students experience?
Although most of our students have access to the internet, data is very expensive in South Africa. Since most of the students are young and unemployed, we can assume that they cannot afford to study fully online. For the same reason, the devices that they will use to study may be limited to a cell phone, or a very basic computer or laptop. South Africa also experiences regular electricity blackouts and, in many areas, access to the internet is not stable.

Since access to technology at most South African government schools is limited, very few of our students have been exposed to online learning. Our challenge is to ensure that our students adjust to the online learning environment and realise that they have to take responsibility for their own learning.

1.5 Design principles based on student characteristics and module aims
Taking the characteristics of our students into account, the following design principles were adhered to:
- We employed a *Universal Design for Learning*, which aspires to design courses that enable each individual student to study in the way that suits that student the best, given their particular learning style.
- We present study material so that it can be used both *online and offline*, depending on the student's access to electricity and the internet. At the same

time, certain tasks must be completed online to ensure that all students are exposed to working in an online environment.
- The module design should enable students to master economic concepts and become *independent learners who take responsibility for their own studies*. A continuous assessment framework with comprehensive feedback to learning activities and assessment is used. The assessment framework is designed to provide students with regular information on their learning and pointers on how to address gaps in their learning.

2. The infrastructure and resources

The learning management system (LMS) that is used is Moodle. In distance education, the LMS is the channel through which students connect with their study material, their lecturer and their fellow students. Research indicates that the effective use of an LMS can increase the intellectual achievement of students, as well as their motivation levels (Al-kreimeen & Murad, 2022; Lumpkin, 2021). Mahmoud (2022) found that the use of an LMS affected self-regulated learning skills positively. Research found that motivation levels are increased by the applicable use of diverse content presentation, such as images, video, voice and interactive activities such as discussion forums and quizzes that provide feedback upon submission, while an advantage of an asynchronous learning management system appreciated by students is the opportunity for flexibility to be able to choose when and where they want to study (Gridina, V., Ryabinova & Chekanushkina, 2021).

High student numbers necessitate a large teaching team to ensure that student-centric teaching will still be possible. The teaching team consists of a module leader, who is an experienced senior lecturer, and a group of young academics who bring vibrancy, enthusiasm and lots of new ideas to the team. Nine tutors and ten external markers are employed, which enables us to provide personal and quick feedback on discussion forums and practice written assessment. An external moderator, who is an experienced academic from another South African university, ensures the quality of the content and assessment.

2.1 How do we ensure that students really engage with the content of the module to reach the learning outcomes?

Learning theory

The learning theory that underlies ECS1500 is andragogy, which is the "art and science of helping adults learn" (Knowles, 1970:55). Part of the purpose of the module is to develop the learner to move from pedagogical learning, which is directed by the teacher, towards heutagogy, which is self-determined learning (Blaschke, 2019), as illustrated in Figure 2.

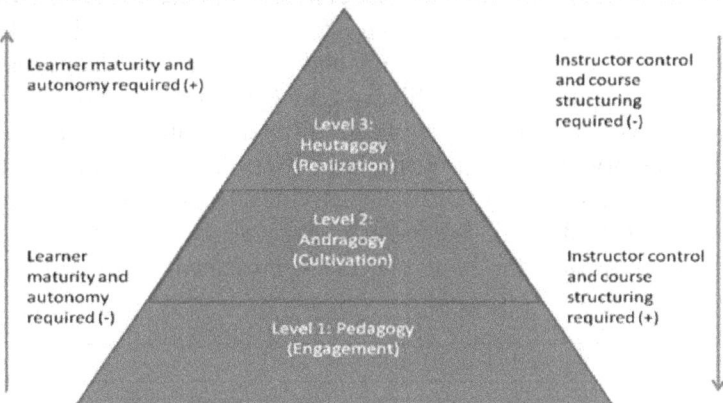

Figure 2: The Pedagogy-Andragogy-Heutagogy Continuum Source: Blaschke 2019

Forrest and Peterson (2006:115) summarised the important characteristics of andragogy as follows:

- Adult learners are aware of their own existing knowledge and their needs, and this informs how they learn.
- Adult learners already possess certain experiences and knowledge that can be used in the learning process.
- Adults' desire to learn originates from their own need to improve the way they interact with society.
- Adults learn to solve specific problems or increase certain performance levels.

To motivate adult learners and to enable them to judge their own competencies against the required skills and competencies, each learning unit starts with a summary of the learning outcomes and an activity that enables students to evaluate their skill levels and knowledge of the content of the learning unit. A summary is also provided to inform students how the skills and knowledge included in that particular learning unit can be applied in the real world and how it will be used in future economics studies.

Employing the VARK model to accommodate various learning styles

To ensure student-centric teaching, it is necessary to consider that not all students learn in the same way (Prithishkumar, 2014) and that our teaching model has to provide for different learning styles (Pérez-Marín, Paredes-Velasco & Pizarro, 2022). The Universal Design for Learning (UDL) is aimed at "designing courses with the intention of helping each student find the approach to acquiring, generating, and using new knowledge that is just right for him or her" (Rogers-Shaw, Carr-Chellman & Choi, 2018). The VARK model distinguishes between different learning styles, namely, Visual, Auditory, Read and Write, and Kinesthetic (Fleming & Baume, 2006), as shown in Table 1. Different activities that appeal to different types of learners are indicated. We include links to examples from the study material to show how the same concept is presented to appeal to different learners.

Table 1: Application of VARK model in ECS1500

Learning Styles	Visual learners Learn by seeing	Auditory Learn by hearing	Read & Write Learn by reading and writing	Kinesthetic Learn by doing
Preferred activities	• Images • Graphs • Diagrams • Icons	• Video • Audio • Group discussion	• Books • Text • Reference guides	• Learning activities • Real-life examples • Demonstrations • Working models
Example from ECS1500	Link to PowerPoint Presentation: Changes in demand	Link to MP4: Changes in demand	Link: Text version A change in demand	Link: Learning Activity 3.4 Link: Feedback learning activity 3.4

Adult learners have knowledge of their own preferences and learning styles, therefore they can choose the type of learning material that suits their abilities and situation best. The module starts with a START HERE section, where we explain to students how to evaluate their own learning style and based on this, how to use the content of the LMS.

Accommodating online and offline learning

Achieving many of the SDGs, including high-quality education for all, requires "inclusive digital transformation" that will ensure access to affordable, safe and scalable technologies (SDG Digital, n.d). Unfortunately, South Africa, like many other developing economies, is experiencing severe challenges with the implementation of inclusive digital transformation. Limited internet access is a reality that has to be taken into account when designing distance learning content in South Africa. Therefore, students who have access should be able to make use of all the affordances that the Internet and online learning offer without disadvantaging students who have limited Internet access. At the same time, we want to ensure that all students are exposed to a digital environment and are afforded the opportunity to develop technology skills, such as searching for and creating electronic content and sharing it with other parties, and, interacting with tools such as online portals, video conferencing and online discussion forums. Such skills prepare graduates to use technology in the workplace and for life-long learning, ensuring they are prepared for the future and the implications of the fourth industrial revolution (Gous 2019).

Therefore, we provide the study material so that students can choose whether they want to study online or download the information and study offline, but all students will still have to access the internet to participate in discussion forums and graded assessments. Table 2 explains how this is done in practice. The assessment components are only available online. However, students can prepare for these offline and only need to be online for the time of the graded assessment. This flexible blended learning approach is a careful balancing act where we try to harness to advantages of digital learning without placing students with limited internet access at a disadvantage, but still ensuring that all students are adequately prepared for the challenges and opportunities of the fourth industrial revolution.

Table 2: Accommodating online and offline study		
LEARNING COMPONENTS	STUDENTS WHO STUDY ONLINE	STUDENTS WHO STUDY OFFLINE
Content of learning units	Work through content online where it is presented in interactive mode	Work through content using a printed/pdf study guide
Videos and PowerPoint presentations that explain difficult concepts	Embedded in online study material	Available as additional resources that students can download to watch offline
Discussion forum learning activities	Participate in discussion forum learning activities as they progress through the study material	Formulate responses to questions in discussion forums offline and post them online when they have access to the internet
Learning activities containing True/false questions, MCQ questions and short questions, with complete feedback	Participate in online quizzes with immediate feedback provided when students submit	Answers questions as they progress through the study material. Feedback is provided in a separate document that becomes available online at the end of the week allocated to a particular learning unit
4 timed formative MCQ assessments with immediate feedback (contribute 32% of total credits). Students can submit each assessment 3 times and receive complete feedback upon submission	Complete assessments online and receive immediate feedback	
1 written summative assessment (contributes 8% of total credits)	Students can submit a practice assessment online and receive feedback from a tutor. Students prepare an answer and post a pdf document for marking on the learning management system. Receive feedback after marking.	
2 timed summative MCQ assessments (contribute 30 x 2 = 60 credits). Students can submit each assessment twice. Limited feedback (only marks and answers) provided upon submission	Complete assessment online and receive immediate limited feedback.	

An assessment framework that supports learning

Since 2022, a **continuous assessment framework** has been introduced to support learning. Assessment tasks are set up at regular intervals in the learning process, to ensure student engagement and active learning. The objective was to design the model so that students feel that they are continuously in conversation with the content, the lecture team and fellow students. Figure 3 explains this conversation.

Cecilia J. van Zyl

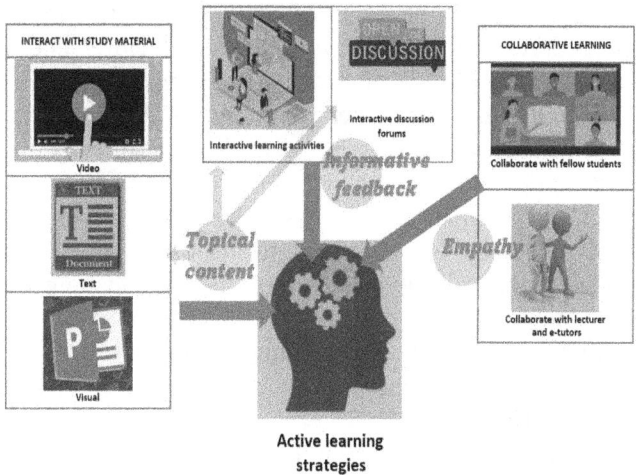

Figure 3: Active learning strategies in ECS1500

The continuous assessment framework allows students to evaluate their own progress and also enables lecturers to identify students at risk, so that gaps in learning can be addressed before students continue with their learning.

Learning is supported by high-quality feedback to learning activities. Assessment *as* learning provides an opportunity for students to master the content by working through learning activities. Formative assessment, or assessment *for* learning, is to enable students to determine if there are still gaps in their learning and how to address such gaps. Students can submit each of these graded formative assessments *for* learning three times over a period of three weeks; thus, opportunity is provided to improve their learning. A lot of effort went into the formulation of the feedback to assessment *as* learning and the assessment *for* learning. Automated feedback on quizzes and short questions is generated upon submission. Feedback to discussion forum activities that are aimed to evaluate crucial learning blocks that students need to have in place to continue with their studies successfully is provided by tutors, using guidelines that are prepared by lecturers. Feedback on learning activities that are included to stimulate interest, debate and creative thinking is provided by peers. These discussion forums are moderated by tutors to ensure that the discussion remains relevant and uplifting. For all the various types of feedback, the utmost care is taken to ensure that an empathetic, conversational tone is maintained.

To ensure the validity and reliability of assessment in this module, quality assurance procedures are in place. A secondary lecturer and an external examiner evaluate both the structure of the assessment plan as well as the content of each individual assessment opportunity. A further way in which the validity of the assessment for this module is controlled is through using the learning analytics that is available on Moodle to identify any multiple-choice, true-false or calculation questions in the question pools that may need to be revised or removed. All questions in which students performed exceptionally well or poorly are identified, as well as questions for which the discriminatory index was lower than 30%. The content of these questions is revised by a panel of lecturers to determine the reason for the high or low success rate, and whether the questions need to be revised or removed from the question pool. The frequency for each of the distractors is also checked to evaluate poor distractors for which the response rate is low compared to the others. Such distractors are evaluated to determine whether they should be revised or excluded.

3. The challenges we experienced

Before Covid-19, ECS1500 students could attend weekly face-to-face tutor classes at regional centres throughout South Africa. The obvious way to replace this was to arrange online classes. However, the lack of access to the Internet resulted in such classes being very poorly attended. To replace the discussion classes, Camtasia was utilised to make videos using PowerPoint presentations. Students regarded the videos and slides as an improvement on the discussion classes, since they can access them at their convenience. These were also incorporated into the study material so that students who prefer to learn by watching a video or working through a PowerPoint, can choose to do this. We feel that this improved the module and ensured that our offering really contributes to addressing the learning needs of all types of learners, especially young learners who prefer watching videos.

An important challenge that was experienced in the first semester when the newly designed module ran on the Moodle platform, was the overwhelming reaction from students. Though this was heartening, the extremely high participation rate was unexpected and we did not have an adequate number of tutors to provide feedback. The lecturing team had to assist, and both lecturers and tutors had to work extremely long hours to provide feedback on time. We have been able to appoint more tutors, but due to budget constraints, it will be necessary to carefully reconsider the number of discussion forums where individualised feedback is provided.

During this first semester, students were also allowed to interact with each other on all discussion forums. We found that this created issues in identifying the posts that tutors had to provide feedback on. As indicated above, some discussion forums still allow for debate and dialogue among students, and tutors mainly play a monitoring role here. For forums where essential building blocks are evaluated, students cannot interact with each other or see each other's feedback. Students also found it difficult to distinguish between fellow students and the teaching team. We created logos to distinguish the teaching team from other participants.

4. How the initiative was received by the users or participants

Figure 4 provides a summary of the results of a student review of this module done in 2020. As can be seen from the statistics, most students agreed or strongly agreed that the module encouraged critical thinking, provided a valuable learning experience, that useful guidance was provided, that learning outcomes were clearly stated, that the content was well structured, that myUnisa was used effectively and that the website was easy to navigate. This sends an encouraging message that our module design is effective.

Many students commented that the module helped them to understand the economy better and that they enjoyed the way in which the theory is applied to real-world situations. The following are comments on the module design from students that were included in open-ended questions in the questionnaire:

- *Interesting, well explained with real situations.*
- *Relevance to the real world. There is always a realistic relevant scenario to use with the aid of the module.*
- *Getting to know and understand monetary policy and seeing the good and bad of the decisions taken by our government in economics. I understand the consequences of our decisions in both economic and personal life.*

Several students' comments indicated that the module design assisted them in mastering the content of the module and becoming self-assured learners:

- *I enjoyed the weekly activities even though I was struggling with how to effectively use the learning management system and the disruption that came with COVID-19 but in the end, I enjoyed doing activities on my own.*
- *The study guide was simple and straightforward. I was able to write my assessment on time and answer all the questions easily.*
- *Having to give my level best and apply what I have studied*

Finally, some students indicated that they enjoyed that the module content and assessment were challenging. We experience this as very positive since we believe that education should open minds and nurture creativity:

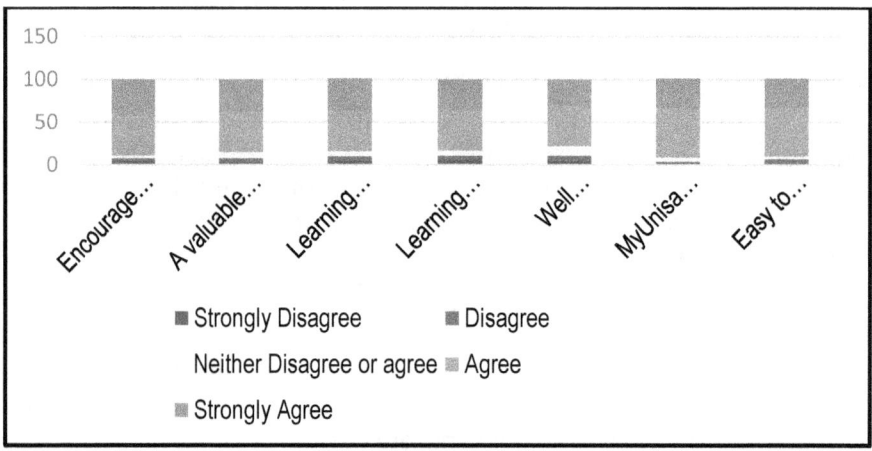

Figure 4: Students' opinion of the ECS1500 module design, *Source*: 2020 Student review done by the Department of Institutional Support and Facilitation of Learning, Unisa.

- *Because this module was very challenging and it needed me to understand the concepts of every unit*
- *I enjoyed the experience and the challenges*
- *These studies and information challenged and opened my mind to how the economy can be improved*

5. The learning outcomes and results

Traditionally, the pass rate for this module was persistently below 40% of the total number of students who registered. The introduction of the online module, with study material being available in different formats, combined with the use of continuous assessment that enables tracking students' learning progress, resulted in the pass rate increasing to 53% in 2022. Previously, many students fell out before the final exam. In 2022, the participation rate increased to 94% of registered students, compared to 79% in 2021 (Department of Economics, 2022).

It is now also possible for lecturers to identify the activities and assessments that students perform poorly in, and in this way, identify the learning outcomes that students have not achieved. Steps can be taken to identify how the learning material can be improved to contribute to more effective learning.

6. Plans to develop the initiative in future

The ECS1500 team continues to monitor the performance of students with regard to the various learning outcomes and improve the study material where required. In the future, we are planning to introduce gamification. This will motivate students to improve their participation and performance, to improve their "game rating". Since students will be able to view their participation and performance graphically, such an approach will also assist students to identify gaps in their own learning more effectively, while at the same time motivating them to address such gaps to improve their performance.

Since preparing feedback is a time-consuming activity, it is necessary to make sure how students experience and engage with the feedback. Such research is currently underway.

7. Conclusion

This case study explains how the online introductory Economics module, ECS1500, was developed taking three design principles into account that would provide the opportunity for all students, regardless of their learning preferences and possible limited internet access, to be successful and become independent learners who take responsibility for their own studies.

We believe that this module design provides a blueprint that can be used to guide module design for open-distance learning in developing economies with limited internet access. Regardless of the subject, adhering to these three principles could contribute to providing maximum access to all students and support the achievement of the United Nations SDG of ensuring inclusive and equitable quality education and promoting lifelong learning opportunities for all.

References

Al-kreimeen, R. & Murad, O. (2022) Using Moodle in university courses and its impact on future anxiety and psychological happiness. *The Electronic Journal of e-Learning*, 20(2):171-179. Retrieved from https://files.eric.ed.gov/fulltext/EJ1333740.pdf on 18 September 2022.

Blaschke, L.M. (2019). The Pedagogy–Andragogy–Heutagogy Continuum and Technology-Supported Personal Learning Environments. In Jung, I. (ed) *Open and Distance Education Theory Revisited*. Singapore: Springer. Retrieved from https://link.springer.com/chapter/10.1007/978-981-13-7740-2_9#citeas on 25 May 2022.

Daniel, J. (2022). Running Distance Education at Scale: Open Universities, Open Schools, and MOOCs. Zawacki-Richter, O. & Jung, I. (eds.). *Handbook of Open, Distance and Digital Education*. Singapore: Springer. https://doi.org/10.1007/978-981-19-0351-9_26-1

Department of Economics. (2022). *Department of Economics Module Reflection Report October 2022*. Unpublished report submitted to the Quality Assurance and Enhancement Committee of the College of Economic and Management Sciences, Unisa.

Fleming, N. & Baume, D. (2006). Learning Styles Again: VARKing up the right tree!, *Educational Developments*, 7(4): 4-7.

Forrest, S.I. & Peterson, T.O. (2006). It's called Andragogy. *Academy of Management Learning & Education*, 5(1): 113-122.

Gous, I. (2019) Yesterday, Today and Tomorrow: The Blossoming Art of Teaching and Learning Required to Prepare Students for the 4th Industrial Revolution. *Proceedings of the European Distance and E-Learning Network 2019 Annual Conference*, Bruges, 16-19 June, 2019. Retrieved from https://www.researchgate.net/publication/349103148_Yesterday_Today_and_Tomorrow_The_Blossoming_Art_of_Teaching_and_Learning_Required_to_Prepare_Students_for_the_4th_Industrial_Revolution on 15 September 2023.

Gridina, V., Ryabinova, E. & Chekanushkina, E. (2021). Designing the learning process for technical university students in conditions of uncertainty. Humanity in the Era of Uncertainty. In E. Bakshutova, V. Dobrova, & Y. Lopukhova (Eds.), Humanity in the Era of Uncertainty, vol 119. *European Proceedings of Social and Behavioural Sciences* (pp. 744-750). European Publisher. https://doi.org/10.15405/epsbs.2021.12.02.92

Knowles, M.S. (1970). The modern practice of adult education: from pedagogy to andragogy. Cambridge Book Company.

Lumpkin, A. (2021). Online teaching: Pedagogical practices for engaging students synchronously and asynchronously. *College Student Journal*, 55(2), 195–207. https://eric.ed.gov/?id=EJ1313926

Mahmoud, E.A. (2021). The effect of e-Learning practices during the Covid-19 pandemic on enhancing self-regulated learning skills as perceived by university students. *Amazona Investiga*, 10(39): 129-135. Retrieved from https://amazoniainvestiga.info/index.php/amazonia/article/view/1579/1597 on 18 September 2023.

Pérez-Marín, D., Paredes-Velasco, M. & Pizarro, C. (2022). Multi-mode Digital Teaching and Learning of Human-Computer Interaction (HCI) using the VARK Model during COVID-19. *Educational Technology & Society*, 25(1): 78-91.

Prithishkumar, I.J. (2014). Understanding your student: Using the VARK model. *Journal of Postgraduate Medicine*, 60(2): 183-186. https://doi.org/10.4103/0022-3859.132337.

Rogers-Shaw, C., Carr-Chellman, D.J. & Choi, J. (2018). Universal Design for Learning: Guidelines for Accessible Online Instruction. *Adult Learning*, 29(1): 20-31. Retrieved from https://journals.sagepub.com/doi/full/10.1177/1045159517735530 on 25 May 2022.

SDG Digital. (N.d). UN High Impact Initiative: Digital Public Infrastructure. Retrieved from https://www.itu.int/initiatives/sdgdigital/digital-public-infrastructure/ on 18 September 2023.

Ukaoha, K.C., Abdullahi, M.B. & Chiemeke, S.C. (2018). Sustainable Development Goals of Education in Nigeria. *Harvard Conference on Preparing Students for an Uncertain Future*, Boston, USA, November 2018, 16(1). Retrieved from https://www.21caf.org/uploads/1/3/5/2/13527682/4._21cef-7094-ukaoha.pdf on 15 September 2023.

United Nations. (N.d.). The 17 Goals. Department of Economic and Social Affairs: Sustainable Development. Retrieved from https://sdgs.un.org/goals on 18 September 2023.

Author Biography

Cecilia van Zyl is a senior lecturer in the Department of Economics at the University of South Africa. She is mainly involved with module development and teaching of first-level Economics and has an interest in ensuring inclusive and open education. Her research involves aspects related to open-distance teaching and learning.

Unlocking Potential: Creating an Innovative Learning Platform to Foster Digital Skills of Educators

Georg Winder, Andrea Kern, Karin Zehetner, Dr. Josef Buchner
St.Gallen University of Teacher Education, St.Gallen, Switzerland

georg.winder@phsg.ch
andrea.kern@phsg.ch
karin.zehetner@phsg.ch
josef.buchner@phsg.ch

Abstract: The development of digital competencies is vital for teachers and principals to harness the potential of digital technology in the classroom. In response, *aprendo*, a learning platform supporting the ongoing growth of digital competencies for more than 12,000 educators in the canton of St.Gallen, Switzerland has been created. The platform offers diverse learning opportunities in synchronous and asynchronous learning formats. Until 2027 it will offer about 100 modules in six competency dimensions. *aprendo* provides flexible and accessible ways for users to develop digital competencies regardless of time and location. Despite initial technological implementation and user adoption challenges, the platform was well-received. Moving forward, *aprendo* will expand and incorporate new modules, along with technological innovations like artificial intelligence to help users find suitable modules based on their interests. By equipping educators with knowledge and tools to navigate the digital landscape, *aprendo* aims to support the ongoing digital transformation of schools and prepare principals, teachers, and students in St.Gallen for the future.

Keywords: digital competencies, teacher development, Switzerland, aprendo.ch, e-Learning, education

1. Introduction

The 21st century is characterized by profound global societal transformation and rapid advancements in technology, which have a significant impact on various aspects of life. These changes bring forth new demands and challenges in the field of education, particularly for teacher education and the teaching profession itself (Falloon 2020; Schweizer 2019). Furthermore, global COVID-19 lockdowns and the increase of artificial intelligence (AI) applications such as ChatGPT, have led to a broad consensus that digital transformation in schools must be advanced (Gašević, Siemens, and Sadiq 2023). As a result, fundamental questions arise regarding the essential competencies required for active and responsible participation in future societies (Caena and Redecker 2019). To ensure that teachers remain effective in their roles and adequately support students' learning journeys, especially the realm of digital competencies requires additional effort for continuous professional development.

Recognizing the need for ongoing professional development in digital competencies among educators, the government of St.Gallen entrusted an innovative project team at the St.Gallen University of Teacher Education, with the task of developing a digital learning platform (KoDiBi 2020). As a result, *aprendo* has been created. The platform aims to strengthen the digital competencies of all teachers and school principals in the canton of St.Gallen.

The platform, designed to fully leverage the potential of digital technology in the classroom, offers a comprehensive range of learning opportunities. It caters to over 12,000 educators across primary, secondary, and vocational schools. This approach distinguishes *aprendo*, as the authors possess no knowledge of alternative continuous education platforms that comprehensively encompass the entire spectrum of digital skills acquisition among educators, spanning from early childhood education to professional development. *aprendo* offers flexible and accessible learning formats, including synchronous and asynchronous fully online and blended modules, empowering educators to enhance their digital competencies at their own pace and regardless of time and location. This user-centric approach acknowledges the heterogeneity of the users, allowing them to individually plan their continuing professional development.

In addition, our developed AI-powered "*aprendo* navigator" supports educators in choosing modules based on their interests and professional development goals. The feature acknowledges the importance of both the acquisition of skills and the promotion of affective-motivational learning of teachers to ensure lifelong learning engagement.

Built on cutting-edge software and featuring a user-friendly interface, *aprendo* overcomes initial challenges related to technological implementation and user adoption. It empowers its users to explore a diverse range of topics across six competency dimensions, which are *ICT*

Application Skills, Instructional Design and Educational Technology, Media Literacy, Computational Education, Digital Professionalism and Digital Leadership. These dimensions are based on DigCompEdu (Redecker 2017) and dig.kompP (Brandhofer and Miglbauer 2020), but combine them to more fully capture the competencies teachers need to shape education in the digital world (Brandhofer et al. 2022).

The platform has already yielded positive results, facilitating significant improvements in users' digital skills. The platform's versatility and adaptability allow for continuous evolution and expansion. Future plans include the incorporation of new modules, e.g., modules that focus on emerging topics in teacher education like AI literacy (Hornberger, Bewersdorff, and Nerdel 2023) or immersive learning with augmented/virtual reality (Buchner and Hofmann 2022), and the integration of further AI features that, for example, consider prior knowledge as another relevant factor for module recommendation.

These advancements will help users identify the most suitable modules based on their prerequisites and preferences and further enhance the learning experience.

2. The infrastructure – people and systems

aprendo consists of three different platform components, although they are not recognizable to users as separate applications. The three main components of the platform are the frontend, the backend, and the Learning Management System (LMS). Additional applications such as *Kaltura*, which is used as videoconferencing tool, are integrated via API (see Figure 1).

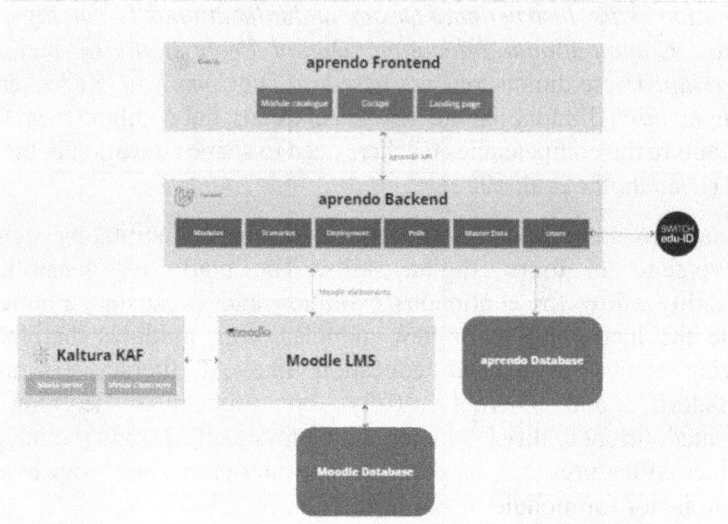

Figure 1: System infrastructure

The frontend has been developed in-house and is the interface that users see and interact with. It includes the essential navigation and interaction elements of the platform, such as module catalog (see Figure 2), personal learning cockpit, support, and personal profile. The frontend is responsible for displaying modules and general platform information and serves as the starting point to access features such as user registration and module content itself. It provides a user-friendly and attractive interface to offer users an intuitive and engaging learning experience. Users have the possibility to personalize their profile and to use filter options available in the catalog. By doing so users actively influence the display of the modules as well as the respective order.

Within a dedicated section of the catalog, users are presented with modules currently under development. This allows users to consider this information while planning their personal training goals. The personal cockpit provides an overview of a users' current, planned, and completed modules. Additionally, it displays the total number of hours already studied on the platform. Future enhancements in this area will incorporate gamification strategies.

Georg Winder et al

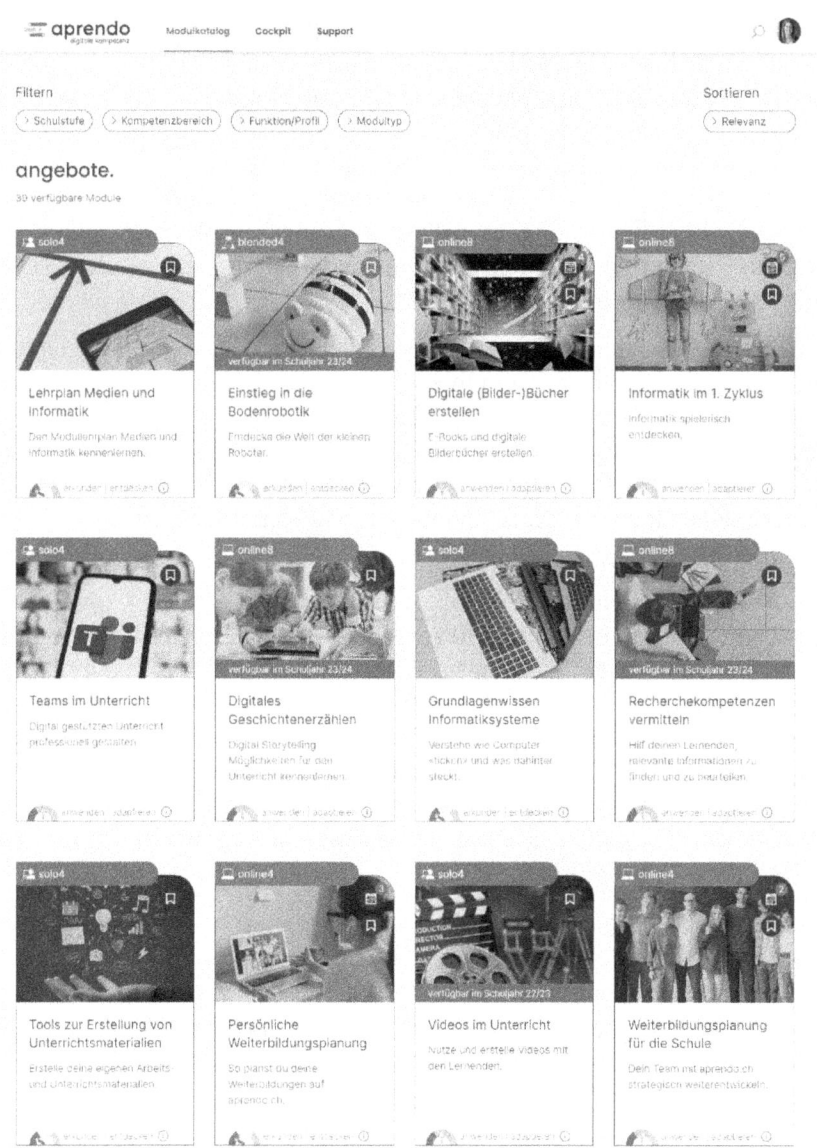

Figure 2: Module catalog

The backend is also an in-house development and is the technical infrastructure that operates behind the scenes of the platform. It includes databases and other components required for storing, administering, and processing all essential data related to offering, implementing, and completing modules. The backend processes user requests, stores user data, learning materials, and other information, manages security and authorization/authentication, enables scalability of the platform, and ensures seamless integration with other surrounding systems and services (LMS, APIs to *Kaltura*, frontend).

he Learning Management System (LMS) is the core element of the learning platform. It is based on a modified version of the open-source software application *Moodle*, specifically developed for the management and organization of learning content. The LMS allows module authors and instructors to create modules, upload learning materials, track the progress of users, conduct assessments, and issue module certifications.

In addition to the software component, *aprendo* is primarily distinguished by its team. Currently, around 30 employees work on the project, divided into three teams that focus on different aspects. The entire software development is done in-house, offering advantages such as customization, quality control, security, and above all high flexibility and speed in implementing new features and user requests. This internal development of all components and integrations allows for tailored solutions, efficient maintenance, ongoing support, and seamless integration. Overall, it ensures a comprehensive and effective platform. The small in-house software development team consists of two full stack developers and one application engineer.

Another team is responsible for the administrative processes of the platform. In addition to coordinating online and blended modules, the team, currently consisting of three employees, handles support cases and public relations. Furthermore, as the team members are power users of the backend they contribute to the continuous improvement of administrative processes within the platform.

The third and largest team within *aprendo* focuses on managing and developing learning content. The team, currently comprising around ten members, is responsible for developing content in the six competency dimensions. They either develop content themselves or coordinate with external module authors and oversee quality management too. To ensure a high quality of the published module, a rigor instructional design process is applied. The process starts with a subject analysis, in which intensive didactic and content research is conducted. Based on the findings, an initial rough planning is made for the respective module. This is followed by detailed planning, in which the concrete content and structures for the module are developed.

The next step is to produce the educational media and embed them in the LMS. This is followed by an initial assessment and test run of the module. If necessary, adjustments are made, otherwise the module can be finally reviewed and released. After this final review, the module is published on the frontend and can be booked by the users. In the further course, the module will be maintained and, if necessary, revised and adjusted after the next feedback phase.

After one year of operation, *aprendo* currently offers 30 modules. By 2027, this offer is planned to grow by approximately 230% to around 100 modules, which equals an average of about 20 new modules per year.

3. Challenges

Developing a continuous learning platform for educators during the COVID-19 pandemic presented several obstacles. These challenges encompassed developing a course program that is catered to a diverse range of stakeholder groups, school types and individual needs, finding new employees, developing a shared culture while dealing with many uncertainties and with tight deadlines at the same time, as well as some technical issues. Here is a more detailed look at these challenges and the successful strategies employed within the project team to overcome them:

Tailored Course Program: Developing a course program that addressed the diverse range of the various stakeholder groups, school types, and individual needs was a substantial challenge. Significant effort has been invested in conducting thorough research and engaging with educators, subject matter experts, and other stakeholders. Several focus groups, surveys, and interviews to gather insights and feedback were conducted. By incorporating a variety of instructional methods, such as interactive modules, video tutorials, and live virtual sessions, the project team created a comprehensive program that is catered to the specific requirements and learning preferences of different target audiences.

Technical Issue Resolution: Like any complex software project, technical issues arose during the development of *aprendo*. The project team established robust quality assurance processes, including rigorous testing procedures at various stages of development. A dedicated team of developers and technical experts promptly addresses and resolves any technical issues encountered. Regular bug fixing and system optimization activities are carried out to ensure the platform's stability, performance, and security.

Creating a team that shares a spirit to succeed: To meet the project's demands, great importance was placed on recruiting professionals with expertise in remote learning and software development. Implementing targeted recruitment strategies, the project lead reached out to individuals experienced in software development, online education, and instructional design. The project's broad scope and significant multiplier effect served as a motivating factor for the team, inspiring them to build something truly exceptional.

Developing educational content while advancing the platform's technical features: Especially during the initial phase the simultaneous development of content and the platform itself presented multifaceted challenges to the project team. The main challenges were resource allocation, the coordination between diverse teams, and the need to balance content quality and relevance with rapidly evolving technical updates.

Managing tight deadlines: The project team effectively handled tight deadlines and the pandemic's uncertainties by embracing agile project management. It broke down the project into manageable tasks, continuously reassessed priorities, and achieved incremental progress. This approach provided the project team with immediate visibility of smaller successes, which greatly motivates the team.

Public project with fixed parameters: It must be emphasized that *aprendo* is not a profit-driven project. Instead, it operates within the constraints of a fixed budget and specific targets for module development (e.g. a fixed amount of modules that need to be developed). This involves a continuous juggling act to strike the right balance between maintaining quality and managing costs. It's important to note that any financial gains resulting from our efforts, in the event of success, won't necessarily translate into increased resources.

4. First Results and Experiences

Following the successful launch of *aprendo* in May 2022, a comprehensive interim assessment was meticulously conducted in April 2023 to gauge its performance. This assessment was executed by a panel of distinguished experts, appointed by the project steering committee due to their extensive knowledge and experience in the field. Their evaluation of the platform resoundingly affirmed its effectiveness and remarkable quality. Furthermore, a series of regular user tests conducted in tandem consistently yielded similar positive results, showcasing users' high levels of satisfaction. These tests not only reaffirmed the platform's intuitive interface but also underscored the exceptional quality of the learning content it offers.

Moreover, the platform's usage statistics have surpassed the initially projected figures, thereby underscoring its burgeoning popularity and widespread adoption among educators. In fact, user engagement with the platform's features and resources has not only met but often exceeded expectations.

The overwhelmingly positive feedback received from users and the growing interest expressed by other cantons and organizations have spurred the government of St.Gallen, the entity that initiated this visionary project, to take proactive measures. To ensure the continued operation and development of *aprendo* and its invaluable content beyond the initial project timeline, a dedicated committee has been established. The primary objective of this committee is to explore sustainable business models that will guarantee the long-term viability and growth of *aprendo*, safeguarding its role as a cornerstone of education and learning excellence.

5. The learning outcomes

During its inaugural year of availability to users, the *aprendo* program witnessed a remarkable level of engagement. More than 9,200 individuals, constituting over 76% of the estimated total of approximately 12,000 teachers and principals, actively registered for the program. These usage statistics are particularly noteworthy, given that only 30 out of the planned 100 modules were accessible at that time. Out of a total of 6,868 module completions, 5,962 modules were autonomously completed through online self-study, while 876 modules were completed in moderated online settings. An additional 30 completions stem from the first blended-learning module offered on *aprendo*. Collectively, these completed modules accounted for an impressive 30,042 hours of professional development, equivalent to an astonishing 4,291 calculated professional development days within the program's inaugural year.

The evaluation of *aprendo* is characterized by a comprehensive and multidimensional approach that incorporates various perspectives and encompasses five key components to assess its overall effectiveness. These components encompass both internal and external factors, ensuring a thorough evaluation of the learning platform:

1. Data-driven analysis: User behavior, module availability, and outcomes achieved are meticulously examined through tools such as backend analytics, *Moodle* logs, evaluation analytics, and *Kaltura* statistics.

2. Standardized user evaluations: Participants willingly provide feedback, offering valuable insights into the user experience and the effectiveness of the training content. This feedback encompasses various parameters, including a "net promoter score" reflecting the recommendation rate. An average rating of 3.22 on a four-point Likert scale indicates a remarkably high level of recommendation, with only three out of the 30 modules receiving a rating below three, prompting subsequent content revisions.

3. Rigorous testing: Multiple test iterations involving small focus groups meticulously assess the module content and the user experience within the learning platform. Observations from participants are diligently reported to the project team, and guided focus group interviews facilitate further discussion and evaluation. Automated regression tests ensure technical functionality, and robust security measures, including professional penetration tests, have been rigorously implemented.

4. External expert evaluation: An external advisory group comprised of independent experts critically evaluates the training offerings and consistently provides recommendations for enhancement based on their domain expertise.

5. External implementation evaluation: This component scrutinizes the utilization of *aprendo* across various school types within the canton of St.Gallen, offering valuable insights into its practical application and effectiveness in real-world educational contexts.

This multifaceted evaluation approach ensures a comprehensive understanding of *aprendo*'s impact, effectiveness, and user experience. By amalgamating data analysis, user evaluations, rigorous testing, external expert perspectives, and real-world implementation assessments, *aprendo* undergoes continuous refinement to provide an engaging, effective, and continuously improved learning experience for its users.

6. Plans for further development

aprendo, encompassing both its individual modules and the technological platform, is still in its early stage of development, with the project scheduled to continue until mid-2027. Both components of *aprendo* will undergo agile development processes, evolving in response to user needs and evidence-based findings in the forthcoming years.

Given the ever-evolving landscape of technological innovations, notably the influence of AI in education, we remain committed to continually monitoring and incorporating these advancements into the platform's ongoing development. Consequently, it remains challenging to foresee all potential future developments at this juncture. However, several noteworthy advancements are already on the horizon, either in an advanced stage of internal prototyping or deemed highly likely for implementation.

As *aprendo*'s module catalog expands from the current 30 modules to an estimated of about 100 modules by 2027, users may encounter increasing complexities in navigating the growing array of module offerings, despite the availability of filter options and automated consideration of personal preferences. To tackle this challenge, we are proactively implementing two specific measures aimed at ensuring efficient navigation.

Firstly, we will introduce various pre-defined module paths that include tailored recommendations based on the competencies of different user profiles. This approach will simplify the user experience, particularly for those less familiar with the platform, by providing clear guidance on accessing modules that align with their specific needs.

Secondly, we just launched the additional access method known as the "*aprendo* navigator." This innovative feature employs specialized weak AI designed explicitly for this purpose. The navigator utilizes six motivational questions to intelligently suggest the most suitable modules to users, further enhancing the platform's user-friendliness and ensuring that learners can seamlessly discover content that resonates with their goals and interests (see Figure 3). These strategic developments underscore our commitment to not only keep pace with technological advancements but also to proactively enhance *aprendo*'s user experience as it continues to evolve.

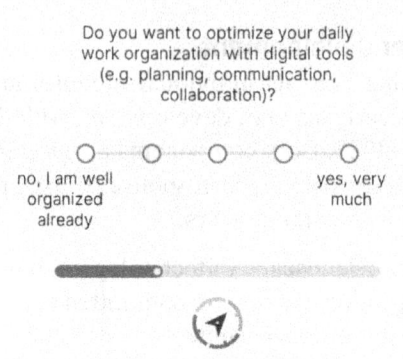

Figure 3: Example question *aprendo* navigator

The navigator primarily considers user interests rather than their existing competencies, following the principle that motivational aspects should be weighted as heavily as current competency levels in professional development, as discussed by Hidi (2006) and proved in a recently published study by Fütterer et al. (2023). The innovative algorithm does not follow a conventional tree structure or if-then logic; instead, it selects the next question from the question pool based on each previous answer of the user to provide the most personalized module recommendation.

Furthermore, to boost user acceptance of the platform, gamification features are being explored. Integrating elements like point systems, rewards, and challenges can significantly enhance learner motivation (see Figure 4). The effectiveness of gamification in increasing motivation has been documented in multiple studies (Huang et al. 2020).

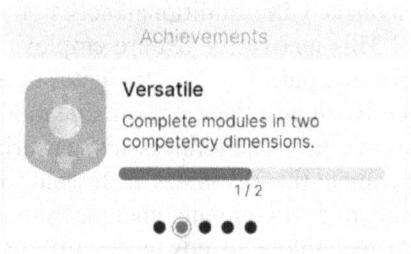

Figure 4: Example gamification badge

Lastly, the aspect of networking and learning from others within and beyond *aprendo* is mentioned. In teacher professional development, the exchange of experiences is particularly important. The introduction of two additional module types, blended learning, and specials will address this aspect. Furthermore, a networking platform developed and integrated into the module design. This will allow teachers to connect with one another, learn from their experiences, and gather new ideas, even after modules have been completed.

7. Conclusion

In our rapidly evolving technological landscape, there is an increasing urgency to equip educators with the essential skills required to effectively navigate the digital realm. The development of *aprendo* represents a significant milestone in addressing this crucial need among teachers and school principals in the canton of St.Gallen. *aprendo* stands as a pioneering platform that offers a comprehensive and user-centric approach, empowering educators to enhance their digital competencies at their own pace and convenience and for teachers of all levels.

What makes *aprendo* truly remarkable is its adaptability and scalability, ensuring that it can meet the evolving needs of educators in an ever-changing technological landscape. The platform's success has reverberated beyond the borders of the canton of St.Gallen, drawing attention from other regions and organizations. This widespread recognition underscores the platform's profound importance and relevance in the broader context of education and digital transformation.

In summary, *aprendo* emerges as a pivotal instrument in supporting educators as they confront the challenges posed by the ongoing digital transformation. It not only equips them with the skills needed to thrive in a digital age but also serves as a beacon of innovation and progress in the field of education.

References

Brandhofer, G. and Miglbauer, M. (2020) 'Digital Competences for Teachers - The Digi.Kompp Model in an International Comparison and in the Practice of Austrian Teacher Training'. *International Journal of Education (IJE)* [online] 8 (4), 55–69. https://doi.org/10.5121/ije.2020.8406

Brandhofer, G., Miglbauer, M., Fikisz, W., Garzi, M., Groißböck, P., Leitgeb, T., and Winder, G. (2022) 'Professionsentwicklung und Kompetenzen von Lehrpersonen in einer Kultur der Digitalität am Beispiel digi.kompP' [Professional development and competencies of teachers in a culture of digitality using the example of digi.kompP']. *R&E-SOURCE* [online] (18). https://doi.org/10.53349/resource.2022.i18.a1085

Buchner, J. and Hofmann, M. (2022) 'The More the Better? Comparing Two SQD-Based Learning Designs in a Teacher Training on Augmented and Virtual Reality'. *International Journal of Educational Technology in Higher Education* [online] 19 (24). https://doi.org/10.1186/s41239-022-00329-7

Caena, F. and Redecker, C. (2019) 'Aligning Teacher Competence Frameworks to 21st Century Challenges: The Case for the European Digital Competence Framework for Educators (DigCompEdu)'. *European Journal of Education* [online] 54 (3), 356–369. https://doi.org/10.1111/ejed.12345

Falloon, G. (2020) 'From Digital Literacy to Digital Competence: The Teacher Digital Competency (TDC) Framework'. *Educational Technology Research and Development* [online] 68 (5), 2449–2472. https://doi.org/10.1007/s11423-020-09767-4

Fütterer, T., Scherer, R., Scheiter, K., Stürmer, K., and Lachner, A. (2023) 'Will, Skills, or Conscientiousness: What Predicts Teachers' Intentions to Participate in Technology-Related Professional Development?' *Computers & Education* [online] 198, 104756. https://doi.org/10.1016/j.compedu.2023.104756

Gašević, D., Siemens, G., and Sadiq, S. (2023) 'Empowering Learners for the Age of Artificial Intelligence'. *Computers and Education: Artificial Intelligence* [online] 4, 100130. https://doi.org/10.1016/j.caeai.2023.100130

Hidi, S. (2006) 'Interest: A Unique Motivational Variable'. *Educational Research Review* [online] 1 (2), 69–82. https://doi.org/10.1016/j.edurev.2006.09.001

Hornberger, M., Bewersdorff, A., and Nerdel, C. (2023) 'What Do University Students Know about Artificial Intelligence? Development and Validation of an AI Literacy Test'. *Computers and Education: Artificial Intelligence* [online] 5, 100165. https://doi.org/10.1016/j.caeai.2023.100165

Huang, R., Ritzhaupt, A.D., Sommer, M., Zhu, J., Stephen, A., Valle, N., Hampton, J., and Li, J. (2020) 'The Impact of Gamification in Educational Settings on Student Learning Outcomes: A Meta-Analysis'. *Educational Technology Research and Development* [online] 68 (4), 1875–1901. https://doi.org/10.1007/s11423-020-09807-z

Redecker, C. (2017) *European Framework for the Digital Competence of Educators: DigCompEdu* [online] ed. by Punie, Y. EUR 28775 EN. Luxembourg: Publications Office of the European Union.

Schweizer, C.R. (2019) 'Kompetenzen Für Eine Nachhaltige Entwicklung – Konzeptionelle Präzisierung Der Nachhaltigkeitskompetenz Über Den Leistungsanspruch' [Competencies for sustainable development – conceptual specification of sustainability competencies via the performance requirement]. in *Bildung Und Erziehung Im Kontext Globaler Transformationen* [Education in the context of global transformations] 1st edn. ed. by Clemens, I., Hornberg, S., and Rieckmann, M. Verlag Barbara Budrich, 111–124.

Author Biographies

Dr. Georg Winder coordinates the IT Educational Offensive at the Institute of Digital and Computer Science Education, St.Gallen University of Teacher Education and leads its biggest project «aprendo». With expertise in early childhood education, professional education and e-learning, his work and research focuses mainly on modernizing teacher education for the digital age.

Andrea Kern works as Head of Content Development of «aprendo» at the Institute of Digital and Computer Science Education, St.Gallen University of Teacher Education. With expertise in teacher and school development, early childhood and media education, her work focuses on supporting teachers and schools in implementing digital media in the classroom and building learners' digital literacy.

Karin Zehetner works as a product owner of «aprendo» at the Institute of Digital and Computer Science Education, St.Gallen University of Teacher Education. She manages and coordinates the maximization of the product's value in the best interest of all stakeholders, with a special focus on user needs and experience.

Dr. Josef Buchner is Head of Research and Development at the Institute of Digital and Computer Science Education, St.Gallen University of Teacher Education. He worked as a teacher and researcher in Austria, Switzerland, and Germany. His research focuses on educational technology, instructional design, multimedia learning, and teacher education in the digital age.

DP Education: Equitable Access to Free Quality Online Learning

Kawshi Amarasinghe[1], Dhammika Perera[1], Dhivyaluckshanna Chandrasegar[1], Loodeesha Ekanayake[1], Rambukka Maha Vidyalaya[2]

[1]DP Education of Dhammika & Priscilla Perera Foundation, Sri Lanka
[2]Rakwana, Sri Lanka
kawshi@dpfoundation.org.lk
chairman@dpfoundation.org.lk
luckshi@dpfoundation.org.lk
loodeeshae@dpfoundation.org.lk
mahabadugedv@yahoo.com

Abstract: Students lack the opportunity for equitable access to free quality education catered in Sinhala, Tamil & English languages in Sri Lanka. With the economic crisis, parents from low/middle-income families struggle to provide their children with quality education. Moreover, unpredictable factors such as pandemics and political instabilities led to learning loss hours. Excluding Western Province, the digital literacy rate in other provinces is at an average of 29% due to limited access to e-learning facilities. With limited free quality online IT-related courses and qualified IT professionals, the current contribution of the IT industry to the GDP is only 1.86%. As a solution, Dhammika & Priscilla Perera Foundation initiated its free digital learning arm, DP Education, which has over 1.5 million app downloads and over 1 billion minutes of YouTube watch time. The content can be revisited to recover learning loss hours. DP Education consists of 19 brands, some of which are below,

Digital School: For students from grades 1-13, covering school subjects in Sinhala, Tamil & English languages, inclusive of test paper discussions, live classes, and virtual lab practical lessons. Over 20,000 lessons are available online for free. The content is developed in collaboration with leading teachers. Since its launch in October 2019, over 32 million unique YouTube viewers are actively engaged.

IT Campus - This incorporates the DP Education Coding School, with 324 coding projects for individuals aged six and above. It enhances learners' creativity, critical thinking, communication skills, and self-esteem. Moreover, funding and assistance in curriculum development are provided to government universities to launch free ICT courses. A noteworthy collaboration is the Trainee Full Stack Developer course with the University of Moratuwa, drawing over 200,000 enrolments in 19 months. The platform equips learners with expertise in software development, UI/UX design, etc. A monumental goal of the IT Campus is to nurture one million young coders, half of whom are girls. To realize this, 331 IT Campuses are being established. Presently, over 70 centres educate 50,000 coding enthusiasts.

Keywords: Equitable access to education, free quality online learning, e-learning

1. Introduction

Since its 2019 inception, DP Education, an initiative of the Dhammika & Priscilla Perera Foundation (DPF), has championed equitable, free, high-quality education, encompassing everything from preschool to lifelong learning, and even health education. Central to its ethos is combating poverty via education, aligning with the DPF's vision of elevating Sri Lanka to a developed nation status with a GDP per capita income of USD12,000.

Boasting over 65 subjects, DP Education's e-learning platform provides more than 21,000 hours of content, crafted by premier educators and available in three languages: Sinhala, Tamil & English. Its digital outreach spans beyond Sri Lanka, evidenced by its 200 million YouTube views and 1 billion watch minutes, touching corners from India to Australia.

Significantly, DP Education nurtures future tech talent with its IT Campus. Working with leading universities, DP Education aims to train 1 million coders (including 500,000 girls) in five years—an investment worth over USD7.5 billion. Beyond tech, DP Education is committed to reducing unskilled labour rates and elevating vocational course completion rates. Furthermore, the language school fosters global communication skills, aiding skill migration by offering English, Japanese, Korean, and Italian lessons.

Additionally, the foundation's Buddhist studies initiative, available in over 400 temples, is enhanced by smart classrooms gifted by the DPF. Meanwhile, Skills for Life brand covers a vast range of skills from hospitality to coexistence. Lastly, DP Education's Public Health initiative addresses comprehensive well-being areas, including maternity and mental health, underscoring their commitment to lifelong holistic development.

2. The Infrastructure

DP Education ensures an uninterrupted learning experience by hosting its videos on YouTube and allowing learners to access and revisit teachings through its apps and websites. This approach fosters self-directed learning and improves skills such as time and self-management, research, and critical thinking. DP Education also promotes digital literacy and competency by teaching users how to access websites, apps, and social media platforms, empowering them to confidently and responsibly engage with digital technologies for learning, work, and participation in society.

DP Education Digital School offers virtual lab practical lessons in physics, chemistry, and biology to enhance science practical learning. The main purpose of delivering these lessons is to ensure that no one is left behind in accessing proper science lab practical teachings, even if they lack access to lab equipment or attend schools without science labs. For recordings, a special camera named SV189 (https://www.svbony.com/sv605-microscope-with-sv189-microscope-camera/) is used. It is a microscope camera attached to a binocular microscope, making it easier to capture micro-organisms. Multiple camera angles also enable students to view these virtual lab practical lessons, ensuring real-life experiences for the student (Figure 1).

Figure 1: DP Education Digital School – Virtual Lab Practical Lessons

DP Education has also established satellite IT centres, a.k.a DP Education IT Campus, equipped with computers, accessories, and internet connectivity (Figure 2). Through collaboration with Microsoft, DP Education offers Office 365 educational licenses to students at their coding centres island-wide. This grants access to various services provided by Microsoft Office educational package, such as; Microsoft Teams, Outlook, Student Notebook, etc. It facilitates effective communication and collaboration within and among centres.

Figure 2: DP Education IT Campus, Nuwara Eliya, Sri Lanka

The DPF funds workshops on robotics and has introduced the "DP Education Python Robot" program, focusing on hardware and software aspects of robotics, including Python programming. Virtual robots are also offered online with free access, allowing students to program and simulate robots remotely through a cloud-based rental system, a.k.a Magicbit Micropython Live (Figure 3).

Figure 3: Magicbit Micropython Live

Innovative EdTech Integration: A Deep Dive into DP Education's Digital Solution

At DP Education, our commitment to bridging digital divides is evident in our main website's architecture, a cutting-edge Progressive Web App (PWA) with an "Offline First Approach". This strategic move ensures that users, even those in areas with limited connectivity, can access educational resources seamlessly. Despite serving over 250,000 daily users, DP

Education has optimized performance, ensuring rapid loading times, minimal data usage, and optimal battery efficiency.

To maintain cost-effectiveness and resource optimization, DP Education's websites are custom-built. Furthermore, eliminating unnecessary user tracking and smartly integrating both client-side and server-side caching techniques, DP Education has ensured consistent offline access. For instance, a student revisiting the websites doesn't expend additional data to reload the page; it's instantly available from their offline cache. While leveraging AWS (https://aws.amazon.com/) for hosting, DPF has adopted a minimalist approach, focusing on scalability in anticipation of DP Education's continuous growth. DP Education has utilized single-page web design with server-side and pre-rendering to enhance user experience and eliminate disturbance to SEO performance.

DP Education hosts online examinations for its learners, one such exam is for fifth-grade students attempting scholarship examinations. Utilizing proprietary technology tailored for MCQ-based evaluations, DP Education introduced features like stratified random sampling for test creation and auto-grading for MCQs. The platform's robustness is evident: in just over a year, it handled 229,000 attempts and 70,000 paper submissions. Live streaming for various classes on YouTube is facilitated through Open Broadcaster Software (https://obsproject.com/), further establishing our commitment to quality e-learning.

In 2021, DPF expanded its digital footprint with the DP Education mobile app. Designed with both older and contemporary Android devices in mind, Android version 4.4 and above, it seamlessly integrates Flutter and Kotlin to serve a wide range of users.

DP Education's venture into the e-learning domain is further enriched by the Moodle Learning Management System (LMS), an exemplar of open-source efficiency (https://moodle.org). Unique features like "My Learning Points" and awarding badges and points to foster a sense of achievement and engagement among students will be introduced. The imminent certificate issuance system further strengthens our promise of tangible outcomes for our learners.

In the quest for an elevated e-learning experience, the introduction of H5P in courses such as Trainee Full Stack Developer (TFSD) stands out (https://h5p.org/content-types-and-applications). H5P, a cutting-edge instrument, equips educators with the prowess to develop diverse content, spanning from interactive video sessions and quizzes to detailed presentations and immersive virtual scenarios. One of its standout features is the adaptive questioning mechanism. More than just pausing the video, this feature, when met with an incorrect student response, astutely redirects them to the relevant content segment, reinforcing conceptual understanding. Furthermore, H5P's design actively discourages content skimming, ensuring learners immerse themselves fully. Upon completing an interactive session, learners receive an in-depth summary, shedding light on their interactions and performance.

DP Education Coding School's website incorporates a bespoke e-certificate generator, awarding certificates to users upon the completion of specific milestones, using our tailored PHP solution for certificate crafting. The above-mentioned methodologies and technologies will soon be integrated into DP Education Language School, further widening our impact.

DP Education partnered with Age of Learning, Inc., USA to cater to early childhood cognitive development. Children can access learning content for math and science through ABCmouse.com and learn drawing, arts, crafts, and educational songs through DP Education Kids. The DP Kids app, a recent introduction, is still in its developmental phase, is developed using Flutter. This app boasts a range of games including colouring activities, math challenges, and memory exercises. All these games are driven by custom-built algorithms (Figure 4).

Figure 4: DP Education Kids App

T-AI, a web extension AI-teaching assistant, elevates interactive learning in video content. Students can seek detailed explanations, clarify grammar lessons, and address comprehension issues. DP Education IELTS offers T-AI integration for free, enabling tailored learning experiences.

3. The Challenges

1. Teaching Style Challenges: Initially struggled to find the best online teaching style for Sri Lankan students.

- First Method: Only voice and visual content, without visible teacher; proved unsuccessful.
- Second Method: Teacher present with interactive digital board; preferred by students and currently used.

2. Parental Concerns: Hesitation from parents about children using digital devices for learning.

- Solution: Online seminars, one-on-one sessions, awareness at exhibitions, and advocating free parental control apps to ensure responsible usage.

3. Content Update Challenges: Ensuring current, globally recognized content.

- Solution: Continuous global curriculum research, vetting by university academics and experts, and collaboration with industry professionals for course relevance and quality.

4. How the initiative was received by the participants

Established before the Covid-19 outbreak in Sri Lanka, DP Education played a pivotal role during school closures that spanned nearly two years since March 2020, impacting roughly 4.2 million students and causing an estimated loss of 10 billion learning hours. Added challenges like fuel crises and teacher strikes further compounded the situation. Nevertheless, DP Education provided an invaluable solution, offering free, quality digital education, enabling students to recover missed content.

The effectiveness of DP Education is evident: the app boasts over 1.5 million downloads, the websites engage over 250,000 daily users, and have accumulated 2 million subscribers across 23 YouTube channels.

Given the economic strain in Sri Lanka, many families grapple with educational access due to rising living costs. Thankfully, DP Education's affordable YouTube-based content, available for under a dollar per monthly data package, ensures continued access for children from all economic backgrounds.

To gain deeper insights into how our learners perceive DP Education's teachings, we conducted two surveys, involving 12,800 students who are utilising DP Education. The surveys incorporated open-ended questions derived from the Delone and McLean (Delone and McLean, 2003) information system success model, as well as the Kirkpatrick model (Kirkpatrick, 1993). These inquiries concentrated on specific areas, and Table 1 showcases the responses we received from the students.

Table 1: Responses from Students

Kirkpatrick	Responses
Reaction What aspects of the course content did you find most engaging and valuable?	1. "The aspect of creating games through simple coding software is the most engaging and valuable content of the course for me" 2. "Their technology amazed me & encouraged me. I personally prefer how they explain everything so clearly!" 3. "Teaching everything A to Z about how we should code and being able to understand the video."
Did the course design and structure contribute to creating a positive learning environment?	Yes - 96.4% No – 3.6%
Learning Were there any topics or concepts that you found difficult to understand?	No – 92.1% Yes – 7.9%
Behaviour What are the main takeaways you will carry forward from this learning experience?	2. "One of the main takeaways I will carry forward from this learning experience is the valuable skill set I have acquired in web development and app creation. This course has equipped me with a strong foundation in programming languages, design principles,

Kirkpatrick	Responses
	and project management, which are essential for a successful career in web development. I've also learned how to work effectively in a team and handle real-world challenges that may arise during the development process." 3. "After completing this coding course and gaining additional knowledge, my goal is to advance and become a teacher at coding school, being familiar with computer proficiency." 4. "Because of the Trainee Full-Stack Developer Course by the University of Moratuwa and DP Education, I'm a Trainee Software Engineer at 99x now."
Results Reflecting on your progress, how has your confidence in the subject matter improved throughout the course?	Yes – 97.5% No – 2.5%
Delone and McLean	
Information Quality – Were you satisfied with the method of delivery? i.e., video materials.	Yes – 97% No – 3%
System Quality Were there any distractions or technical issues that took your focus away?	No – 96.3% Yes – 3.7%

Kirkpatrick	Responses	
Were there any issues with the visibility of on-screen text or small details?		No – 90.6% Yes – 9.4%
Service Quality – How would you rate the instructor's communication and clarity in explaining concepts? (1 being poor, 5 being excellent)		5 – 74.8% 4 – 16.4% 3 – 3.8% 2 – 2.1% 1 – 2.9%
Intention To Use – Is using our learning site align with your long-term educational or career goals?		Yes – 96.6% No – 3.4%
User Satisfaction – Would you recommend this course to others?		Yes – 96.9% No – 3.1%
Did the course content meet your expectations?		Yes – 97.5% No – 2.5%

Kirkpatrick	Responses
Net Benefits – On a scale of 1 to 5, how satisfied are you with your overall learning experience in this course? (1 being poor, 5 being excellent)	5 – 75.5% 4 – 15.4% 3 – 4.1% 2 – 1.8% 1 – 3.2%

Further, positive feedback from our online learners (Figure 5) demonstrates the effectiveness and positive reception of DP Education's offerings in providing accessible and quality digital education to learners nationwide.

Figure 5: Positive comments from our learners

DP Education's impact is evident from the performance of learners in the 2021 Advanced Level Examinations in Sri Lanka. Three out of the top 10 island rankers were learners who utilized DP Education's digital school content. The students are; Neranda Dilhara for Engineering Technology, Ishara Lakmal for Arts, and Isuri Pabasara for Biosystems Technology.

These achievements are few examples to reflect the effectiveness of the platform in helping students succeed academically.

DP Education has received positive feedback from the best rankers who have sat for GCSE examinations (Figure 6). Furthermore, students have accessed online resources of DP Education such as revision, past paper and model paper discussions, and live classes for exam preparation. These resources enable students to independently assess their subject knowledge and improve their performance.

Figure 6: Positive comments from students who sat for 2021 GCSE Examinations

In university collaborations, digital certificates are offered after learners are assessed online through assignments, quizzes, and assessments. The use of automated grading through CodeRunner software and manual grading ensures the authenticity and accuracy of evaluations. The TFSD course offered by the University of Moratuwa, which received over 200,000 enrolments, exemplifies the success of DP Education's collaboration with universities. DP Education funded the full project along with providing research input on global curriculum analysis, and best technologies that can be adapted for e-learning.

In summary, DP Education's initiatives have positively impacted learning outcomes, as demonstrated by improved examination results and learner feedback. DP Education's commitment to providing accessible and quality education is evident in its comprehensive approach and the positive responses received from the learners. In analysing the trajectory of DP Education's impact, the voice of the students stands paramount. The recent surveys, encompassing feedback from 12,800 active learners, shed light on the ground realities of how the initiative has revolutionized digital education amidst adversities. The Kirkpatrick model results underscore the positive reception of course content, with students highlighting the engaging nature of game creation through coding and the clarity in instructional delivery. A telling testimony came from a participant who, thanks to the TFSD Course, is now a Trainee Software Engineer at a reputable organization. The Delone and McLean inquiries echoed similar sentiments; participants noted the high quality of information, minimal technical disruptions, and strong satisfaction rates. This feedback paints a holistic picture of the success of DP Education, reiterating its indispensable role in bridging educational gaps during these unprecedented times. As we move forward, these invaluable insights will guide our commitment to ensuring quality, accessible education for all.

5. The Learning Outcomes

DP Education, in collaboration with academic institutions, has meticulously curated digital courses emphasizing key tech skills, such as machine learning, cybersecurity, app development, data science, and more. DP Education also offer unique programs through their TVET Studies brand on topics like caregiving, fish farming, and tiling. Moreover, in an alliance with Sri Lanka's Department of Technical Education & Training, 500 tilers will be enhanced with skills needed for local and international job markets.

Emphasizing the expansive reach, DP Education has established IT campuses in all 25 districts of Sri Lanka. This initiative aims to foster a workforce that's not only tech-savvy but also ready to excel on the global front, significantly contributing to the digital economy. Their educational journey starts at the DP Education Coding School, which boasts a rich curriculum of 324 projects and related assignments. Here, students cultivate:

- Modern-day skills, encompassing analytical thinking, innovation, efficient communication, and bolstered self-esteem.
- Enhanced mathematical capabilities, creative thinking, and an ingrained ability to remain focused and organized.
-

In coding education, DP Education Coding School (Figure 7) leverages global platforms such as Code.org, to teach. The Coding School covers various subjects such as app & web development and other skills as shown on Figure 8.

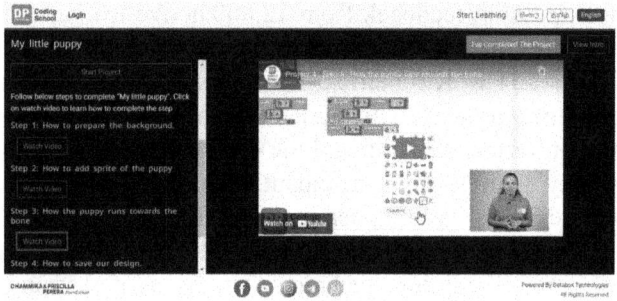

Figure 7: DP Education Coding School web – www.dpcode.lk

Platform	Learning Outcomes
Code.org	UI/UX Design, Database Connectivity, App Development
Thunkable	Block Coding, Database Connectivity, Loops and Conditions in Coding
Pictoblox	AI, Face Detection, Object Moving, Sound Detection, Machine Learning, Augmented Reality, Virtual Reality
Microbit	AI, Robotics, Self-Detecting and Responding, Machine Learning
COSPACES	3D Objects, 3D Games

Figure 8: Learning Outcomes of Each Platform taught via DP Education Coding School

As students advance, they're introduced to the TFSD program, a collaboration with the University of Moratuwa. This program equips them to:

- Analytically approach and untangle intricate tech challenges.

- Implement top-tier programming concepts to real-world problems.
- Develop web platforms utilizing current tools.
- Scrutinize an array of ICT tools.
- Improve communication skills within genuine software environments.
- Ensure they're job-ready for the tech sector.
- Uphold a continuous learning ethos, aligning with the swift tech advancements.

Furthermore with 16 diverse brands under its belt, DP Education amplifies its reach, enabling students to master languages, enhance collaboration skills, personal growth, digital understanding, and holistic knowledge centred on health and mental wellness.

We conducted a third survey to assess how 180 teachers perceived student learning outcomes after integrating DP Education into their lessons. The open-ended questions were rooted in the RAT model (Hughes, 2005). These inquiries honed in on specific domains, and Table 2 captures the feedback from these educators.

Table 2: Feedback from Educators

Questions	Responses
Replacement	
1. How has the use of DP Education in your teaching replaced traditional methods or tools? Can you provide examples of specific instances?	1. "A 7th grader who struggled made an app after a month of coding lessons. Students now prefer solving problems. I thought tech might create distance, but it brought us closer. We can learn in fun ways that weren't possible before." 2. "This approach let me teach deeper topics without the usual papers and board, something old ways couldn't do."
2. What benefits have you observed in terms of efficiency or time-saving when using DP Education to replace manual tasks?	1. "Students now challenge themselves instead of competing with each other. With DP Education's great resources and quick fixes for broken equipment, they achieve more and make their dreams come true." 3. "To be a good entrepreneur, you need hands-on experience in many

Questions	Responses
	areas quickly. This also teaches how to manage time and money well."
3. How has DP Education helped you deliver content more effectively compared to traditional methods?	4. "DP Education allows me tailor lessons for each student using varied materials. This helps them learn better and faster."
Amplification	
1. In what ways has DP Education amplified your teaching strategies, making them more impactful for student learning? Can you share any success stories?	1. "In one month, students have become more excited about learning. Their thinking and problem-solving skills are better. They're doing much better in ICT, Math, English, and Science." 5. "Recently, some students struggled with the human heart's structure. After watching the video on DP Education, they quickly understood the whole circulatory system."
2. How has DP Education allowed you to provide personalized learning experiences for your studies?	1. "I value how DP Education supports many languages, including Sinhala, English, and Tamil. It's great for our diverse community. They also help students of all ages and boost English skills with DP IELTS." 6. "We group children by age for learning. This helps every child get the right lessons. We also give them hands-on activities to learn better."
Transformation	
1. How has the integration of technology transformed the way you design and deliver your lessons? Can you describe a lesson that was significantly different due to technology?	1. "As an ICT teacher in the government sector, I have many experiences. The grade 10 Logic Gates lesson was earlier done using a whiteboard only. Now, with the aid of a smart class, I am able to demonstrate the logical behaviour of logic gates through actual circuits.

Questions	Responses
	Using IDEs to demonstrate programming in Pascal for Grade 11 is another example. Using apps like Limo, I am making interactive content for students, like image hotspots, making learning content a fun game for them." 7. "Studying from regular textbooks takes kids more time and effort. Even after understanding a topic, they often need to spend a lot of time on it."
2. How has DP Education enabled you to foster creativity and innovation among your students?	1. "Students come up with fresh ideas and talk about them. In one month, they've built over 15 apps, some very special. DP Education lets them join events like Awrudu Kreeda and Digital Thoran. I push them to be more creative, improving their thinking and knowledge." 8. "The development of children's cognitive abilities is influenced by the structure of the teaching pattern. This approach enables students to acquire the capability to generate the knowledge necessary for fostering innovation on their own."

6. Plans to further develop the initiative

DP Education has ambitious plans for the future. Some of the key projects include:

- Tech Job Hubs: Envisioning 1,000 hubs in remote Sri Lankan areas to tap into IT and Tech opportunities, advocating for remote work and home-based employment.
- Precision Poverty Reduction: An online job bank will be introduced, merging potential employers with candidates. Geotagging learning communities, they'll enable socio-economic upliftment and poverty eradication.

- Inclusivity: Special emphasis on disabled learners, integrating scripts in three languages, and embedding assistive technologies, ensures education is accessible to all.
- Coding Expansion: Collaborating with the government, coding education will reach 1,000 schools, equipping students with pivotal IT skills.
- Olympiad Prep: Specialized video content is under development for global Olympiads, like IMO and IOI, promoting excellence in math and informatics.
- Enhanced Learning: An AI-backed LMS will deliver custom content, incorporating digital assignments for self-assessment.
- DP Education Kids: Collaborate with more global early learning content providers to improve children's reading and digital literacy skills, and cognitive development. Expanding digital content with the Age of Learning Foundation will further enhance education initiatives.
- Public Health Initiative: Launching a health website covering well-being topics, enhancing public health services and mental well-being outreach. This project will also involve upskilling and reskilling the midwives' community, providing them with digital devices and resources to offer higher-quality services. A digital platform will also facilitate forming of support groups for mental health, expectant mothers, new parents, suicide prevention, substance addiction, and overall well-being.
- Senior Citizens: A digital guide tailored for seniors will encompass caregiving, finance, health, and legal advice, ensuring enriched, informed lives.
- TVET Studies: In alliance with TVET bodies, DP Education will refine courses for high-demand jobs. Certified graduates will get employment assistance through a job bank.
- Environmental Sustainability: Partnering with TreeTag India, kickstarted a reforestation project targeting endangered trees, with over 1,600 plants being geotagged, underscoring DPF's commitment to conservation.

In conclusion, DP Education's future plans demonstrate its commitment to expanding its impact and addressing diverse educational needs in Sri Lanka. DP Education's focus on precision poverty reduction, job generation, inclusivity, coding education, Olympiad preparation, enhanced learning journeys, early childhood education, public health, support for senior citizens, TVET studies, and environmental sustainability reflects its holistic approach to education and development.

References

ABCmouse.com. (n.d.). ABCmouse.com. [online] Available at: https://www.abcmouse.com/redeem?code=DPKIDS.

Age of Learning FoundationTM. (n.d.). Age of Learning FoundationTM. [online] Available at: https://www.aoflfoundation.org/ [Accessed 20 Sep. 2023].

Amazon Web Services, Inc. (n.d.). Free Cloud Computing Services - AWS Free Tier. [online] Available at: https://aws.amazon.com/free/?trk=14a4002d-4936-4343-8211-b5a150ca592b&sc_channel=ps&ef_id=CjwKCAjwsKqoBhBPEiwALrrqiCOxjhmp9b_Y-qZV3bEWqIqBrKbvvInDZhJ1WWLFW66GSnuZ-eOiqxoC5-sQAvD_BwE:G:s&s_kwcid=AL [Accessed 20 Sep. 2023].
code.org (2011). Code.org: [online] Code.org. Available at: https://code.org/.
coderunner.org.nz. (n.d.). CodeRunner. [online] Available at: https://coderunner.org.nz/ [Accessed 20 Sep. 2023].
Cospaces.io. (2018). CoSpaces Edu: Make AR & VR in the Classroom. [online] Available at: https://cospaces.io/edu/.
DailyFT (n.d.). Moratuwa Uni., DP Education Launch World's First Free Online Project Management Skills Learning Platform | Daily FT. [online] www.ft.lk. Available at: https://www.ft.lk/front-page/Moratuwa-Uni-DP-Education-launch-world-s-first-free-online-Project-Management-skills-learning-platform/44-749978 [Accessed 20 Sep. 2023].
Databox. (n.d.). #1 Business Analytics Platform & KPI Dashboards. [online] Available at: https://databox.com/?origin=20231 [Accessed 20 Sep. 2023].
DeLone, W. and McLean, E. (2003) 'The DeLone and McLean Model of Information Systems Success: A Ten-Year Update', J. of Management Information Systems, 19, pp. 9-30. doi: 10.1080/07421222.2003.11045748.
DP IELTS. (n.d.). DP IELTS. [online] Available at: https://dpielts.lk/t-ai [Accessed 20 Sep. 2023].
GitHub Docs. (n.d.). Quickstart for GitHub Educators. [online] Available at: https://docs.github.com/en/education/quickstart [Accessed 20 Sep. 2023].
H5P (2019). H5P. [online] H5p.org. Available at: https://h5p.org/.
H5p.org. (2019). Examples & Downloads. [online] Available at: https://h5p.org/content-types-and-applications.
Herbarium (n.d.). This Publication Is Sponsored by the Biodiversity Secretariat of the Ministry of Environment in Technical Collaboration with the National THE NATIONAL RED LIST 2020 Conservation Status of the Flora of Sri Lanka. [online] Available at:
http://www.neic.cea.lk/assets/img/The%20National%20Red%20List%202020-The%20Conservation%20Status%20of%20the%20Flora%20of%20Sri%20Lanka.pdf.
Hughes, J. (2005). The role of teacher knowledge and learning experiences in forming technology-integrated pedagogy. Journal of Technology and Teacher Education, 13(2), 277-302.
ioinformatics.org. (n.d.). International Olympiad in Informatics. [online] Available at: https://ioinformatics.org/.
Kirkpatrick, D.L. (1993). 'Techniques for evaluating training programs', Evaluating training programs
Magicbit. (2019). Magicbit. [online] Available at: https://magicbit.cc/.
Microbit.org. (2019). Micro:bit Educational Foundation. [online] Available at: https://microbit.org/.

Microsoft (n.d.). Free Microsoft 365 Education. [online] Microsoft Education. Available at: https://www.microsoft.com/en-us/education/products/microsoft-365.

Moodle (2019). Moodle - Open-source Learning Platform | Moodle.org. [online] Moodle.org. Available at: https://moodle.org/.

OBS Project (2012). Open Broadcaster Software | OBS. [online] Obsproject.com. Available at: https://obsproject.com/.

pictoblox.ai. (n.d.). PictoBlox: Learn Coding and Program Robots Online. [online] Available at: https://pictoblox.ai [Accessed 20 Sep. 2023].

Stories, M. (2023). Microsoft and DP Education Joins Hands to Empower Sri Lankan Youth with Digital Skills. [online] Microsoft Stories Asia. Available at: https://news.microsoft.com/apac/2023/05/23/microsoft-and-dp-education-joins-hands-to-empower-sri-lankan-youth-with-digital-skills/ [Accessed 20 Sep. 2023].

Thunkable.com: Drag and Drop Mobile App Builder for iOS and Android. (2019). Thunkable.com: Drag and Drop Mobile App Builder for iOS and Android. [online] Available at: https://thunkable.com/.

Treetag.in. (2023). Treetag. [online] Available at: https://www.treetag.in/ [Accessed 20 Sep. 2023].

University of Kelaniya (n.d.). The University of Kelaniya and DP Education Join Together to Build a Knowledge Economy in Sri Lanka through a Free Online Program in ERP. [online] Department of Marketing Management. Available at: https://fcms.kln.ac.lk/dep/dmm/index.php/news/310-the-university-of-kelaniya-and-dp-education-join-together-to-build-a-knowledge-economy-in-sri-lanka-through-a-free-online-program-in-erp [Accessed 20 Sep. 2023].

University of Moratuwa (n.d.). UoM - Open Learning Platform. [online] open.uom.lk. Available at: https://open.uom.lk/ [Accessed 20 Sep. 2023].

uom.lk. (n.d.). University of Moratuwa. [online] Available at: https://uom.lk/.

Weerasooriya, S. (2023). Dhammika Perera Launches DP Education Coding and Robotics Campuses Islandwide. [online] The Island Online. Available at: https://island.lk/dhammika-perera-launches-dp-education-coding-and-robotics-campuses-islandwide/ [Accessed 20 Sep. 2023].

www.adaderana.lk. (n.d.). Best Results of 2021 GCE A/L Exam. [online] Available at: https://www.adaderana.lk/news.php?nid=84595#:~:text=Ishara%20Lakmal%20Heenkenda%20of%20Kendagolla [Accessed 20 Sep. 2023].

www.dialog.lk. (n.d.). UNLIMITED YouTube for All Unlimited Dialog Power Plan Customers. [online] Available at: https://www.dialog.lk/unlimited-youtube-for-all-dialog-power-plan-customers [Accessed 20 Sep. 2023].

www.imo-official.org. (n.d.). International Mathematical Olympiad. [online] Available at: https://www.imo-official.org/.

www.svbony.com. (n.d.). SV605 Microscope with SV189 Microscope Camera. [online] Available at: https://www.svbony.com/sv605-microscope-with-sv189-microscope-camera/ [Accessed 20 Sep. 2023].

www.youtube.com. (n.d.). 2021 Neranda Dilhara, the island in Engineering Technology. [online] Available at: https://youtu.be/EJc9bm9h-4k [Accessed 20 Sep. 2023].

www.youtube.com. (n.d.). 2021 Isuri Pabasara, the island first in Biosystem Technology. [online] Available at: https://youtu.be/5hVNYhKm9Kc [Accessed 20 Sep. 2023].

www.youtube.com. (n.d.). Ishara Lakmal, the island first in Arts. [online] Available at: https://youtu.be/R_1HJ364o3g [Accessed 20 Sep. 2023]

Author Biographies

Kawshi Amarasinghe: Chief Executive Officer, Dhammika & Priscilla Perera Foundation. Executive Director, Vallibel One PLC.

Dhammika Perera: Founder and Chairman of the Dhammika & Priscilla Perera Foundation. He is also the author of "Sri Lanka 2030: A Developed Nation" book, and is the visionary behind Vallibel One PLC, where he previously served as Chairman.

Dhivyaluckshanna Chandrasegar: Senior Project Associate, Dhammika & Priscilla Perera Foundation

Ms. Loodeesha Ekanayake: Project Associate, Dhammika & Priscilla Perera Foundation

Other Contributors

Mr. Dushyantha Mahabaduge: Director and Maths Tutor, Dhammika & Priscilla Perera Foundation

Mr. Kalana Thathsara: Head of Operations, Dhammika & Priscilla Perera Foundation

Mr. H.M. Wijewardena: Information Technology Teacher, Rambukka Maha Vidyalaya

Ms. Ridmini De Silva: Content Developer: DP Education Coding School, Dhammika & Priscilla Perera Foundation

Mr. Harsha Randeny: Country Manager, Microsoft Sri Lanka

Mr. Abdul Qadir Anas: Product Specialist, Microsoft Sri Lanka

Mr. Prabath Perera: Chief Executive Officer, Databox Technologies

LivePBL Liking Vocal Education through Project-Based Learning: A Music-led Hybrid Sino-International Social Learning Community

Ying Liu[1], Andy Hogg[1], Yuanyuan Li[2], Lian Sun[3], Ting Zhao[4], Jing Geng[5] Xiang Li[6], Zhinan Zhu[7], Yasmin Mirza[8]
[1]NCFE CACHE Learning Centre, The Support School, Liverpool, UK
[2]Music College, Capital Normal University, Beijing, China
[3]Kede College, Capital Normal University, Beijing, China
[4]Beijing Youth and Politics Vocational College, Beijing, China
[5]High School, Capital Normal University, China
[6]Beijing Chaoyang Children's Palace, China
[7]Beijing Mentougou District Children's Palace, Beijing, China
[8]Capital Case, London, UK

1. Introduction

LivePBL, short for Linking Vocal Education through Project Based Learning, is a platform that has been innovating hybrid learning pedagogies to engage music education with Sino-International local family communities and cultures. This paper reflects on the history of LivePBL research and development.

The platform was initiated in 2019 and then developed in 2020 in response to the Covid-19 pandemic. The aim was to provide accessible and engaging eLearning experiences for students and families to overcome the most difficult time they were facing. Since then, LivePBL has undertaken research and development, offering a range of hybrid programs, supporting training and learning in

1) Digital literacy of multimedia design for children
2) Sino-international cloud family visit communication
3) Pre-service teacher students to assist in online teaching

4) In the near future, homestay entrepreneurs and project managers will explore music and art, sport, cooking, food and health

These programs are not just for music education but also explore music education to promote family intergenerational learning, English communication skills, digital literacy skills, and cross-cultural exchange. Participants from China, Nepal, and the UK have already participated in the platform, benefiting from the unique approach to music and digital community education. The impact of LivePBL has been significant in terms of participants who have demonstrated learning outcomes with increased motivation and engagement.

The platform has been recently CPD accredited, validating its impact and effectiveness in promoting inclusive online family home learning. LivePBL leadership team and student teaching assistants from China and Nepal. LivePBL has also organised two independent international workshops and published several journal papers and articles, highlighting its impact in the field of eLearning.

Another significant aspect of LivePBL is its self-motivated, self-organised, and low-cost-effective approach to e-Learning. This approach has enabled LivePBL to reach a wider audience of learners, regardless of their socio-economic background or geographical location. Therefore, the platform is all-inclusive, promoting a sense of community and belonging among participants, while also providing opportunities for cultural exchange and enrichment.

We believe that LivePBL has the potential to transform the way we think about music education and online learning more broadly. We are excited to share our work with the wider community and to continue our mission of promoting innovative and inclusive e-Learning practices.

2. The infrastructure

LivePBL leadership team consists of

1) Professors and lecturers based in universities and colleges
2) Headteachers based in schools, kindergartens and children's clubs, and recently joined
3) Dalian Shuxiang social community of parents and children
4) An entrepreneur innovating capital cases

The leaders are from UNIC, i.e., UK, Nepal, Ireland/India and China. Learners are diversified by the following groups:

1) Under- and post-graduate students led by the professors and lecturers
2) Children learners led by headteachers from schools and children's clubs
3) Parents and children learners led by parents based in the local social communities

LivePBL programmes are running on Zooms. Teaching, learning and activity-related materials are administrated by The Support School's Learning Management System. Our infrastructural development of LivePBL will continue to focus on the "e-learning ecology". E-learning ecology is a metaphor (Cope & Kalantzis, 2017) that undertakes "learning ecology" as lenses to consider e-learning on the facets of online socio-cultural activities in teaching and learning contexts. Such convergence of e-learning ecologies will be further piloted in February 2024 by launching LivePBL programme training Homestay managers by the theme of music, sport, food and health.

3. The challenges

3.1 From 2019-2021: Established a hybrid intergenerational family and local community model

Before Covid started in 2019, LivePBL was initiated in working together with a local Chinese community called Tulip Community Academy. As a social service organisation, Tulip shares its successful experience on how to undertake the social responsibility to engage and motivate children to learn through a new model of Family Education. LivePBL enabled Tulip and regulated its organisation to have achieved the accreditation awarded by British NCC Education Digi Programmes (www.nccedu.com) as a partner centre based in Dalian City, China. The innovation began with digital literacy delivery for 5-9 years old together with their parents. Some of their parents are mothers who used to be teachers but have not been back to work since their childcare commitments; some are fathers who work in IT/Software industries. LivePBL also encountered some disadvantages of China's Family Education.

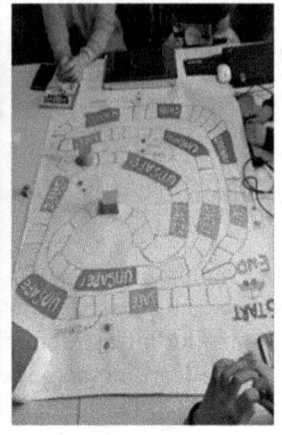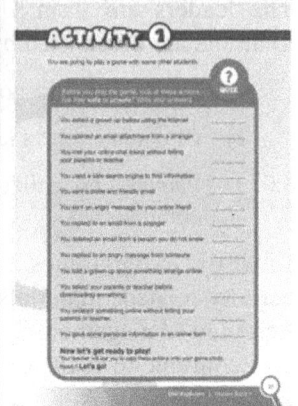

It is well known that China has undertaken an enormous scale of change at astonishing speed and from many aspects. Amongst many, sometimes challenging problems that education reform encounters are caused by the increasing and widespread commercialism that has been heavily influencing the national education policies and overall school pedagogies and management. By collaborating with Tulip, LivePBL tackled two challenging issues.

One challenging issue is that there are still many schools' traditional normative assessment systems, where the aim of teaching and learning practices is only to get children prepared to undertake the national school admission exams. This has led to flourishing commercial classes of tutorials out of schools paid for by the parents. The expectations of parents for their children and their financial affordability to the classes drive such commercial development. Children's own interests and motivations in learning needs are, by and large, underdeveloped, or even neglected.

The other challenging issue is that the relationships between schools and parents have become more complex because the tutorial class out of school should play as a partner to facilitate the engagement with children, parents and schools, rather than a mere medium connection that parents expect from the commercial market. In respect of digital literacy education, the national curriculums of digital literacy have not been fully developed. Whilst a massive scale of commercial courses led by AI robots coding is on sale, both schools and parents have already taken a commercial stake. All this is causing a great amount of anxiety - Parents only expect and believe what technical coding skills as sold by the commercial classes; they have been unable to realise how digital literacy will impact their children's future in many ways.

3.2 From 2020 to 2022 on the resilience of the Covid-19

Trying to be at the heart of the local community during a pandemic presented many challenges. During periods of full and part school closures, it became apparent that childcare issues were very stressful for families, with serious financial implications at what was already a very scary and trying time. LivePBL response was through international collaborative communities in China across Tulip networks in Beijing, Dalian, Qingdao, Taiyuan and Xiamen. LivePBL also collaborated with a college in Nepal and in the UK to continue the NCC Education programme online.

The leadership team recognised the importance of supporting parents by offering a safe caring environment for their children online. To suddenly need English support, LivePBL collaborated with The Support School online, and Dibyabhumi Multiple College based in Nepal. LivePBL offered virtual internships for Nepalese students to join us to assist parents and children in English. The following images illustrate the learning activities that were carried out.

3.3 From 2022 up to today: Developed a cost-effective and sustainable non-formal hybrid teaching and learning approach

LivePBL had been facing a new challenge, i.e., the leadership critically needed to standardise its online activities to re-collaborate with colleges and universities. This is because, at the end of 2021, Tulip Community Academy decided to carry out its own development with NCC Education. LivePBL leadership is determined to further develop the collaborative partnerships. LivePBL started to work together with The Support School in collaborating with NCFE CACHE qualification body. The Support School has been successfully accredited by and established as an NCFE CACHE learning centre.

Local community and cross-international cultural learning

LivePBL leadership re-focused on the teaching and learning practices in non-formal educational settings that could shed light to facilitate learning. Colleges and universities students have been centred to learn, as well as assisting teaching to engage with local social communities and families. Thanks to The Support School (UK) and Dibyabhumi Multiple College (Nepal) who stayed and continued to collaborate with LivePBL.

LivePBL delivered hybrid classes to deliver digital literacy creative art design for beginners' online classes. These classes were designed in line with NCFE standards. Families and communities could explore Storyboard, Comic, Animation, Sound, Music, and Filming tools to present and exchange their ideas of design. For teacher trainee students in particular, LivePBL has been providing such situated observations on how teaching and learning took place.

As a constructivist practitioner, LivePBL focuses on hybrid and situated teaching and learning practices, which embrace teaching together with learners as individuals construct cognitive thinking, previous experience, attitudes, and beliefs (Karwasz and Wyborska, 2023). In supporting such a construction, the use of technology is of

"Recent efforts to solve the problems of education—created by neoliberalism in and out of higher education—have centred on the use of technology that promises efficiency, progress tracking, and automation" (Koseoglu et al, 2023).

LivePBL's digital capacities not only reflect the necessary digital competency of teaching and learning-related activities in a non-formal educational setting. Garrison raised four critical issues concerning digital technologies:

"Shifting social presence from socio-emotional support to a focus on group cohesion...; concerns the progressive development of cognitive presence (inquiry) from exploration to resolution ...; moving the discussion beyond the exploration phase...; do with how we conceive of teaching presence (design, facilitation, direct instruction)" (Garrison, 2023)

LivePBL's teaching and learning practices foremost are in applying the relevant digital roles to enable role-based teaching and learning activities. LivePBL designed projects in multidisciplinary areas including academic and vocal education, academic and school music education, music profession, music and social development, where everyone within the LivePBL framework has a clear mindset to have a role to play. Moreover, contextualising the use of digital tools must be associated with the design of roles and switching roles. Many argued that the current blended teaching and learning design is still based on a framework that has been originally developed in pure online contexts, which has ignored the dynamics of multiple teaching and learning roles (Armellini and Stefani, 2016).

On the digital sphere – where we are on connecting LivePBL with non-formal education

Digital sphere exists and is often understood as the totality of the infosphere over the internet (Dawson, 2021; Fuchs, 2021; Ritzi, 2023). However, when emerging digital technologies and platforms are advanced to enable teaching and learning, that sphere has a clear boundary between formal and non-formal education.

"Formal education refers to teaching that happens in schools, following an official curriculum.... Non-formal education is 'any organized, systematic, educational activities carried on outside of the formal system to provide selected types of learning to particular groups .... '" (Johnson and Majewska, 2022).

The formal digital sphere on, for instance, JISC, FutureLearn, or Universities' VLE Moodle, significantly limits itself to connecting individuals' *experiences* with teaching and learning processes, or in other words, these VLEs are "one size fits all", which are not originally constructed to adapt social and collaborative teaching and learning. The Human-

Computer Interactive (HCI) interfaces are not designed to apply to different digital roles in teaching and learning but are dedicated primarily to role-based public or private data/information access controls.

The teaching and learning practices in LivePBL have been encouraging different teaching and learning roles to develop and formulate their own projects, so as to relate or share their experience in teaching and learning. LivePBL first designed online seminars where individuals presented their music-related experiences. LivePBL then set up different projects, roles, and responsibilities for leading professors to work together with their own student teams. We have now set up five projects:

1) Bel Cando, Chinese music, and culture
2) Folk/Pop music from Nepal and China
3) Individual singing performances from Nepal and China
4) Education and social work development
5) LMS LivePBL websites, digital tools, promotion materials administration

LivePBL has enabled shared teaching and learning leadership and responsibilities. LivePBL has provided an additional critical dimension to the digital sphere where individual projects have been formulated to embrace individuals' experiences.

LivePBL personalisation collaborated with TSS LMS (Learning Management System)

In a formal educational organisation, class differentiation is strongly emphasising personalisation. When individuals use social media digital tools, they have their individual social presence and transform their roles in the "real world" in digital social contexts. The LivePBL projects have created personalised dimensions in the digital sphere. Such personalisation has become a critical pathway to support individual learning. However, because the digital capacity of a formal educational organisation is not scalable to personalisation, institutional in-services should be developed and partnered with non-formal educational organisations.

LivePBL has been collaborating with NCFE CACHE Learning Centre at The Support School based in the UK. The personalisation is constructed by the project role-based learning registration, and digital links toolbox including Padlet, Thinglink, and other Comic, Animation, Sound, Music, and Image multimedia editing tools. LivePBL has been using project templates to guide learning processes including project specifications, project role-based registration forms, lesson plans, semi-structured learning journals, and learner feedback forms.

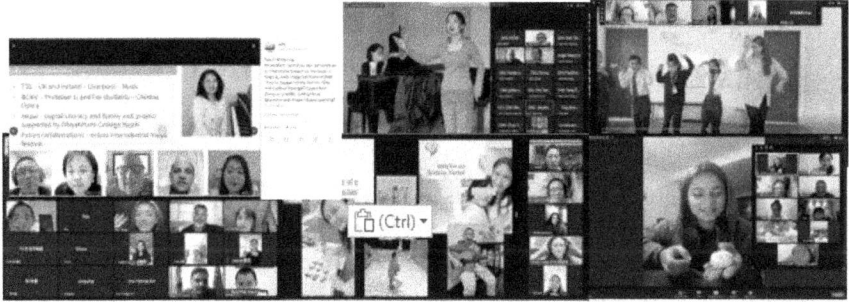

Connecting learning with all-round skills development

Extensive R&D exists to understand "all-round skills" to prepare students for the 21st century; moreover, one of the Higher Education (HE) values that are still underdeveloped is about HE capacities to equip students with the skills, and such development is severely limited in social mobility (Barrie, 2006; Universities UK, 2023). Collaborative learning, community learning, home learning, or family intergenerational learning should have better been explored through hybrid teaching and learning. Teaching and learning practice in LivePBL settings has been carried out by Sino-International Family Visit, where professors, lecturers, teachers, undergraduates, postgraduates, parents, and children were all getting together online to share their learning experiences from their life, work, family, community, festival event, etc. One case was Miss Luge Zhang presented her experience of organising and conducting a team of students' choir and observed what and how students had developed various skills through the singing activities.

Another case was a mum teacher based in Malaysia who brought her son and joined a LivePBL; her son was learning Mandarin, playing the guitar and singing a song in Mandarin; he communicated with others bilingually. LivePBL has been engaging with LinkedIn from several aspects:

1) That encourages learners who have little international communication skills to develop an online social presence. Students can explore digital integration functions such as presenting with photos and video

2) That enables teachers to design assignments by using LinkedIn as a research tool to be inspired by other researchers. LinkedIn has a good variety of professional groups and communities that provide specific topics

3) That facilitates students to design posting activities and share individual learning experiences with others

6) 3.3.5 Critical digital pedagogy – hybrid macro- and micro-teaching practices connecting pre-service teachers

LivePBL has applied critical pedagogy (Stommel et al. 2020) by encouraging students to set up their own projects and understand their roles and role-switching in learning processes. However, while LivePBL has been centred on technological applications, the uses of digital tools need pedagogical care to reflect relationships with teaching and learning design with these tools in an online environment. LivePBL has advanced project-based learning pedagogy trans-formatively onto macro and micro-teaching, and hybrid webinar that is a combination of online webinar, offline seminars, and workshops.

4. How the initiative was received by the users or participants

CPD has certified LivePBL training programme, and appraises:

"[This] Hybrid programme is a unique learning opportunity for Sino-international music teachers; student teachers; and local community schoolteachers to develop music education projects through such virtual social project practices. Participants will benefit from macro-teaching seminars; micro-teaching workshops; and cross-cultural team-working through digital LMS platform."

Lecturers based in the Education Faculty, London University of Greenwich, had attended and observed LivePBL training sessions; they highly endorsed LivePBL, which can be seen in appendix A & B:

1) Feedback from perspectives of teaching and learning practice

"Dear Ying, thank you so much for inviting me to your session where you discussed how to link vocal education through project-based learning. In our debrief you mentioned how participation has been a problem for you in these webinars and that you were thinking about working with UK-based academics to bring new approaches to the delivery of this programme. I will focus on participation in my feedback based on our debrief.

Overall, you supported learning really well. You set clear expectations at the beginning and noted that one of your objectives was to help participants identify their roles in this project. You were approachable and clear throughout the session - I really enjoyed seeing how you bridge formal education with non-formal education through the examples you have given. The idea that academic learning does not need to be confined to formal education institutions is a powerful message, which was clear in your session".

2) Feedback from perspectives of critical pedagogy in non-formal learning settings

"You demonstrate a good understanding of hybrid and online learning with plenty of examples from practice. The case studies you included were engaging and demonstrated the impact of the programme on participants. I also liked your focus on pedagogy - everything you do in this programme is driven by clear values and visions."

5. The learning outcomes

Learners demonstrated excellent learning outcomes via academic performances. Many of them had experience in publishing papers and receiving their CPD certificates for the very first time. LivePBL publications include:

1) The First Model of Family Education on the Delivery of Bilingual British NCC Digital Literacy Qualifications in Dalian, China – Engaging and Motivating Children, 16:38-49, 2020 The Eurasia Proceedings of Educational and Social Sciences, http://www.epess.net/en/pub/issue/55066/755951

2) China's Cases of LivePBL: Linking Vocal Education with Project Based Learning in Aesthetics of Life, Ireland International Conference on Education (IICE-2022) and International Conference on Information Society (i-Society 2022), Page(s): 89 - 92

3) Think Globally and Act Locally: Higher Education Can Make Critical Change of Collective Mindset on SDGs, The Frontiers, 1(1), 2023

4) A Hybrid and Non-Formal Music Education Connecting China's Local Family Communities and Cultures with Nepal, International Journal for Infonomics (IJI), 15(1), 2023

5) Student Choirs and Virtual Social Practices by LivePBL: Linking Vocal Education with Project Based Learning, Literacy Information and Computer Education Journal (LICEJ), 13(1), 2023

6) Student Virtual Social Practices between China and Nepal, International Journal of Technology and Inclusive Education, 12(1), 2023

LivePBL has the advantage of giving students feedback (Lipnevich and Panadero, 2021). As LivePBL is in a non-formal educational setting, student feedback is sensitive in certain contexts. We often ask for feedback to be "consistent, clearly outlined and specific". Because of LivePBL in scalable contexts, LivePBL can realise feedback in a more meaningful contributing to understanding the digital competency in teaching and learning, and more effectively enhancing the teaching and learning confidence.

In the formal educational approach, student academic learning outcomes are observed through formative and/or summative feedback, like in the case of Philo. LivePBL brought undergraduates and graduates together participated in online international conferences, and organised an independent workshop on LICE-2022 London International Conference on Education. Student academic learning performance was observed by their group teamwork, presentations, and participation in workshops, more effectively and interestingly by student papers published. In a digital sphere, a digital social presence and role-based learning activity both can be connecting learner's social and academic mobility, contributing to teaching, and learning materials.

6. Plans to further develop LivePBL

The LivePBL uses educational technologies for teaching and learning in non-formal settings. The digital capacities in a non-formal educational setting would be usefully scalable to individuals' contexts that connect, reflect and/or individuals' experiences by their project designs, hence, present themselves in a digital social presence. These non-formal educational digital capacities would be not just on connectivity and accessibilities, but also enable diversified and dynamic roles in teaching and learning within the project contexts, whereby adding a new and meaningful artefact to the digital sphere dedicated to teaching and learning. Such LivePBL project role-based teaching and learning practices are cost-effective to facilitate training and learning, for pre-service teacher students, because non-formal education technologies are to their social mobilities and, hence, can share hybrid experiences within and off schools.

LivePBL undertakes critical and interesting ethical challenges. Regulating non-formal education organisation services with professional and/or qualification bodies is highly feasible. For instance, CPD and NCFE have been collaborating with LivePBL. LivePBL would continue to provide non-formal educational services collaborating with local communities, learners can cross different ethical backgrounds intergenerationally and have different expectations to meet their individual and beneficial goals.

In February 2024, LivePBL will pilot training homestay managers jointly with Eco-Home-Stay Nepal. The main aim is to train project innovators from both China and Nepal. The trainees can come from families, schools, colleges, unemployed, homestay or hospitality business staff. At the end of the training, trainees from both China and Nepal could present their homestay projects. If we can have one college join in from Nepal and China, we shall further provision the training towards joining China's national competition of Internet+ Innovation in 2024. We hope Homestay will be able to find a place that has an internet connection, a group of trainees can share a computer or laptop, a vocational school or college or a group of staff who are interested in collaborating with China and the UK.

The future workshop will have 12 sessions. Hence, the workshop is equivalent to 12 credits. The pedagogy is hybrid Project Based Learning. By doing so, the workshop enables individual participants to innovate, pilot, present and share with others' homestay project initiatives.

LivePBL will have the following three tracks:

1) Track One: Music and Art,
2) Track Two: Mountaineering, and
3) Track Three: Food and Health.

LivePBL will be the pedagogical method to facilitate training and learning through "doing the projects". PBL here is different from Problem-Based Learning or Inquiry-Based Learning. Trainees complete PBL to meet the project's objectives, while trainees complete Problem-Based Learning by providing a solution for the problem. Moreover, PBL is a pedagogical approach to engage trainees with well-defined, managed, and sustainable projects with clear end products for trainees to develop and learn. To be able to train effectively, the presenter is an expert and coach who is responsible for the training delivery on his/her track to

1) Emulate the skills of Digital Literacy and Teamwork Communication in a socio-cultural environment and results as part of the group-work project
2) Create digital connections and conversations to promote information exchange between group members through online meetings, emailing, etc
3) Manage the communication "content and context" to enable training communicative and organisational knowledge and direct groups to accomplish PBL deliverables, and therefore to enable trainees to meet the learning outcomes
4) Enable trainees to carry out key reflections, e.g., how trainees emulate real-world homestay practices, and how trainees help each other develop transferrable skills, while trainers are able to observe

The presenter will adapt LivePBL model on the track respectively, see Figure 1 LivePBL Homestay Model.

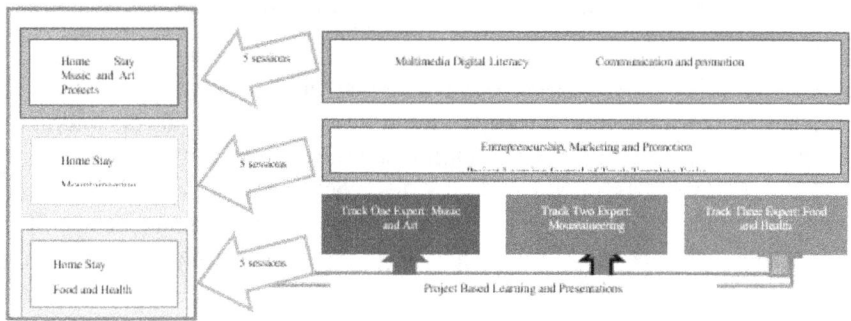

Figure 1 LivePBL Homestay Model

Sessions are delivered via Zoom with the following supporting documents:
1) Presenter Note
2) Session timetable
3) Lesson (session) Plan
4) Session PPTs
5) Project task template for Sessions 1-12
6) Workshop feedback form

A webinar is a type of online seminar that is conducted over the Internet. It typically involves a presentation or lecture by a speaker, which is broadcast live to a remote audience through video conferencing software. Webinars often include interactive features, such as live polls, Q&A sessions, and chat rooms, to facilitate engagement between the speaker and the audience.

A seminar is an academic or professional gathering where participants meet in person or online to discuss a specific topic or issue. It usually involves a lecture or presentation by an expert in the field, followed by discussion and interaction between participants. Seminars are often used in academic settings, such as universities, but can also be used in corporate or professional settings. LivePBL Seminar is typically used to facilitate Webinars to support trainees in completing the project tasks. The presenter needs to make sure the trainees can use the templates provided to discuss or present their work in such a seminar. There are various situations when they prefer or have to do so offline, e.g., cost-effectively using internet accessibility. Moreover, project tasks will be specified by various templates only. Trainees should lead the seminar with their presentations, discussion, reporting teamwork, etc.

Online learning is a form of education that takes place entirely over the internet. It can take many forms, including self-paced courses, interactive tutorials, and virtual classrooms. Online learning is often used in both formal and informal settings, such as universities, vocational schools, and corporate training programs. LivePBL combines Webinars with different forms of PBL to enable trainees to online learning including online observations, presentations, teamwork, and group discussions, to complete project-based tasks.

The Presenter in LivePBL is not just one person. There are various different presenter roles. At present, we have

1) Presenter for training to use digital tools and demonstrating such training practices (Responsible for delivering *Lesson Plans* by Webinars)

2) Presenter in enabling trainees to understand generic project-based learning methods and tools

3) Presenter for the expert on the track to facilitate trainees to complete project-based tasks (Responsible for supporting trainees to complete templates of *Learning Journals*, design and present project tasks)

4) Presenter for supporting trainees to write research papers based on their PBL experience

References

Armellini, A. and De Stefani, M (2016) Social presence in the 21st century: An adjustment to the Community of Inquiry framework. British Journal of Educational Technology, 47(6), 1202-1216.

Barrie, S. C (2006) Understanding what we mean by the generic attributes of graduates, Higher Education, 51(2):215-241

Caprara, L., Caprara, C. Effects of virtual learning environments: A scoping review of literature, Educ Inf Technol 27, 3683–3722 https://doi.org/10.1007/s10639-021-10768-w [accessed by 01-06-2023]

Cope, B. and Kalantzis, M. (2017) e-Learning EcologiesPrinciples for New Learning and Assessment, Routledge

Cordella, A. and Shaikh, M (2023) Actor Network Theory and After: What's New For IS Research? https://personal.lse.ac.uk/shaikh/ANT%20ECIS%20FINAL%20VERSION%2031%20March.pdf [accessed by 01-06-2023]

Dawson, M (2022). The accountability of non-governmental actors in the digital sphere: A theoretical framework, European Low Journal, 27 May https://onlinelibrary.wiley.com/doi/full/10.1111/eulj.12420 [accessed by 01-06-2023]

Fuchs, C (2021) The digital commons and the digital public sphere: how to advance digital democracy today, *Westminster Papers in Communication and Culture* 16(1), 9-26. doi: https://doi.org/10.16997/wpcc.917 [accessed by 01-06-2023]

Garrison, D. R. (Online Community of Inquiry Review: Social, Cognitive, and Teaching Presence Issues https://files.eric.ed.g [accessed by 01-06-2023]

https://www.universitiesuk.ac.uk/what-we-do/policy-and-research/publications/graduate-employment-its-limits-measuring [accessed by 01-06-2023]

Johnson, M., and Majewska, D (2022) Formal, non-formal, and informal learning: What are they, What are they, and how can we research them? Cambridge University Press & Assessment Research Report

Karwasz, G. P. and Wyborska, K (2023) How Constructivist Environment Changes Perception of Learning: Physics Is Fun. Educ. Sci. 13, 195. https://doi.org/10.3390/educsci13020195

Koseoglu, S., Veletsianos. G., & Rowell, C. (2023). Critical Digital Pedagogy for Higher Education. Athabasca University Press. Open Access version is available at: https://www.aupress.ca/books/120310-critical-digital-pedagogy-in-higher-education/ [accessed by 01-06-2023]

Lipnevich, A. A. and Panadero, E. (2021) The Development of student feedback literacy: enabling uptake of feedback. Assess. Eval. Higher Education, 43(8):1315–1325

Ritzi, C (2023) The hidden structures of the digital public sphere, Constellations, 30(1):55-60

Stommel et al. (2020) Critical Digital Pedagogy: A collection https://hybridpedagogy.org/critical-digital-pedagogy/ [accessed by 01-06-2023]

Universities UK (2023) Graduate employment: its limits in measuring the value of higher education https://www.universitiesuk.ac.uk/what-we-do/policy-and-research/publications/graduate-employment-its-limits-measuring [accessed by 01-06-2023]

Ying Lui et al

Appendix A University of Greenwich observation feedback from perspectives of critical pedagogy in non-formal learning settings

What you did well:

You demonstrate a good understanding of hybrid and online learning with plenty of examples from practice. The case studies you included were engaging and demonstrated the impact of the programme on participants (for example the case of Philo). I also liked your focus on pedagogy - everything you do in this programme is driven by clear values and visions.

What you can improve/work on:

I thought perhaps you could have explored more TEL frameworks relevant to what you're doing and a bit more in depth. I was looking for more explanation and critical analysis in some parts. For example, here when you mention actor network theory, I was curious to know how you see this network through the lens of ANT.

Appendix B: University of Greenwich Observation feedback from Perspectives of teaching and learning practice

Observer notes

Key relevant UKPSF dimension elements are included below, to help with mapping to the reflective mapping document.

Category	Notes	Category	Notes
Number of students present			see in what ways you could facilitate these presences in the live sessions and beyond.
Planning and preparation	Excellent		I wondered if there are any asynchronous activities you're doing with this group to draw more participation?
Overall structure	Maybe use different tools to encourage participation? Please see more on this below.		I hope this is useful feedback for you. Good luck with this fascinating project, and let me know of the results of the interventions you are planning on doing in the near future!
Communication and Interaction	This was done well, please see more on student engagement below	Relationships	Good, limited opportunities to observe this
		Summary	See above.
Monitoring and supporting learning	Dear Ying, thank you so much for inviting me to your session where you discussed how to link vocal education through project based learning. In our debrief you mentioned how participation has been a problem for you in these webinars and that you were thinking about working with UK based academics to bring new approaches to the delivery of this programme. I will focus on participation in my feedback based on our debrief.

Overall, you supported learning really well. You set clear expectations at the beginning and noted that one of your objectives was to help participants identify their role in this project. You were approachable and clear throughout the session - I really enjoyed seeing how you bridge formal education with non-formal education through the examples you have given. The idea that academic learning does not need to be confined to formal education institutions is a powerful message and this message was clear in your session.

I wondered if it would be a good idea for you to use an audience response system like a mentimeter or perhaps an interactive board like padlet before or during the session to encourage more active participation from the audience. another strategy could be in the ground rules you state at the very beginning perhaps make active participation an expectation. This shouldn't mean turning on cameras but that everyone should be willing to and should have the means to participate, whether via chat or audio or another method.

The communities of inquiry framework might be helpful for you to frame the online sessions. You could explicitly introduce this framework or you can simply think about the different presences (teaching presence, social presence, and cognitive presence) and | Participant reflection (max 500 words in total)
Please refer to the checklist of criteria when writing up your reflection.

Reflection
As a constructivist believer and practitioner, I designed this lesson as a continuous session embracing teaching together with learning, because learners as individuals construct cognitive thinking, previous experience, attitudes, and beliefs. I had students' brief presentations in the last session, then using their music preferences, experiences and skills to suggest the project developments. The students are of a mixed group of professors, under-/post-graduates, school, and kindergarten teachers. The focus is to use the music projects that are associated with their own experiences, so as to motivate and encourage them to learn from each other. On the digital sphere, a teaching role on a digital network is often digitally multifaceted, and that makes significant and critical impacts on this lesson's teaching and learning activities.

Successes
This lesson has laid good initiatives to motivate and engage with students to meet the learning outcomes to acquire various skills. The contextualising digital roles have been clearly designed by the projects that have been developed by themselves. The project learning tasks are formulated by the templates, which was explained well. The lesson also tried to enable shared teaching and learning leadership and responsibilities but provides an additional critical dimension to the digital sphere where individual projects have been formulated to embrace individuals' own experiences.

Actions
Although the above initiatives were made successfully, there are several areas for further improvement, particularly in utilising digital interactive tools to engage with students more effectively. |

Author Biographies

Dr Ying Liu is a Country Director for the International Higher Education Teaching and Learning Association; and a former Advisor to China's Education Ministry at the Schooling Plan and Development Committee. He is teaching at the London School of Science and Technology, UK.

Professor Yuanyuan Li is at the Music College, Capital Normal University, Beijing, China. She is a member of China's National Music Academy, Beijing Music Academy, and the International Society for Music Education.

Dr Andy Hogg is CEO of The Support School and a learning centre of the Northern Council of Further Education. He has over 25 years of experience in supporting pupils with additional needs. Research is an important aspect of Andy's professional practice. He believes that only through practitioner research can we fully understand the pupils with additional needs.

Dr Yasmin Mirza is CEO of Capital Case Ltd, presently a faculty member at The London School of Science and Technology. She takes a keen interest in wider learning participation. She has earned her MBA from HULT International Business School, London, UK and her PhD in Microbiology from Kurukshetra University, Kurukshetra, India.

Inclusive e-Learning for Marginalized Communities:
The Mobile Learning Center Initiative

Mahmoud Hawamdeh, Bayan Shoubaki, Nisreen Awadallah, Saeda Abu Halaweh
Al-Quds Open University, Ramallah, Palestine
mhawamdeh@qou.edu
bshobaki@qou.edu
nawadallah@qou.edu
sabuhalaweh@qou.edu

1. Introduction

The 1995 Oslo II Accord introduced an administrative division of the Palestinian West Bank, categorizing it into areas A, B, and C, as an interim measure until a final status agreement could be reached. This segregation of land persists today, with area A falling under the governance of the Palestinian Authority, area C under the control of Israel, and area B being jointly managed.

Area C, encompassing approximately 62% of the total land area of the West Bank, is home to an estimated 300,000 Palestinians residing in 532 residential areas, which are partially or entirely situated within this region. Unfortunately, area C remains subject to stringent military orders and regulations enforced by the Israeli Occupying Forces (IOF). These measures severely curtail the daily activities and rights of the Palestinian population. The IOF restricts the construction of crucial social infrastructure in vital sectors such as education, healthcare, and agriculture, as well as various other aspects of daily life.

This dilemma has dire consequences for the communities in Area C. Shockingly, over one-third of Palestinian communities in this region lack a primary school[4], compelling children to undertake difficult journeys to reach the nearest educational facility. Compounding the issue, existing roads, if any, are often unpaved and in a state of disrepair, making mobility a considerable challenge. Consequently, young students are compelled to embark on lengthy walks each morning to reach their schools, repeating the process in the evening after their classes conclude[5].

The limitations imposed by the IOF extend beyond infrastructure and basic services. Palestinians in Area C face restrictions on their freedom of movement, affecting their ability to commute, access essential services, and engage in economic activities. The presence of checkpoints, roadblocks, and other physical barriers further exacerbates these challenges[6], impeding the movement of people and goods and stifling economic development.

Furthermore, the strict planning regulations enforced by Israel within Area C virtually render it impossible for Palestinians to obtain the necessary permits for constructing essential infrastructure, including adequate housing and educational institutions. This impediment obstructs the development of crucial facilities that are imperative for the well-being and progress of the population.

Considering these formidable challenges, Palestinians are left with no choice but to consider alternative arrangements. Some contemplate leaving their children with relatives in communities where schools are located for the duration of the week. In more distressing cases, families may opt to withdraw their children from school altogether. Regrettably, this phenomenon predominantly affects girls, reflecting the prevailing social norms and the hardships they face.

The right to education[7] is recognized as a fundamental human right by international human rights instruments such as the Universal Declaration of

---

[4] area_c_key_humanitarian_concerns.pdf (ochaopt.org)

[5] OCHA report for Area c United Nations Office for the Coordination of Humanitarian Affairs occupied Palestinian territory
https://www.ochaopt.org/sites/default/files/area_c_key_humanitarian_concerns.pdf

[6] Access to education in Area C of the West Bank | United Nations Office for the Coordination of Humanitarian Affairs - occupied Palestinian territory (ochaopt.org)

[7] Universal Declaration of Human Rights | United Nations

Human Rights and the Convention on the Rights of the Child. However, in certain regions, such as Area C, there can be significant challenges and limitations to accessing quality education.

These restrictions on access to education in Area C highlight the importance of addressing the educational needs of the population and striving for equitable opportunities. Education plays a crucial role in empowering individuals, promoting social and economic development, and fostering a sense of dignity and self-determination.

To address the education challenges faced by the marginalized communities in the Palestinian territories, al-Quds Open University (QOU) has taken a proactive approach. One of the University initiatives involves the establishment of two Mobile learning centers. These centers aim to overcome obstacles such as the lack of computer labs in schools and mobility issues.

The objective of this initiative is to provide access to quality education, digital learning tools, and resources to schools in the marginalized areas, particularly in Area C of the West Bank.

Being the largest University in Palestine with 18 branches covering all districts, the Mobile Learning Centers extend their reach to areas that are not easily accessible through the existing branches. Specifically, the centers operate in the Jordan Valley through the Tubas branch and in South Hebron through the Yatta branch. All activities conducted are closely coordinated with the local community, education directorates in Tubas and Yatta, as well as the local governance in the marginalized areas of the Palestinian Territories.

QOU has partnered with higher education institutions to develop an innovative mobile learning center, which can be accessed through the website (http://cec.qou.edu/trcenter/), ensuring open access to educational, social, and digital learning tools and resources for all schools. The project not only provides valuable digital learning resources to schools and communities in underserved areas but also offers opportunities for skill development. By prioritizing a quality e-learning experience, QOU establishes itself as a key partner in educational collaboration.

2. The infrastructure

To support the initiative, QOU has collaborated with the Ministry of Education directorates, local governance, and community-based organizations to establish two mobile centers in Tubas and South Hebron. These centers serve as training hubs for teachers, providing them with access to digital learning tools and resources. Moreover, the centers offer students the necessary IT equipment to complete their school tasks and participate in IT lessons.

Each mobile center is staffed by two individuals—a driver and a technical support person responsible for equipment maintenance and user assistance. Additional staff may be present for specific activities held at the centers

The hardware and software equipment in each center include 20 laptop computers, desks, chairs, headphones, a projector, printer, LCD monitor, smart board, generator, sound system, and air conditioner Internet connectivity is available, allowing access to a library of 1,500 books in physical and eBook formats. The centers also provide virtual labs for Physics and Chemistry, such as "Crocodile," and contain educational multimedia materials on the laptops. Wheelchair accessibility is ensured through the presence of a lift. The challenges (how and when they were encountered, how they were overcome)

Within the mobile learning center, individuals are introduced to and granted access to the OSOL Repository for Digital Content. OSOL stands as an open-access digital repository extended by QOU, dedicated to capturing, storing, organizing, indexing, preserving, and facilitating access to a wide spectrum of digital assets and intellectual creations. This encompasses a diverse range, from QOU's scientific journals, scholarly papers, theses, articles, and projects, to books, digital learning materials, SMART courses, and various other valuable resources.

By integrating the e-learning service provided by the Center for Continuing Distance Learning (CDL), QOU demonstrates its commitment to inclusive education and lifelong learning. The CDL serves as a transformative platform that leverages technology to ensure equal access to quality education, regardless of geographical constraints. Through the CDL's e-learning service, QOU empowers students in marginalized areas, helping them overcome educational barriers and unlock their full potential.

Furthermore, the two mobile learning centers have facilitated a substantial number of training opportunities for individuals in Area C. These initiatives have been orchestrated through the Continuing Education Center (CEC) at QOU, which has organized a diverse array of training programs, including:

- Comprehensive training in ICDL (International Computer Driving Licenses) tailored for both students and teachers.
- Specialized training sessions on conducting online teaching, designed specifically for school teachers, particularly in light of the closures enforced during the COVID-19 pandemic.
- Workshops focusing on 21st-century skills, encompassing vital proficiencies like media literacy, information literacy, technology literacy, and digital marketing. Participants were equipped with all requisite training resources.
- Entrepreneurship training sessions, expertly conducted at the centers. These sessions provided students with foundational knowledge in entrepreneurship, covering aspects such as initiating a business and crafting a business plan, inclusive of financial and marketing strategies.
- Targeted training in basic information security, especially tailored for teenagers in the designated areas.

This initiative directly addresses the pressing challenges encountered by schools in Area C, including inadequate classrooms, insufficient sanitation facilities, and substandard road infrastructure. These hurdles not only curtail educational opportunities but also infringe upon the fundamental right to education. Through the establishment of mobile learning centers and the provision of digital learning resources, QOU effectively surmounts these challenges, ensuring that marginalized communities gain unfettered access to quality education. These centers play a vital role in empowering students and teachers, fostering digital literacy, and fostering lifelong learning opportunities. This novel initiative has garnered significant attention from both local and Arab news agencies. The innovative nature of the project, coupled with its potential to bring about positive change, has made it a topic of interest and discussion in media circles.

3. How the initiative was received by the participants

The resounding success of Mobile learning Centers initiative is evident in the positive response from teachers, students, and communities within the designated areas. The provision of digital learning tools, resources, and valuable training opportunities has not only empowered teachers but also significantly enriched the learning experience for their students. Notably, the centers have transformed into inclusive spaces, conscientiously catering to the diverse needs of all learners, including those with disabilities.

In the current era, the role of educational technology in teaching has never been more pivotal, owing to the rapid advancements in information and communication technologies. Technology serves as an invaluable facilitator of learning, nurturing creativity, and heightening engagement levels within the classroom environment.

A noteworthy aspect is the way in which educational technology empowers teachers to exercise greater control over the learning process. It facilitates the meticulous monitoring of student progress, allowing for the customization of lessons tailored to the unique needs of each student. Additionally, it enables timely and constructive feedback, serving as a powerful motivator to keep students engaged and invested in their educational journey.

Moreover, the data-driven capabilities of educational technology empower teachers with comprehensive insights into student performance. This includes the ability to track progress over time and readily identify students who may require additional support or resources. Armed with this data, teachers are better equipped to provide precise and targeted feedback, ensuring that every student receives the necessary guidance to remain motivated and deeply engaged in their learning endeavors. This personalized approach to education stands as a cornerstone in nurturing a thriving and inclusive learning environment.

In essence, the integration of educational technology through Mobile learning centers represents a paradigm shift in education, transcending traditional boundaries and opening up a world of possibilities for students and educators alike. It not only prepares students for success in a technology-driven world but also empowers them to become lifelong learners, critical thinkers, and informed global citizens.

Through our prior engagements, it became evident that the beneficiaries expressed a strong demand for extended sessions and visits from the mobile learning center. For instance, during the COVID-19 pandemic, the education directorate in Yatta collaborated with QOU to conduct specialized training sessions for teachers in schools facing persistent threats of destruction by the Israeli Occupying Forces (IOF). Due to the high demand, we organized three distinct training sessions for different target groups. This pattern held true for various other training programs and courses.

Furthermore, the centers served as vital hubs for online courses and examinations over the past years. QOU carefully devised schedules for each center to visit targeted schools in partnership with local governance. These visits aimed to conduct e-learning sessions for teachers, students, and members of the local community.

In tandem with these efforts, the Center for Digital Learning (CDL) within QOU assumes a crucial role in amplifying the reach and impact of our educational endeavors. The CDL extends an extensive suite of e-learning services to students in remote areas. It encompasses an array of digital learning tools and resources, including interactive modules, multimedia presentations, e-books, and video lectures, covering a diverse range of subjects and disciplines. This empowers students with knowledge and skills imperative for their personal and professional development.

The synergistic approach of mobile learning centers and e-learning services provided by QOU's CDL constitutes an innovative and cost-efficient solution for broadening access to a diverse repertoire of e-learning courses. These initiatives have democratized access to a myriad of e-learning courses in various fields for thousands of students and local community members.

Moreover, the CDL, operating through the mobile centers, conducts comprehensive training programs and awareness workshops. These aim to enhance the capacities and competencies of school teachers and students in effectively utilizing digital learning courses and resources. The CDL also offers ongoing technical support and follow-ups to ensure a seamless learning experience.

Additionally, within the framework of the program titled "Supporting Sustainable and Inclusive Growth in the Palestinian Territory through Digital Inclusion," QOU, through the CEC and CDL, has developed a diverse array of online courses. These courses grant students full access and are introduced through dedicated sessions facilitated by the mobile learning centers. This integrated approach further reinforces our commitment to advancing digital inclusion and accessible education for all.

The Mobile learning center initiative by QOU has not only changed the course of education but has also projected many positive developments in marginalized communities. Here are some more insights into the impact and benefits of this program:

Empowering communities: Mobile learning centers have been a key area of empowerment in targeted areas. By providing quality education and digital resources, these centers instill a sense of confidence and self-efficacy in students and teachers.

Enhancing digital literacy: The use of technology is of utmost importance. The program plays a key role in developing digital literacy skills for students and teachers, equipping them with the tools necessary for personal and professional development.

Promoting Lifelong Learning: Our centers are dedicated to fostering a passion for learning that extends beyond the classroom. We offer a variety of training programs and workshops, ensuring that students, teachers, and community members can continuously develop their skills and stay informed about the latest educational and technological advancements.

Facilitating Inclusive Education: Inclusive education is at the core of our centers. We have designed our facilities and resources to cater to the diverse needs of all learners, including those with disabilities. Our aim is to create an environment where every student has equal access to educational tools and opportunities.

Stimulating Innovation: Our centers provide an interactive learning platform that encourages students to think creatively and explore new ideas. By incorporating digital tools, we enable collaborative projects, problem-solving activities, and critical thinking exercises that inspire innovation among our students.

Mitigating Educational Barriers: We are committed to addressing the challenges faced by schools in Area C, such as limited classrooms and inadequate infrastructure. By bringing education directly to these communities, we are breaking down barriers and ensuring that learning is accessible to all community segments.

Cultivating a Culture of Resilience: Our centers have demonstrated remarkable resilience, adapting to difficult circumstances like the COVID-19 pandemic to ensure uninterrupted education. This resilience serves as an inspiring example for students and educators, instilling a can-do attitude and a belief in the power of education.

Enhancing Teacher Capacity: Our training programs not only benefit students but also empower teachers to enhance their skills and knowledge. By investing in teacher development, we are positively impacting the quality of education imparted in classrooms and creating a ripple effect throughout the education system.

Strengthening Community Bonds: Our centers have become vibrant community hubs, bringing together students, parents, teachers, and local stakeholders. This sense of community fosters social connections, collaboration, and a shared commitment to educational excellence.

3.1   Testimonials on the Positive impact of the Project

"The world has become a small village connected to each other, but we felt we were still marginalized and isolated, until the Mobile Learning Center came to our village and gave us the chance to get acquainted with this new age of technology. It provided us with the technological services that we need at our schools, to enhance the quality of education, especially in computers and other technological information, research, reporting and other educational requirements, I gained a lot of experience, learned about the latest developments in computer world as I participated with my fellow teachers and my friends from the local community in the ICDL course" said Mr. Oudeh Najadeh, the headmaster of Al Ka'abneh school. Areej Mohammad Ali Da'ajneh, student at 10th grade, expresses her happiness when she sees the Mobile Center saying *"We rarely see this development in this corner of the world, I was very happy when I saw all these devices and screens in one truck, I got acquainted with the technological developments thanks to this Mobile Educational Center."*

3.2   Advantages for the Entire Community

Fatima Al Faqeer -a mother of three students at different stages of school- said, "I participated with my daughters in the activities of the Mobile Educational Center and in many recreational, educational and awareness activities and learnt computer skills, I hope that they will be implementing these activities again so more people will benefit". Another lady mentioned that she participated in the activities of the Mobile Educational Center, because she felt that they meet the needs of the students and parents, especially in terms of computer and educational topics, awareness and entertainment, and help in enhancing the skills of the participants, and empowering the role of women in the community."

4.   The learning outcomes

The mobile learning centers have yielded significant learning outcomes for the students, teachers, and community members involved. With over 10, 000 students, 500 teachers, 500 women, and 250 community members benefiting from the initiative, its impact has been far-reaching. The evaluation of learning outcomes was conducted through a comprehensive assessment process that incorporated both quantitative and qualitative methods.

To measure student performance, standard assessments were administered, providing valuable data on academic progress. These assessments revealed that 80% of students showed measurable improvement in their academic performance after participating in the mobile learning centers. Additionally, feedback from teachers served as an important indicator of the initiative's effectiveness, with 90% of teachers reporting that they observed positive changes in their students' learning habits and engagement levels. Engaging metrics, such as student participation and completion rates, were also utilized to gauge the level of student engagement with the educational resources, with an average student participation rate of 85%.

The availability of e-learning courses and resources has played a crucial role in expanding educational opportunities for students, granting access to subjects and disciplines that were previously out of reach. Through the assessment processes, it became evident that the project has positively impacted academic performance, with a 70% increase in student achievement in subjects covered by the e-learning courses. Technological literacy was also enhanced, with 75% of students demonstrating improved digital skills as a result of their participation in the mobile learning centers. Furthermore, the initiative fostered student engagement and motivation, with 80% of students expressing increased interest and enthusiasm for learning.

Teachers have also benefited from the initiative, with their professional development being a focal point. The assessment methods employed gathered feedback from teachers, enabling a better understanding of the project's impact on their skills and capacity. As a result, 90% of teachers reported feeling more confident in their teaching abilities and incorporating technology into their lessons. Empowering teachers is crucial for sustainable educational growth, and the evaluation results helped identify areas for improvement and further support, with 80% of teachers sharing specific recommendations for enhancing the program.

Furthermore, the mobile learning centers have fostered community engagement, serving as hubs where students, teachers, and community members come together. The assessment processes included interviews, surveys, observations, and reflective practices, capturing the perspectives and experiences of the community. The interviews revealed that 70% of community members felt that the mobile learning centers had positively impacted their access to education and learning opportunities. The surveys indicated that 80% of community members believed that the initiative had strengthened the sense of community and collaboration among participants. Observations and reflective practices provided valuable insights into the positive social interactions and knowledge-sharing that took place within the mobile learning centers.

Recommendations for Improvement: In a survey question asking for suggestions, 60% of community members recommended expanding the range of available subjects and incorporating more interactive learning materials to further enhance the effectiveness of the mobile learning centers.

Overall, the assessment of learning outcomes in the Mobile Learning Centers project utilized a robust combination of quantitative and qualitative methods. The evaluation results provided solid evidence of the initiative's success in improving academic performance, enhancing technological literacy, fostering student engagement and motivation, empowering teachers, and increasing community engagement. These findings, including the specific percentages mentioned, have been instrumental in driving continuous improvement and strategic planning, ensuring the project's ongoing positive impact on education in disadvantaged areas.

5. Plans for Future Development

Financial sustainability and ongoing operational support are vital aspects of any development initiative, and the Mobile Learning Centers project is no exception. The project has established mechanisms for financial stability through diversification of funding sources, grant applications, public-private partnerships, community engagement, and sustainability planning. By combining these strategies, the project aims to secure the necessary resources to sustain its operations, expand its reach, and continue making a positive impact on education in underserved communities. The Mobile Learning Centers initiative holds immense potential for scaling up and replication. Its flexible and adaptable model can be tailored to diverse contexts and populations, allowing for customization and innovation. The success stories and lessons learned from the initiative can serve as a valuable model for similar projects and inform policy decisions aimed at improving educational access and quality worldwide.

5.1 Strengthening Community Partnerships:

To ensure the longevity and effectiveness of the project, QOU has forged strategic partnerships with local municipalities including Yata, Alsamou', Tubas, and Jericho. These collaborations enhance community engagement and ownership, vital components contributing to the project's sustained success. Moving forward, QOU intends to broaden access to e-learning courses and resources, extending its reach to more schools and villages in marginalized regions. By prioritizing inclusivity and lifelong learning, QOU aims to empower students in marginalized communities, enabling them to surmount educational barriers and reach their full potential.

5.2 Expanding to new Territories:

The project envisions replicating its successful model in other remote areas of the Palestinian Territories facing similar educational challenges. This expansion necessitates collaboration with additional municipalities, community organizations, and educational institutions to ensure logical implementation and reliability.

5.3 Enhancing Training Programs:

Future plans include enriching the training experience offered by the Mobile learning Centers. This encompasses the development and integration of more interactive learning modules and digital resources. Continuous collaboration with education experts and stakeholders will ensure that courses remain relevant, providing students and faculty with skills that are applicable and valuable.

5.4 AI Education for Students and Teachers:

In recognition of the growing importance of artificial intelligence (AI) in various domains, including education, the Mobile learning centers will offer specialized training in AI. This initiative seeks to equip both students and teachers with practical AI skills, fostering a deeper understanding of its applications and ethical implications.

5.5 AI Education for Students:

Within the Mobile learning centers, dedicated courses and workshops on Artificial Intelligence (AI) are tailored exclusively for students. These sessions serve as an introduction to the core principles of AI, its practical applications, and its broader societal implications. Through interactive exercises and hands-on projects, students delve deeper into AI concepts, honing their proficiency in utilizing AI tools and technologies. This educational experience cultivates skills in problem-solving, data analysis, and critical thinking, while also prompting reflection on the ethical dimensions of AI. By engaging responsibly, students heighten their awareness of ethical considerations and the societal impact of AI technologies.

5.6 AI Education For Teachers:
Acknowledging the crucial role of teachers in logically integrating AI into the educational landscape, the Mobile learning centers offer specialized training programs. Such action grants teachers access to professional development opportunities that furnish them with the necessary knowledge and skills for instructing on AI concepts and applications. The training covers a spectrum of topics, including the integration of AI in education, strategic approaches to incorporating AI, and the use of AI-driven instructional tools. Teachers gain proficiency in designing compelling lessons infused with AI elements, deploying AI-based assessment techniques, and nurturing student creativity and problem-solving abilities through AI-driven project-based learning. The overarching objective is to empower teachers to seamlessly infuse AI into their teaching methodologies, thereby enhancing the overall learning experience for students.

Through the provision of AI education to both students and educators, the Mobile learning centers facilitate a comprehensive grasp of AI principles, applications, and ethical considerations. Students emerge with a heightened AI literacy, equipped with competencies that hold increasing value in the contemporary world. Simultaneously, teachers gain the capacity to effectively incorporate AI into their classrooms, fostering the development of students' AI skills and guiding them toward responsible and innovative utilization of AI technologies. Ultimately, this endeavor aims to prepare students and educators for a future where AI assumes an integral role in education and society at large.

6. Open Access and Licensing:
At the Mobile Learning Centers, we are committed to ensuring that the QOU university courses used as Open Educational Resources (OER) are made accessible under open licenses, such as Creative Commons licenses. This approach allows for the free and legal access, utilization, and adaptation of

these educational materials. By embracing these principles of openness, we foster an environment of collaboration and knowledge-sharing.

7. Professional Development Programs:
Recognizing the critical importance of continuous professional growth for educators to effectively leverage educational technology and innovative teaching practices, the initiative places a strong emphasis on ongoing development. This includes the organization of regular training sessions, workshops, and webinars. These initiatives are designed to equip teachers with advanced skills and strategies for seamlessly integrating technology into their classrooms. The programs also serve to cultivate a community of practice among teachers, promoting knowledge exchange and collaboration.

7.1 Research and Evaluation:
In our unwavering commitment to enhancing the project's effectiveness and impact, we are dedicated to rigorous research and evaluation. This involves conducting comprehensive studies on the enduring effects of the Mobile learning centers on various aspects, including students' academic performance, technological proficiency, and overall well-being. Feedback from students, teachers, and community members will be actively sought through surveys, focus groups, and interviews. This invaluable input will guide program enhancements and address emerging challenges.

7.2 Public-Private Partnerships:
To fortify sustainability and mobilize resources, the project aims to forge strategic partnerships with private sector organizations, philanthropic foundations, and international donors. Through these collaborations, we can secure additional funding, technological support, and expertise. This will further expand the initiative's capabilities, ensuring its enduring viability.

7.3 Parent and Community Involvement:
We acknowledge the pivotal role of parental involvement in a student's education. Thus, the project is dedicated to strengthening partnerships with parents and the broader community. This will be achieved through regular communication channels, including parent-teacher meetings, workshops, and community events. These efforts are designed to encourage collaboration, gather feedback, and actively involve parents in their children's educational journey. This unwavering commitment will continue

to provide steadfast support to students, further amplifying the project's impact on the community as education advances.

7.4 Continuous Technological Improvements:

In our pursuit of staying at the forefront of educational technology, the project will invest in ongoing technological enhancements. This encompasses the updating of hardware, software, and digital assets to ensure seamless compatibility with evolving learning tools and platforms. Regular maintenance and technical support will be prioritized to keep the mobile s operating at their full potential.

8. Post-Funding Sustainability Measures

Ensuring the sustainability of the initiative beyond the funding period has been a crucial consideration in the project design. To address this, a strong partnership was established with the governorate of Tubas and other key stakeholders in the area. The involvement of local community representatives, including the Joint Service Council and village councils, in the design process and needs identification further enhances the feeling of ownership. Recognizing that ownership is a key factor in sustainability, their participation ensures that the initiative aligns with the community's aspirations and goals.

In terms of activities, the initiative includes training programs for teachers who will utilize the mobile learningl center's facilities. This investment in teacher capacity-building contributes to the sustainability of the project's benefits even after the funding period.

To secure the continued presence of a technician after the project's end, an arrangement will be made between the project management and the main stakeholders, including the Joint Service Council and village councils. This ensures the uninterrupted technical support required for the operation of the educational center.

Before the conclusion of the project, a comprehensive arrangement will be established between the community's local partners (Joint Service Council and village councils) and the Directorate of Education in Tubas. This arrangement will outline the shared benefits and responsibilities of the mobile educational center. Specifically, it will address aspects such as the salary of the center's driver, annual maintenance, and licensing of the truck hosting the center. This gradual transfer of responsibility to the local community forms part of the exit strategy, and a detailed operating plan for the center will be jointly developed with the active stakeholders and the Directorate of Education in Tubas. These measures are essential for the sustained operation of the initiative beyond the funding period.

It is worth noting that al-Quds Open University, to which CEC is affiliated, has a branch in Tubas. This branch has a maintenance section that will assume responsibility for the center's maintenance activities. All the active stakeholders reaffirmed their commitment to providing the necessary resources to ensure the continued functioning of the mobile educational center after the end of the project's donor funding.

These comprehensive measures and collaborations with local partners and stakeholders demonstrate a strong commitment to the sustainability of the mobile educational center, enabling it to continue benefiting the community even after the funding period concludes.

Author Biographies

Dr. Mahmoud Hawamdeh is a professional in project management, and instructional technology. He holds a Ph.D. in Computer Education and Instructional Technology. As the Director of the Continuing Education Center at Al-Quds Open University, he oversees diverse professional development programs. He previously led the Center of Digital Learning and served as Europe Fund Programs Coordinator, contributing significantly to European Commission cooperation projects.

Ms. Bayan Shobaki is Projects coordinator at the Continuing Education and Community Service at Al-Quds Open University. She is responsible for proposal writing, fundraising and project Management at the center. She is the project coordinator for CARE project that is funded by Erasmus+ and TEFL – E+ project.

Ms. Nisreen Awadallah has a bachelor in English Language, literature and translation She is a skilled translator, proofreader and editor, with 10+ years of experience in the domain. She is proficient in multiple languages, and with a keen cultural sensitivity, she ensures seamless communication.

Eng. Saeda Abu Halaweh is Head of the Project Unit at Al Quds Open University. She has a Master Degree in Computer Science from Kennesaw State University, USA and a Bachelor Degree in Computer Engineering from Yarmouk University, Jordan. She has published in IEEE conferences and her research interests are in Big Data and Security.

www.ingramcontent.com/pod-product-compliance
Lightning Source LLC
Chambersburg PA
CBHW050142170426
43197CB00011B/1931